Business Ethics

Packed with examples, this book offers a clear and engaging overview of ethical issues in business.

It begins with a discussion of foundational issues, including the objectivity of ethics, the content of ethical theories, and the debate between capitalism and socialism, making it suitable for the beginning student. It then examines ethical issues in business in three broad areas. The first is the market. Issues explored are what can be sold (the limits of markets) and how it can be sold (ethics in marketing). The second is work. Topics in this area are health and safety, meaningful work, compensation, hiring and firing, privacy, and whistleblowing. The third area is the firm in society. Here readers explore corporate social responsibility, corporate political activity, and the set of ethical challenges that attend international business.

Issues are introduced through real-world examples that underscore their importance and make them come alive. Arguments for opposing positions are given fair hearings and students are encouraged to develop and defend their own views.

Key Features

- Introduces each topic with a real-world example, which is referenced regularly in the subsequent argument.
- Contains a critical evaluation of capitalism and socialism, with a focus on private property, the market system, and the welfare state.
- Explores the limits of markets and encourages students to ask what should and should not be for sale.
- Explores the phenomena of corporate political activity and ethical consumerism.
- Includes initial chapter overviews and – at the end of each chapter – study questions and suggested additional readings.

Jeffrey Moriarty is Professor of Philosophy at Bentley University and currently serves as Executive Director of its Hoffman Center for Business Ethics.

ROUTLEDGE CONTEMPORARY INTRODUCTIONS TO PHILOSOPHY

Series editor
Paul K. Moser
Loyola University of Chicago

This innovative, well-structured series is for students who have already done an introductory course in philosophy. Each book introduces a core general subject in contemporary philosophy and offers students an accessible but substantial transition from introductory to higher-level college work in that subject. The series is accessible to non-specialists and each book clearly motivates and expounds the problems and positions introduced. An orientating chapter briefly introduces its topic and reminds readers of any crucial material they need to have retained from a typical introductory course. Considerable attention is given to explaining the central philosophical problems of a subject and the main competing solutions and arguments for those solutions. The primary aim is to educate students in the main problems, positions and arguments of contemporary philosophy rather than to convince students of a single position.

Recently Published Volumes:

Philosophy of Action
Sarah K. Paul

Animal Ethics
Bob Fischer

Philosophy of Time
Sean Enda Power

Philosophy of Perception
2nd Edition
William Fish

Business Ethics
Jeffrey Moriarty

For a full list of published Routledge Contemporary Introductions to Philosophy, please visit https://www.routledge.com/Routledge-Contemporary-Introductions-to-Philosophy/book-series/SE0111

Business Ethics

A Contemporary Introduction

Jeffrey Moriarty

NEW YORK AND LONDON

First published 2022
by Routledge
605 Third Avenue, New York, NY 10158

and by Routledge
2 Park Square, Milton Park, Abingdon, Oxon, OX14 4RN

Routledge is an imprint of the Taylor & Francis Group, an informa business

Library of Congress Cataloging-in-Publication Data
A catalog record for this book has been requested

ISBN: 978-1-138-49813-6 (hbk)
ISBN: 978-1-138-49812-9 (pbk)
ISBN: 978-1-351-01687-2 (ebk)

DOI: 10.4324/9781351016872

Typeset in Times New Roman
by Apex CoVantage, LLC

Contents

Acknowledgments

Like many of my peers, I got into business ethics by chance. There was a need for someone to teach a course in the field, and having a background in ethics and political philosophy, I seemed a suitable candidate. My thanks to Edwin Hartman for showing me the ropes and encouraging me to take it seriously. I did and have never regretted it. Business ethics, I hope you'll come to agree, is fascinating.

My next thanks go to my students – first at Rutgers University; then California State University, Long Beach; Bowling Green State University; and now Bentley University. Business ethics can be challenging to teach. It is often taught by philosophers, but to students whose primary focus is something else. My students helped me to see (with bracing candor) what's interesting about the field to them and what the best ways to teach it are. Special thanks go to Bentley University for giving me the time and resources to work on this project.

When I first started to do serious work in business ethics, I began attending meetings of the Society for Business Ethics (SBE). It is a stimulating and collegial group from which I have learned much. My thanks to the members of the SBE – many of whom are now friends and collaborators – especially those who have taken time from their own research and teaching to manage the organization.

I started writing this book a few years ago – too many years ago. I thank Andrew Beck at Routledge for inviting me to contribute to this series and for his exemplary patience as I found the time to complete the project.

I had help. Thanks go to students Juliette Smieszek, Augustine Peprah, and Harshpreet Singh for locating examples to illustrate the ideas discussed in the book. Without their assistance, it would have been much less lively.

The full manuscript was read by Alan Strudler and two anonymous reviewers for Routledge. Alan saved me from many errors, and the reviewers helped me to figure out what was working in the manuscript and what wasn't. I am grateful for their time and attention.

My family has been a constant source of comfort and support. My mother Karen read the entire manuscript, identifying countless grammatical infelicities and collecting $.25 for each typo. My brother Kevin helped me with some of the facts in Chapter 6, and my father Daniel has been an eager participant in philosophical conversations through the years. My wife Kelly and our children Henry and Jack have been more than patient with me as I worked out some of the arguments in this book aloud, wandering the house. They know more about business ethics than they ever wanted.

Jeffrey Moriarty
Bentley University
March 2021

1 Business, Ethics, and Business Ethics

What is business ethics? It is hard to define a field in the abstract. The best way to learn about business ethics is to read what's in books and articles that claim to be about business ethics or to listen to businesspeople talk about the ethical dilemmas they face. But you might want to know what you are getting into, so here goes. Business ethics can be understood by understanding its component parts: business and ethics.

1. What Is Business?

'Business' has two meanings, both connected with exchange. 'Business' can mean an exchange activity or an activity in which one party exchanges some of what it owns for some of what someone else owns. I do business with Walmart when I exchange some of my money for a pair of its shoes. I do business with my corner store when I purchase a cup of coffee before class. 'Business' can also mean an individual, group, or organization that offers goods or services for exchange, that is, that sells things. Walmart is a business. So is the corner grocery store from which I get my coffee. To talk of business ethics, then, is to talk of the ethics of the activity of exchange and of the ethics of individuals, groups, and organizations that offer things for exchange.

The claim that a business is any individual, group, or organization that offers goods or services – occasionally I will simply say "things" – for exchange might seem too broad. It implies that organizations like art museums, professional associations, and universities are businesses, since they offer things for sale, including tours, memberships, and degrees. In fact, these types of organizations face many of the same challenges that we will discuss in this book. Art museums and universities need to think about how to advertise their products and how to treat their employees, just as Walmart and the corner store do. So it makes sense to think about them as businesses. But a business is typically understood in a narrower sense, as an individual, group, or organization that offers things for sale with the goal of making a profit. Businesses seek to bring it about that their revenues exceed their

DOI: 10.4324/9781351016872-1

expenses. Art museums, professional associations, and universities do not usually seek profits. Following this convention, in this book, we will be focusing on for-profit businesses, but many of the conclusions we reach apply to businesses in the broader sense.

Businesses come in many forms. Sometimes they are just one person. You might have already started a business in your apartment, and you may be its sole employee. Sometimes they are hundreds of thousands of people, spanning the globe, like Amazon or Walmart. Businesses take many legal forms as well. They can be sole proprietorships, partnerships, cooperatives, and corporations. We will not concern ourselves with the differences among types of businesses here. The issues we discuss are almost always common to all types of businesses. In the rare cases where they are not – for example, in discussions of corporate social responsibility – this will be made explicit.

A quick note about terminology. The main term we will use for an entity that sells things is 'business'. This is a book about business ethics after all. But we will sometimes refer to these entities as firms, corporations, companies, or organizations. When we talk about ethical issues involving employees, we will often refer to them as employers. You shouldn't read anything into this. Scholars in different disciplines refer to "entities that sell" in different ways, and where our discussion overlaps with theirs, it becomes convenient to use their terminology.

We have said that business is all about exchange. Business is the act of exchange or an entity that offers things – goods and services – for exchange. Ethical questions can be raised about business in each of these senses.

Consider first the activity of exchange. We might ask what can be sold. Tables, chairs, cups, beds, fruits, and vegetables seem appropriate for sale. But what about energy drinks that have a lot of caffeine in addition to a lot of alcohol? Some believe that people should be able to purchase these drinks so long as they know the risks. Others believe that people shouldn't be given this choice, because if they have it, some will make a bad choice. We can also ask questions about *how* things can be sold. Suppose you are considering purchasing a membership in a weight loss program. It is wrong for the seller to tell you that it is common for people to lose 60 pounds on the program when they normally lose only 20 pounds. But suppose you mistakenly believe that people normally lose 60 pounds on the program. Does the seller have an obligation to try to correct your error?

Consider next entities that offer goods for sale. In many cases, a business will have an owner and this owner will employ several people to produce those goods. We might ask questions about the nature of the work that employees perform. Should it be safe? Meaningful? What does it mean to say that work is safe or meaningful? We might also ask questions about what the enterprise should be doing. Is it enough for it to make goods and services? Or should it provide some additional benefit to the community? That is, should firms engage in acts of corporate social responsibility? Employers may wish to know all sorts of facts about their employees – not just whether they have the skills and credentials that they say they do, but how much they exercise or whether they smoke. Should employers be allowed to ask for this sort of information?

As these questions reveal, when we study business ethics, we are concerned not just with exchange itself. We are also concerned with activities relating to exchange, such as the production, distribution, marketing, sale, and consumption of goods and services. We are concerned with how business organizations operate in the wider world.

2. What Is Ethics?

We have said what the business part of business ethics is. What about the ethics part? The previous section contained hints. Business ethicists are concerned about how activities of exchange *should be* conducted.

Many people engaged in the study of business think about how business should be conducted. Accountants tell us how financial information should be reported. Marketers tell us how products should be promoted. What's the difference between what you learn in accounting and marketing, and what you learn in business ethics?

Very roughly, the 'should' of business disciplines like accounting and marketing (and management and finance) is an *instrumental* 'should'. These disciplines tell us the effective means to achieve certain ends. In marketing, the goal is to sell the firm's products. In marketing classes, you learn the techniques and strategies to accomplish this. In accounting, the goal is to provide an accurate picture of the firm's financial position. In accounting classes, you learn the rules and practices that enable you to do so. And so on for the rest of the business disciplines.

The 'should' of business ethics is *non-instrumental*. When we do business ethics, we ask not just whether certain actions are the right ones to achieve certain ends, but whether they are the right ones, period. That is, we are asking whether they are the right actions independent of whether they are effective at achieving the specified business objective. Our answers will draw upon concepts such as good, bad, just, unjust, virtuous, vicious, and so on. We might learn that we can maximize profit by charging customers higher prices for necessary goods in an emergency. But is this the right thing to do? Is it good? Is it fair? We might also learn that it is cheaper for a firm to make an extortion payment (e.g., to a corrupt government official) than not to do so. Is this right, or good, or fair?

Two clarifications are in order. First, business ethics is not only about what means should be used to achieve business ends. It can include analysis of the ends themselves. A firm might decide that it wants to make as much money as possible. We can ask: is this an appropriate end for a firm? Or should the firm sacrifice some profit in order to provide benefits to society?

Second, business ethics is not only about right action. It is also about right character. That is, we can ask what it would mean for a person to be a good businessperson. Of course, we might mean by "good businessperson" a businessperson who is effective at achieving business objectives. But if we understand "good" more broadly than this, as including ethical considerations, we are doing business ethics.

We have described the 'should' of the business disciplines (e.g., accounting and marketing) as instrumental, as asking what the effective means to achieve business objectives are. We have said that this 'should' is not the same as the 'should' of ethics, which is non-instrumental. We need to be careful here. Ethics and effectiveness are theoretically distinct. We can ask of a business practice that is effective whether it is also ethical. Similarly, we can ask of a business practice that is ethical whether it is also effective. This does not mean that ethics and effectiveness are practically distinct. In some cases, the most effective course of action may be the most ethical. In other cases, the most effective course of action may not be the most ethical. In these cases, firms and businesspeople will have to make a choice between doing the effective thing and the ethical thing.

We have been talking about business ethics. You might wonder where morality fits in. What's the connection between ethics and morality? We will use the terms 'ethics' and 'morality' interchangeably in this text. For us, these are the same concepts. If you look at other texts, you will see that some people use the terms 'ethics' and 'morality' differently. Sometimes ethics is understood to have two components: morality, which is concerned with how we relate to others, and prudence, which is concerned with how we relate to ourselves. Sometimes morality is understood to be personal, while ethics is understood to be interpersonal or social. It is not important for our purposes to catalog the various possibilities or try to defend one against the others.

When in doubt, we can remember Plato, who said that ethics is the study of how to live. We are asking how we should live in the business arena.

3. Business Ethics and Business Law

In business ethics, we are concerned fundamentally about the ethical aspects of exchange in society. We are interested in questions like these: is it ethically permissible for employers to ask their employees whether they are smokers? Should businesses set aside a portion of their profits to donate to charity? Sometimes we will think that things are perfect as they are now. But other times we will think that things need to be different than they are now.

When we think things should be changed, it is natural to think that the laws need to be changed. You might think it is permissible for an employer to offer, and an employee to accept, a wage that is less than the minimum wage. (In the U.S. the federal minimum wage is $7.25 per hour.) The law, however, does not permit this arrangement. You might think that the law should be changed to allow people to work for less than the minimum wage.

Or suppose we become convinced that it is morally wrong for employers to ask their employees about their salary history. (There is evidence that this perpetuates an unfair pay gap between men and women.) Then we might say that a law needs to be written that forbids employers from asking employees about their salary histories.

The conclusion that "things should be different than they are now" may require changes in laws and regulations. Perhaps we need to either abolish the minimum wage or create laws prohibiting employers from asking employees how much money they made in previous jobs. But it may not. Sometimes things should be left up to individuals.

Suppose we become convinced that corporations should do more good for society by giving more of their profits to charity. It's not clear that this moral judgment can or should be encoded into law. This is so for at least two reasons. First, the law is a blunt instrument. It is easy enough to write a law that directs employers not to ask employees about their salary history. It is a lot more difficult to write a law directing firms to donate more of their profits to charity. How much of their profits? And which charities? When it comes to philanthropy, what the firm should do depends on what it can do, and what society needs, and this is going to vary from case to case. Second, the law has both financial and moral costs. Financially, it costs money to construct the legal apparatus – including inspectors, courts, judges, and more – necessary to enforce the law. All of these people need to be paid. Morally, the law is intrusive and bothersome. Consider why we don't have laws against adultery (or why in the few jurisdictions that still have them, they are never enforced). The reason is not that adultery is not morally wrong. It is that we don't want government officials spying on us in our bedrooms.

Even if a moral judgment could be encoded into law and enforced with minimal costs, you might think that it should not be, since it gives expression to your personal values. Moreover, you might think that, while these values are important to you, they are values that others may reasonably not embrace. Chik-fil-A closes all of its stores on Sunday in order to give its employees time to spend with their families. Patagonia gives 1% of its sales to environmental causes. These companies might see these behaviors not as a moral requirement that all companies should observe, but simply a requirement for their firms, given the values to which they are committed.

One lesson to be drawn from our discussion is that business ethics concerns both individual morality and public policy. Business ethics is "about" how individuals engage in activities of exchange (and related issues). The question is what individuals should be like, and what they should do, in the business arena. But business ethics is also "about" how we as a society want these activities of exchange to be structured by law and policy. When we decide that things should be different than they now are, we may give expression to this decision in a change to law or policy.

Another lesson to be drawn is that ethics and law are different. Laws *can* track moral judgments. For example, it is illegal for firms to lie about the characteristics of their products. It is also immoral for them to do so. It is illegal for employees to steal from their employers. It is also immoral for them to do so. You can think of countless examples like this, where what is legally impermissible is also morally impermissible. But in some cases the law and morality can come apart. We see this in some of the examples given earlier.

The law might forbid you to act in a way that you think it is morally permissible to act. Consider the minimum wage case. You might think it is permissible to offer or accept a wage that is lower than the legal minimum, but the law does not allow this to happen. The law might even forbid you to act in a way that is morally required for you to act. Nazi-era laws required Jews to wear gold stars on their clothing to publicly identify them as Jews. The fugitive slave act in the U.S. required people to help return escaped slaves to their masters. We also noted that the law might permit you to do something that it would be morally wrong for you to do. In most circumstances, it is wrong for you to lie to or cheat on your spouse. But the law often permits you to do so.

The point is this. When thinking about issues in business ethics, we will sometimes focus on the actions and character of individual people engaged in business. We will also sometimes focus on laws and policies. We must do both, since laws and policies shape individuals' actions and even their characters. But we also should not suppose that there is a one-to-one mapping between ethics and the law. We should not assume that what the law forbids you to do is immoral, and we should not suppose that what the law permits you to do is morally permissible.

4. Why Study Business Ethics?

We have said in a general way what business ethics is. A further question is why anyone should study it. One reason you might have is this: I need to pass a class I am taking on business ethics. If this is the only reason you have, studying business ethics will be a slog. So it is worthwhile thinking about other, more powerful, reasons for studying business ethics.

4.1. Knowledge of Business Ethics as Valuable

One reason for studying business ethics is that doing so provides a way to learn more about the world that you live in. The study of business ethics helps us to understand the ethical aspects of our shared reality. It helps you to see ethical problems that may have been invisible to you and to discern the rightness or wrongness of certain traits, behaviors, and policies. According to some philosophers, knowledge of this sort, especially about matters of substance, is non-instrumentally valuable. That is, it is valuable in itself, even if we do not put it to use.

Why, for example, should you take a course on ancient Egyptian civilizations? One answer is that learning about Egyptian literature, history, culture, mathematics, and more is valuable. Moreover, according to some philosophers, it is valuable for you even if it doesn't add to your professional skill set or help you to earn more money in your career.

This answer is important and should not be discounted. But it will be unsatisfying to many people. This may be especially true in a business setting. When people take a course with 'business' in the title, they expect to learn skills that they can deploy in the business world and that will help them to advance their professional goals. At a minimum, they expect to learn something that will help them to guide their actions. For these people, there is good news. The study of business ethics gives us more than simply knowledge of the world, however valuable that may be.

4.2. Ethics, Right Action, and Self-Interest

Another answer to the question of why study business ethics is because it helps you to *act* ethically – do the right thing – in the context of business. When you study business ethics, you learn how to see ethical aspects of situations, and you acquire a set of concepts and tools for assessing the ethical status of certain behaviors and policies. You can then use this knowledge to figure out what the right thing is to do and then do it. Or at least you can use your knowledge to avoid doing the wrong thing.

Now to this you might reply: "What good is that?" You might mean something like "Ethics. What's in it for me?" What might be said to this?

One thing that might be said is this: "You are confused. You are asking for reasons to do what ethics requires you to do. But ethics itself is a source of reasons. You should do what you are ethically required to do, because you are ethically required to do it."

The 18th-century German philosopher Immanuel Kant seemed to have held something like this view of ethics. For him, asking what reason you have to do what you are ethically required to do is like asking what reason you have to believe a truth of logic (e.g., that it can't be both raining and not raining at the same time and in the same place). As a rational person, this is what you are required to do.

Some people will be satisfied with this answer. At some point, reasons run out, so why not here? But others will not be satisfied. They might find this answer mysterious or odd, or perhaps they just want to know whether ethics is valuable to them in any other sense. Now perhaps these people are being unreasonable, and we should not engage. But can anything else be said to them? According to a popular argument, something more can be said. According to this argument, in business, ethics pays. This is sometimes called the "business case" for business ethics.

4.3. Does Ethics Pay in Business?

When people say that "ethics pays" in business, they mean that doing the right (ethical) thing in business leads to conventional business success, in the form of increased sales, profits, promotions, and the like. To this claim is sometimes added the converse claim that doing the wrong thing in business will lead to business failure or at least a lack of business success. This argument is sometimes used on two levels: the level of the firm and the level of the individual.

Look at what happened, some will say, to BP's stock price after the Deepwater Horizon explosion and resulting oil spill, which caused the deaths of 11 workers and allowed 4.9 million barrels of oil to flow into the Gulf of Mexico. Better ethics – in the form of better safety precautions and procedures – could have prevented this tragedy. Or look at Patagonia's continued success. This is the result, it might be thought, of the loyalty of Patagonia's customer base, which is due in part to Patagonia's contribution of 1% of its gross revenues to environmental causes. On this view, people should study business ethics because it helps firms make money or at least not lose money.

The view that ethics pays for the firm may be correct, but it may not be. The question of what causes some firms to succeed, or to do better than other firms, is incredibly complex. Just ask people who work on organizational strategy. It cannot be solved by pointing to a few examples where ethical or unethical behavior (apparently) led to good or bad results. We need a lot of data. In fact, scholars have tried to collect a lot of data to determine whether ethics pays – or in academic terminology, whether corporate social performance is correlated with corporate financial performance – but have not arrived at a definitive answer. Current research seems to indicate that there is a slight positive correlation between corporate social performance (roughly, ethics) and corporate financial performance (roughly, payment). But it is exceedingly difficult to tell whether there is a causal relationship between these factors, and if so, which way the causality goes. One possibility is that firms that are more ethical are able to make more money, because their being more ethical helps them to attract more customers. But another possibility is that firms that are already more successful have more money on hand, which they feel free to spend on ethical causes. Just because two events (ethics, financial success) are correlated, doesn't mean that they are causally related in a certain way.

A second version of the "ethics pays" argument appeals to your individual self-interest. It says that if you do something unethical, you will get caught and punished, and this will be bad for you personally. The flipside of this argument is that if you do something ethical, you will be noticed and rewarded, and this is good for you personally. After the Deepwater Horizon oil spill, Tony Hayward lost his highly lucrative job as CEO of BP. In the early 2000s, several high-ranking executives from Enron (Jeff Skilling, Andrew Fastow) and Worldcom (Bernard Ebbers) were convicted of financial crimes and went to prison. Many universities try to convince their students of the importance of business ethics by having people who committed crimes come to campus and tell their stories. Fastow, now out of prison, does this routinely. You don't want to go to prison, do you? According to this argument, you better figure out what ethics requires in business.

This argument is confused on at least two fronts. First, while it is true that if you do something illegal, there is a chance that you will be caught and punished, there is no guarantee that this will happen. The worldwide financial crisis of 2007–2009 cost millions of people their jobs and homes and resulted in financial losses of trillions of dollars. Large banks were deeply in debt and were hiding this information from the public. When their true condition was revealed, markets crashed and financial catastrophe ensued. However, in the U.S. only one banker – Kareem Serageldin – went to prison for his role in the financial crisis. In contrast, the U.S. government prosecuted more than 1000 individuals for their role in the savings and loan crisis in the 1980s, a much smaller financial disaster. Of course, it is possible that only one banker did something illegal during the financial crisis of 2007–2009, but this seems unlikely. A more likely possibility is that many bankers did something illegal and got away with it. Second, business ethics is about much more than obeying the law. As we saw, the law sometimes permits you to engage in unethical behavior. So if you want to do the right thing, you will have to think about more than just what is legally permitted. Moreover, as we also saw, in business ethics, the law is *itself* a subject of evaluation. We will ask whether our laws are correct or should be changed.

It is tempting to try to motivate the study of business ethics by connecting it with business success. If you are studying business, you probably want to be successful in business. Minimally, you want to avoid failure. So this way of motivating business ethics, if it could be substantiated, would be very powerful. But this connection, given what we know now, cannot be relied upon. If this is the reason you are studying business ethics, then your commitment to it will be tenuous.

4.4. What Kind of a Person Are You?

Does this mean that nothing more can be said to the person who says: "Ethics. What's in it for me?" Not quite. Being ethical in business might not promote conventional business success in the form of increased profits or promotions, but it might nevertheless be something that promotes your self-interest and something that you care about.

To see how, ask yourself a simple question. Am I a good person who wants to do the right thing? In particular, am I a good person who wants to do the right thing in business? If your answer to these questions is 'yes', then we have discovered a reason that the study of business ethics is useful to you. In order to do what you want – which is to be a good person and do the right thing in business – you need to study business ethics. That is, you need to become aware of the ethical issues that attend business activity, and you need to acquire the tools necessary to figure out what the right thing to do is. You need to do these things to accomplish your own goals.

This reason is underappreciated and more powerful than you might think. It is true that people care about conventional business success: getting promoted, making money, and all the rest. But people care about a lot more than this. They care about how they appear in the community, to their friends and neighbors, and to themselves. People sometimes explain why they didn't do something by saying "I wouldn't be able to look at myself in the mirror if I did that" or even "I wouldn't be able to live with myself if I did that." The source of this self-concern or self-regard could be many things: religious or philosophical commitments, parental conditioning, or even a sense of moral vanity. The point is, people think of themselves in a certain way, and this self-conception is a significant source of motivation. Bringing people to recognize that they see themselves this way, I am suggesting, helps them to see a reason why they should study business ethics. Studying business ethics can help people to become the person they want to be. This reason to study business ethics appeals to people's self-interest, though not in the narrow way that the "ethics pays" argument does. It claims that studying business ethics helps you to get what you want, where what you want includes being the kind of person you want to be and living the kind of life you want to live.

Two qualifications are in order. First, I do not claim that every person thinks of themselves as a good person who wants to do the right thing. There are probably some people out there who do not think of themselves this way (but good luck getting them to admit this). Perhaps they think of themselves as bad people, or perhaps they don't think of themselves in moral terms at all. For these people, the argument that I am making will have little traction. This qualification has the effect of shrinking the pool of people to whom this argument applies. But the second qualification will have the effect of expanding it. That is, thinking of yourself as a "good person who wants to do the right thing" is compatible with thinking that the ethics for business activities will be different than the ethics for ordinary life. A commitment to being a good person who does the right thing in business does not mean treating your competitor in business exactly as you would your neighbor or a member of your family. Most businesses operate in competitive markets. Consumers have a choice of products, and if not enough of them choose yours, then you will go out of business. This might license a different sort of behavior – a "sharper" or "tougher" kind – than would be acceptable among friends, around the dinner table, or at church.

This section asked why anyone should study business ethics. One answer is that, by studying it, you will learn something about the world. At the very least, you will learn something about the ethical aspects of business activity and what thoughtful people have said about the ethics of business. But more than this, you will learn something you can put into practice. You will learn how to avoid moral error, and how to do what's right, in business. This is relevant information for you both as a person who engages in business activity and as a citizen who helps to shape business law and regulation through political activity (e.g., voting). As for why you should care about that: it is not clear that any answer needs to be given to this question. You should do what's right, because it is right, and that's it. Some people try to provide an additional reason to study business ethics by claiming that doing what's ethical will pay off for you or your firm. While there is some evidence for this view, it is not conclusive. We might do better by appealing to people's self-conception as good people who want to do the right thing. If you think of yourself this way, and many people do, then this book will be valuable to you.

5. What Is This Book Meant to Do and Not Do?

You now have a better sense of what this book is about and why its subject is worth caring about. Now let me refine its content a bit further.

5.1. How to Recognize and Think About Ethical Issues

You play, or will soon play, various roles in the business world. You will make goods and provide services, you will sell them, you will manage people, you will buy things, and more. You will also help to shape the business world through your political activity, for example, by electing leaders who will adjust relevant laws and regulations. In these roles you will be confronted with ethical problems. You will make decisions that will be regarded as ethical or unethical, by others and by yourself. This book's goal is to help you recognize and think through ethical issues in business in order to make better decisions.

Now you might think: "I don't need a business ethics book to recognize ethical issues." In some cases, you would be right. Some ethical issues hit you over the head. When the Rana Plaza building in Bangladesh collapsed in 2013, killing more than 1100 workers and injuring hundreds more, it seems correct to think that *something* went wrong here.

But other issues are more subtle. You see thousands of advertisements for consumer products every day and think little of them. But they have important effects on our preferences and behavior. It is the job of a good businessperson – and citizen – to recognize both the obvious moral issues and the non-obvious ones. Reading this book is, I hope, like walking through an art museum with a knowledgeable guide. You would have noticed some interesting things for yourself, but you will learn new things too.

In addition to increasing your awareness of ethical issues in business, this book's goal is to help you think through them in a rational way. Consider again the Rana Plaza collapse. The collapse of the building may have been due to lax building codes, or perhaps the building codes were ignored. But who is responsible for the disaster, and what should be done about it? Do we blame the construction company that built the building? Do we blame government regulators for failing to enforce building codes? Do we blame the factory owners who failed to confirm that the building was safe for industrial use? What was being produced in the Rana Plaza were clothes for Western companies, like Walmart, Primark, and The Children's Place. Do these companies have any responsibility for the working conditions in their suppliers' factories? In fact, many of these companies decided to *take* responsibility and require their suppliers' factories to conform to certain health and safety guidelines. But that itself raises ethical questions. Who are firms like Walmart and Primark to tell countries like Bangladesh how to regulate their economies? What about you and me? People worked in the Rana Plaza because people like to buy cheap clothes, and the cheapest place to make clothes is in developing countries like Bangladesh. Part of the reason that clothes are so cheap to produce there is that they have weak health and safety regulations. If these regulations were strengthened, then Western multinationals might decide to source their clothes from suppliers in other countries, and workers in Bangladesh would be unemployed. Would that be better? These problems do not admit of easy answers, but after reading this book you will be more confident in addressing them.

5.2. Not Telling You What to Think or What to Do

I have said that this book will help you to recognize and think through ethical issues in business so that you can make better decisions. One thing this book will *not* do is tell you what to think about ethical issues in business or what to do. This is so for two reasons.

The first and most important is that there is no consensus on many of the issues that we discuss. This is not because consensus is unobtainable or that there is no such thing as truth in business ethics. (More on this in the next chapter.) It is because many of the issues discussed here are difficult. We don't bother to discuss the easy problems. Is it permissible to gain an edge on your competitors by burning down their factories? Is it permissible to threaten your employees with physical violence if they don't meet their production quotas? The answers to these questions are 'no', and obviously so. But it is much more difficult to determine – to return to the Rana Plaza case – whose responsibility it is to ensure that workers have a safe environment to work in or even what counts as a safe environment for workers. Reasonable arguments can be found for different, conflicting positions. Please do not throw up your hands in despair. Consider it instead a challenge and an invitation. Ethical issues in business are difficult, but they are pressing – they demand answers – and you are invited to take part in solving them.

Second, there is a very real sense in which no book on business ethics can tell you what to think or do about ethical issues in business. This is because ethical reasoning is very much a contextual process. You have to think in the moment about all the relevant facts, relationships, histories, social contexts, possible futures, and more. These are going to vary from case to case. Perhaps some employers – for example, healthcare providers – should be permitted to ask their employees whether they smoke. But perhaps other employers – for example, accounting firms – should not be permitted to ask. Perhaps firms in some countries – those with weak or corrupt political institutions – should be permitted to lobby the government for reforms. But perhaps firms in other countries – those with high functioning political systems – should stay out of politics. The point is, business ethics – and probably ethics in general – is not about learning certain things to think and do in certain situations, and then doing them when you find yourself in those situations. Chances are, you will never find yourself in those exact situations. To be an ethical businessperson, you need to learn to become aware of ethical issues, to have at your command a set of concepts for thinking through them, and to have an ability to apply them to the unique situation in which you find yourself. In short, you need to learn to think for yourself. The goal of this book is to give you the tools that you need to be a better thinker when it comes to business ethics.

5.3. Normative Ethics, Not Descriptive Ethics

Here are two types of questions you might have about ethical conduct in business. One is what is the right thing to do. A second is how can we get people to do the right thing. The first type of question is a question in normative ethics. It is answered primarily by philosophers and others who think about the normative dimensions of human behavior (what should be done). The second type of question is a question in descriptive ethics. It is answered by psychologists, sociologists, and others who think about the causes and effects of human behavior (what is done).

This is a book in normative business ethics. It is a work in philosophy, not psychology or sociology. While we will say a few things about the causes and effects of right action, we will focus mostly on what right action in business is.

Before moving on, it is a good idea to say something more about this distinction, because it is important, and forgetting it can lead to confusion or error. The first thing to be said is that, because we are focusing on normative business ethics, we are not going to say a lot about some of the most popular business scandals of the last 20 years. When people hear you are taking a course in business ethics, they might say: "Oh, so you are going to spend time talking about Jeff Skilling, Ken Lay, and Andrew Fastow at Enron, or Bernard Ebbers at WorldCom, or Kweku Adoboli at UBS – people who went to prison for the crimes they committed at their companies." The answer is no; we will not be spending much time on the likes of Skilling, Lay, Fastow, Ebbers, or Adoboli. We don't need to spend a lot of time thinking about the moral dimensions of these cases. This is because what these individuals did was obviously wrong. They were all convicted of securities fraud, which is a kind of deception.

This is not to say, of course, that there is nothing interesting to be said about Skilling, Lay, and the others. It would be very interesting to think about why these people did what they did. Was there a flaw in their characters? Were they subject to irresistible temptations? Did they rationalize away the immorality of their behavior? All of the above? It would also be interesting to think about how organizations can be designed so that less wrongdoing occurs. Would it be helpful for firms to train their employees in ethics? Or reduce temptations to cheat by offering smaller bonus payments? We might want to think that Skilling and Lay were moral monsters, and we would never do something like that. I hope that's right. But in similar circumstances you and I might also be tempted to cheat and lie. Then the question is how those circumstances can be adjusted so that the temptations are removed or that we can more successfully resist them. These are all questions in descriptive ethics. They are questions about why people engage in wrongful behavior and how organizations can be designed so that less wrongful behavior occurs, not whether the behavior is wrongful in the first place. Descriptive questions are not the sorts of questions that we are going to be examining.

The second thing to be said is that, in focusing on normative business ethics, I am not downplaying the importance of descriptive business ethics. To do so would of course be ridiculous. Adoboli's crimes cost UBS billions of dollars. The crimes of Skilling, Lay, Fastow, and Ebbers cost investors billions more dollars and caused thousands of employees to lose their jobs. It is a vital matter to discover what caused these individuals to do what they did and how a repeat of their actions can be prevented.

So, you might add, why aren't we discussing descriptive questions alongside normative ones? The short answer is that there is only so much space in this book.

To cover adequately descriptive issues with as much care as we are discussing normative issues would require a book that is twice as long as this one. Limiting ourselves to normative issues is what allows us to keep our project manageable. While this may seem disappointing, it should not be. There is a lot to learn about our world, including the business world, and so it is natural that not all of it can fit into a single book. Moreover, normative issues in business ethics are no less important – and may in fact be more important – than descriptive ones. Before it makes sense to discuss why people do the wrong thing in business, or how to get them to do the right thing, first we must figure out what the wrong and right things are. That is, the study of normative business ethics is, in this sense, more fundamental than the study of descriptive business ethics. We have to figure out what is right first and then we can begin to think about how to do right.

6. Plan of This Book

This book is meant to offer a reasonably comprehensive introduction to the field of business ethics. We cover a lot of ground.

The next three chapters address foundational issues. Whole books have been written about these issues; we will move quickly. In Chapter 2, we consider the reality of ethics. Very few people say that business doesn't exist or is all an illusion. But some say this about ethics. We begin by addressing this worry. I will try to convince you that it's not something you are truly worried about. We move on in Chapter 3 to consider what ethics requires. We conduct a whirlwind tour of four important ethical theories – consequentialism, deontology, virtue ethics, and Buddhist ethics – asking how we might reconcile the different instructions these theories give us, and more generally, how we make progress in ethics. Our final chapter in this group, Chapter 4, is on political and economic conditions of business. We compare capitalism and socialism, considering what can be said in favor of each system. Much of the business activity we will be concerned with takes place in the context of capitalism. We can only understand why that is if we have a good grasp of arguments for and against both capitalism and socialism. Moreover, few people think that the political and economic system in which they now find themselves is perfect. To understand how it might be improved, we need to understand what the alternatives are and what can be said for them.

Our next group of chapters examines ethical issues in markets. Business is about selling. In Chapter 5, we ask what can be sold. You can buy many things in markets, things like computers, pencils, shoes, cars, houses, and much more. But other things you can't buy, like drop-side cribs, caffeinated alcoholic beverages, bombs, sex, and human embryos. There are some things that are for sale that you might think shouldn't be, like the services of psychic mediums. We ask when an item is the sort of thing that should be sold and when it is not. We next consider, in Chapter 6, how things can be sold. Here our focus is on advertising. We consider ethical issues in deception and persuasion. Most think that deception is wrong, though it can be hard to say what exactly deception is and why it is wrong. We also consider the techniques that advertisers use to persuade us, comparing rational and non-rational persuasion. We conclude this chapter with a brief discussion of pricing, asking whether and when restrictions on prices can be justified.

Having discussed ethical issues that arise in business as an activity, we next consider ethical issues that arise in business as a thing, that is, an entity that sells. We look "inside" the firm to examine ethics in the employment relationships. Chapter 7 starts with a description of working in an Amazon warehouse. We use this description to explore issues of health and safety, meaningfulness, control and participation, and pay. Work in an Amazon warehouse can be dangerous. We consider how safe workplaces should be and who should decide. Many workers in Amazon warehouses perform tedious and boring tasks, over which they have little or no control. We ask whether this is a problem, and if so, who should solve it. Work at Amazon can be incredibly lucrative – just ask Amazon's founder and former CEO, Jeff Bezos, the richest person in the world – but it also can be very poorly paid – just ask the pickers in one of its many warehouses. We consider different views about justice in wages. We remain inside the firm in Chapter 8 to explore additional ethical issues in employment relationships. We begin with ethics in hiring and firing, considering what are good reasons to hire (or not hire) someone, and what are good reasons to fire them. Then we consider privacy at work. Before you hire someone, you probably want to know certain things about them. What things should you be allowed to ask about, and what things are off limits? Our final subject in this chapter is whistleblowing. If your employer is up to no good, when is it permissible to tell someone? When are you required to tell someone? These issues – hiring and firing, privacy, and whistleblowing – are distinct, but they are united by a common theme, and that is information. We are asking what information is relevant for making choices about employment, and what information can pass between employers and employees.

In our final group of chapters, we zoom out from the firm and consider ethical issues that arise from its engagement in society. Chapter 9 examines the classic question of what firms' social responsibilities are. Some believe that they should be focused on making profits for owners or, in the case of corporations, for shareholders. Others believe that this is not required and that businesses managers should attempt to benefit a wider range of stakeholders. We ask what can be said for each approach and then show how the question of whether firms have duties to promote social welfare can sometimes come apart from the question of what goals they should be managed to achieve. Chapter 10 covers the collection of issues that attend firms' engagement in the political arena. Firms exercise political influence not just through lobbying and giving money to political candidates, but by stating what they will do if certain laws are passed (or not passed) and agreeing to systems of private regulation. We consider what can be said for and against such behavior. We close the chapter with a discussion of ethical consumerism, which can be understood as an attempt by consumers to use economic power for political purposes. In Chapter 11, we consider ethical issues that arise when business is conducted across national borders. We consider ethical relativism, sweatshops, corruption, and divestment, all through the lens of the Rana Plaza tragedy. When we do business across borders, we find that people do things differently than us. When do we accept these simply as differences, and when do we object to them as wrong? When they are wrong, what are we supposed to do about it?

I said that this book offers a *reasonably* comprehensive introduction to the field of business ethics. It is not exhaustive. It cannot be; there is too much ground to cover. But it may be worthwhile flagging some of the topics that you might have thought would be discussed in detail, but will not be.

One is the environment. Business activity can affect the environment in profound ways, and it can be evaluated in ethical terms. This book contains no standalone chapter on the environment. But this does not mean that it offers nothing of relevance to environmental issues. Much of the discussion in Chapter 9 on corporate social responsibility can be applied to these issues. Firms' obligations to the environment are structurally similar to their social obligations. In both cases, the question is whether and to what extent firms should try to make the world a better place. The difference is whether they do so by addressing social problems or environmental ones. A second topic that does not receive separate treatment is finance. Financial institutions play a critical role in the world economy, as the financial crisis of 2007–2009 demonstrated. What role they should play is a matter worthy of careful study. Here again, though, the attentive reader will find much in this book of relevance to issues in finance. Some of the drivers of the financial crisis were (1) dishonesty in the marketing of financial products, (2) poorly structured compensation packages for financial executives, and (3) excessive political influence by financial institutions. Food for thought about (1) can be found in Chapter 6 (on marketing), about (2) can be found in Chapter 8 (on employment), and about (3) can be found in Chapter 10 (on politics).

In addition to the environment and finance, you may have hoped that more would be said about accounting, artificial intelligence, conflicts of interest, data security, insider trading, leadership, sales, and other topics. These are all worthy of discussion but regrettably could not be addressed in this limited space. I have focused on what I think are foundational issues in business ethics. These are important in themselves but also prepare you to think through other issues.

7. Chapter Summary

This is a book about business ethics. This chapter explained what business is: 'business' can refer to an entity that offers goods for sale (like Walmart or

Amazon) or an exchange activity (I prefer to do business with Walmart over Amazon). We will consider ethical issues that attend both aspects of business. We then explained what ethics is: we are doing ethics when we ask what we should do, and we don't mean simply "what we should do to achieve business objectives." The 'should' of ethics is non-instrumental. In our study of business ethics, we will have to consider both laws and individual actions. In some cases, we will think that laws are wrong and need to be changed, but thinking that "things should be different than they now are" does not necessarily mean laws should be changed – sometimes laws should be left alone and people should behave differently.

Some people try to make a "business case" for studying business ethics. They claim that acting ethically in the business arena will pay off for you or your firm. This is an empirical thesis, and our best evidence does not confirm it (or show that it is false). But ask yourself the question: "Am I a good person who wants to do the right thing?" If the answer is 'yes', and for many of you it will be, then you already have a strong reason to study business ethics. This book will help you to fulfill your goal by making you more aware of ethical issues in business and giving you the concepts and tools necessary to determine what to do. This book does not tell you what to do, because the problems discussed here are difficult, and consensus does not exist. Even if it did, you need to learn to think through things for yourself, because the problems you encounter in business will be unique – they will depend on facts, circumstances, obligations, and consequences particular to the situation in which you find yourself. This is a book in normative business ethics – it focuses on discovering the right thing to do. Questions in descriptive business ethics – questions like 'why do people do the wrong thing?' and 'how can we design firms so that less wrongdoing occurs?' – are important, but they will not be our main focus. We concluded with an outline of the chapters of the book. We are ready to get going.

8. Study Questions

1. People use 'business' in two ways. What are these ways?
2. What is ethics?
3. The 'should' of ethics is different than the 'should' of marketing. Explain the difference.
4. When studying business ethics, you will think about both laws and individual actions. Give an example of one law and one action that might be the subject of debate in business ethics.
5. Some people think that if an action is morally wrong, it should be prohibited by law. Why might this not be a good idea?
6. Some people say that we should study business ethics because "ethics pays." What do they mean by this? Can you think of an example in which

being ethical paid off? Can you think of an example in which it didn't? In general, what should we make of this claim?

7. What reasons – other than being professionally successful – might a person have for studying business ethics? What reasons do you have for studying business ethics?
8. Why might it be impossible for a book in business ethics to tell you what to think or do when you are faced with an ethical dilemma?
9. What is the difference between descriptive ethics and normative ethics? Is this book primarily a work in descriptive ethics or normative ethics?
10. Based on what you know now, what do you think is the most important issue in the field of business ethics?

Additional Readings

Bazerman, M. H., & Tenbrunsel, A. E. (2011). *Blind spots: Why we fail to do what's right and what to do about it*. Princeton, NJ: Princeton University Press.

Crisp, R. (2003). A defense of philosophical business ethics. In W. H. Shaw (Ed.), *Ethics at work: Basic readings in business ethics* (pp. 1–14). New York: Oxford University Press.

Dunfee, T. W. (1996). On the synergistic, interdependent relationship of business ethics and law. *American Business Law Journal*, *34*(2), 317–325.

Goodpaster, K. (2007). *Conscience and corporate culture*. Malden, MA: Blackwell Publishing.

Marcoux, A. M. (2006). The concept of business in business ethics. *Journal of Private Enterprise*, *21*(2), 50–67.

Margolis, J., Elfenbein, H., & Walsh, J. (2009). Does it pay to be good . . . and does it matter? A meta-analysis of the relationship between corporate social and financial performance. Available at SSRN: https://ssrn.com/abstract=1866371 or http://dx.doi.org/10.2139/ssrn.1866371

May, J. (n.d.). Psychological egoism. *Internet Encyclopedia of Philosophy*. https://iep.utm.edu/psychego/

Schmidtz, D. (1993). Reasons for altruism. *Social Philosophy and Policy*, *10*(1), 52–68.

Vogel, D. J. (2005). Is there a market for virtue?: The business case for corporate social responsibility. *California Management Review*, *47*(4), 19–45.

2 Skepticism About Ethics

Our subject is business ethics. No one would say that business is unreal, or fake, or just an illusion. But some people say something like this about ethics. So it would be a mistake to go any further without addressing skepticism about ethics. By 'skepticism about ethics' I mean doubt about whether ethical claims can be true or false and doubt about whether any ethical claims can be proven true or false.

There are lots of ways to be skeptical about ethics. What I want to do is to consider one big skeptical challenge to ethics: the claim that there are facts and opinions, and ethics belongs to the realm of opinions. It turns out that this challenge is more complex than it may at first appear and can be used to state several distinct skeptical challenges to ethics. In this chapter we will unpack and analyze them. I will provide some reasons for thinking that we should not be skeptical about ethics in the way this challenge suggests – and I will argue that you think this too.

1. Facts Versus Opinions

When business ethics – or ethics more generally – comes up, it is common to hear something like "it's all a matter of opinion." On this view, there are no facts about business ethics (or ethics generally), just opinions. Perhaps you have said this yourself. If ethics, including business ethics, is just a matter of opinion, then it might seem that it's not worth thinking hard about. You've got your opinion, and I've got mine, and we can't say one is better than the other.

This is a misguided way of thinking and speaking. Seeing exactly how it is misguided is going to take some work, so you're going to need to be patient. At the end of this chapter, I will provide a replacement for the language of facts and opinions.

On the standard definition, factual statements are statements that are true and can be proved to be true. '2 + 2 = 4' seems like an example of a factual statement. So do "the earth is a sphere" and "my dining room table is made of wood."

What might people be saying when they say that ethics is just a matter of opinion? The standard definition of a fact has two components: one that makes a point about what is the case (the earth is a sphere) and another that makes a

DOI: 10.4324/9781351016872-2

point about what we can prove (we can prove the earth is a sphere). Philosophers would call the first a point in *metaphysics* and the second a point in *epistemology*. So if you said that ethics is not a fact of matter, and is instead merely a matter of opinion, you might be denying either the metaphysical point or the epistemological point. That is, you might be denying either that ethical statements can be true (this is the metaphysical point) or you might be denying that we can prove the truth of ethical statements (this is the epistemological point). I will say something about each of these concerns.

2. Truth

Let us start with the first concern – the worry that ethical statements can't be true. What should we make of this?

This is a really important question. If ethical statements can't be true, then ethics is in trouble. In a world in which ethical statements aren't true, we could still engage in some "ethics-like" inquiries. We could, for example, ask what values people actually have. We could try to determine whether the values people say they have are the values that they act on. We might be able to align people's actions with the values that they say that they have. But we could not ask whether people have the correct values or whether the ethical statements they make are the correct ones. Ethics would still exist, but it would have a much more limited content.

Now a confession. I can't demonstrate that there are ethical truths. Philosophers spend their careers investigating this question. Instead, what I will try to do is give a clearer explanation of why you might think that ethical statements cannot be true and then provide some reasons for thinking that ethical statements can be true. Moreover, I will try to show you that *you already* think that ethical statements can be true. You might try to claim that there is no ethical truth to get out of a debate (e.g., in a business ethics class), but deep down, you don't think this.

It will be useful to have an example in mind for our discussion. Let us use this:

1. Burning down your competitors' factories is wrong.

What could it mean to say that this statement is not true? This question can be answered in various ways. First, you might say that ethical statements don't really try to tell us something that is true or false. Second, you might say that ethical statements try to tell us something true but fail, because they are all false. I will consider these possibilities in turn.

2.1. Neither True nor False?

Some people think that ethical statements – statements like (1) – don't really try to tell us something that is true or false. According to these people, statements like (1) are merely disguised expressions of emotion or perhaps disguised commands.

According to the first of these possibilities, the person who says, "It is wrong to burn down your competitors' factories," is just expressing a negative feeling about this. They are saying something like this: "Boo! Burning down your competitors' factories." This statement is neither true nor false. In the same way, when I cheer for my team – "Woo-hoo Celtics!" – my cheering is neither true nor false. It is simply an expression of how I feel. (Of course, if I said, "I like the Celtics" or "The Celtics will win the NBA championship," *those statements* could be true or false, depending on how I feel and what happens in the future.) Philosophers have a name for this view. They call it 'emotivism'.

According to the second of these possibilities, the person who says, "Burning down your competitors' factories is wrong," is giving us a command or telling us how we should live. She is telling business owners "don't burn down your competitors' factories." This is another type of utterance that cannot be true or false. It would be like a parent telling his child not to do drugs. The parent is not saying it is true (or false) that the child *will* do drugs. The parent is not even saying that he *wants* the child not to do drugs, though that may also be true. He is issuing a command: don't do drugs. Philosophers also have a name for this view. They call it 'prescriptivism'. Are ethical statements really like this? I want to say 'no', and I think you want to say 'no' too.

In the first place, it certainly looks like (1) – burning down your competitors' factories is wrong – is trying to tell us something that is true. (1) has the same grammatical structure as familiar true claims like "the earth is a sphere" and "my dining room table is made of wood." In each case, there is a thing (the earth, my dining room table, burning down your competitors' factories) that is supposed to have a certain property (sphericalness, woodenness, wrongness). Either the thing has this property, or it doesn't. You are saying the thing has that property. If ethical statements were simply expressions of emotion or commands, then this sort of analysis would not make sense. Mere expressions of emotions or commands do not attempt to describe the world.

A second reason for thinking that emotivism and prescriptivism aren't the correct views about ethics comes from thinking about *justification* in ethics. Everyone might agree with the claim that burning down your competitors' factories is wrong. But consider a claim about which there might be reasonable disagreement, like this one:

2. It is wrong for employers to ask their employees whether they smoke.

You might think that it is impermissible for employers to ask employees whether they smoke. I might think it is permissible for them to do so. What then? Well, we might explain to each other our *reasons* for our (opposite) points of view.

You might say something about how all employees deserve to be able to keep their private lives private. I might say something about how smokers take more sick days and employers deserve to be able to hire the steadiest employees. That is, we try to justify our points of view to each other. This wouldn't make sense if we didn't think we were saying something true. "Woo-hoo Celtics" doesn't require a justification. It is simply an expression of emotion. And while I might have reasons why I want my children not to do drugs, and why doing drugs is a bad idea, my command to them, "Don't do drugs," need not be supported by reasons. It is simply a command. Insofar as we think it is appropriate to provide reasons for our ethical claims, or to try to justify them to each other, then we are offering them as claims that can be true or false.

2.2. *All False?*

In the previous section we considered views that say that ethical statements do not even try to tell us something that is true about the world. Understood properly, the emotivists and prescriptivists say that ethical statements are neither true nor false. They are, respectively, expressions of emotion or commands. We then considered some reasons for thinking that these views are false.

Another form of skepticism about truth in ethics says that ethical statements do try to tell us something that is true about the world but fail to do so. Ethical statements always tell us something that is false, this form of skepticism says, because ethical properties do not exist. Philosophers call this view 'error theory', because it says we are in error about the existence of ethics.

Consider again (1) – burning down your competitors' factories is wrong. According to error theory, this statement tries to say something true – that burning down your competitors' factories has the property *wrongness* – but fails to do so, because there is no such thing as *wrongness*. Error theory says that ethical statements are like statements about witches (of the sort that cast spells on people and ride around on broomsticks). Consider the claim "Hagatha is a witch." This claim tries to say something true – that Hagatha has the property of *being a witch*. But it says something false, because Hagatha does not have the property of *being a witch*. No one has this property, because there are no such things as witches (no people who cast spells or ride on broomsticks).

Error theorists make a claim about what is in the world – or more precisely, what isn't. The question is, why believe them? You might believe them because you can't perceive anything in the world that seems like a moral property. If I light a match and set my competitor's factory on fire, we can point to the match, the factory, and the fire. We can perceive the heat that comes off the blazing building and see the color of the flames. But it's not clear where the "wrongness" is in all this. You might think, more generally, that there is nothing in the world that is even *like* a moral property. Moral properties are supposed to be action-guiding. When we perceive the wrongness of lighting a competitor's factory on fire, you know you shouldn't do it. But that doesn't seem to be the case. There doesn't seem to be anything in the world that demands that we act in a certain way.

Yet there is room for doubt about the error theorist's claims. It is possible that moral properties do exist but are in fact identical with other properties. Perhaps the wrongness of lighting your competitor's factory on fire consists in the fact that it makes your competitor very sad. Sadness is surely a real thing. Perhaps moral properties are identical with "natural" properties like sadness or happiness, or perhaps the satisfaction or frustration of desires. Or perhaps moral properties are not identical with natural properties but are somehow "non-natural." The question here is whether the only things that exist in our world are natural things (whatever "natural" might mean).

We cannot hope to solve this problem here. To solve it we'd have to learn a lot more about what moral properties (wrong and right, good and bad) are supposed to be like and about what kinds of things are in the world. We would need to study a lot more metaphysics. For our purposes, the key takeaway is that error theory is still very much in doubt. Error theorists have not provided us good reason for thinking that all ethical statements are false.

2.3. Why You (Probably) Think Some Ethical Claims Are True

This might seem like cold comfort. We have said that error theory – the view that there are no moral properties, so all ethical claims are false – is in doubt. Don't you want to know that error theory is *false* – and in particular, that some ethical claims *could be true* – before spending your time studying business ethics? In business ethics we will be supposing that some ethical claims could be true and trying to figure out which claims these are.

Let me say two things about this. First, every inquiry – like this inquiry into business ethics – has to start somewhere, and in particular, by making a set of assumptions. If you tried to justify all of your assumptions, you would never get to where you wanted to go. This is true as a general matter. Here is a thing that you might be wondering about right now: what should I eat for dinner tonight? Should it be chicken, or fish, or maybe tofu?

In devoting time to this inquiry, you are making certain assumptions. You are assuming mundane things like the grocery store will be open, and they will sell you food. You are also assuming less mundane things like you will not be abducted by aliens, and you will not be called up to pitch for the Yankees this evening. Should you put your inquiry into what you will have for dinner on hold until you can justify your assumptions about the grocery store, aliens, and the Yankees?

The first thing we might observe is that people don't do this. They think about what to have for dinner all the time without justifying their assumption that having dinner will be a possibility for them. The second thing is that all of this seems quite reasonable. We live in a world in which people routinely have dinner. Given this, it seems reasonable to think about what to have for dinner, even if it is also the case that, due to unforeseen circumstances, you might not have dinner. The same is true, I am suggesting, about business ethics. It is true that an inquiry into business ethics assumes that "right" and "wrong" exist in some fashion and that some writers contest this assumption. But this should also not bother us too much, because many of our inquiries – like an inquiry into what to have for dinner tonight – make certain assumptions, which seem reasonable but which we cannot easily justify.

Now you might say: "Well, it seems reasonable to assume that I will have dinner tonight, because I have had it so many times before. But why think it is reasonable to suppose that ethical claims can be true?" Again, I can't prove that there are ethical truths here. I would simply point out that you probably think and act as if there are ethical truths across a wide range of human activities. An inquiry into business ethics asks you to make the same assumptions about the reality of ethics in business that you are already making about the reality of ethics in the rest of your life. Let me explain.

Navigate to your favorite news website, and you will be inundated with ethical commentary – about the morality of abortion and euthanasia, the justice of the tax code, fair play in sports, and much more. In saying things like "abortion is wrong" or "women should have the right to choose," the talking heads are assuming that ethical properties exist, and attach, as it were, to certain actions. You have probably heard your parents and friends make ethical claims too, claims like "it is wrong to waste your time partying when you should be studying" or "it is wrong to ghost a romantic partner." The talking heads, your parents, and your friends are trying to convince you that what they are saying is *true*, and you should believe it too. I suspect you find nothing odd or confused about these claims. But you would if you thought that ethical properties do not exist. It would be as if the talking heads, your parents, and your friends started talking about who was and who wasn't a witch. Instead, I think that you evaluate what they say with a view to assessing its truth. You might come to agree with them or you might disagree. But in doing so, you are assuming that what they say could be true.

In fact, you don't have to navigate to your favorite news website, or talk to your parents or friends, to observe this phenomenon. Your instructor could produce it for you right now. Suppose you are a conscientious student who works hard on their assignments. Suppose that your instructor now says: "Grading is a pain. Instead of reading your assignments and assessing their merits, I'm just going to pick a grade out of a hat for each of you." You think: this is unfair. And while this may sound redundant, you think it is *true* that this is unfair. Suppose that when you complain to your instructor, she says: "Well, that is your view. My view is different. I think that it is not unfair to assign grades this way." Would you respond: "Ah, I see we have different views, and since there is no truth here, I guess the discussion ends." I bet not! I bet you would say: "We have different views, but your view is *wrong* and my view is *right*. More precisely, it is *true* that assigning grades by drawing numbers out of a hat is unfair. Your view is false."

What does this mean for our current inquiry into business ethics? When you start to think hard about the foundations of ethics, it is easy – and in fact even desirable – to question its existence. But leave this inquiry alone for just a moment, and you are immediately snapped back into a rich and complex moral life. You assume across a wide range of human activities – abortion, euthanasia, romance, grading – that there are such things as ethical truths. When people make ethical statements, you do not think that they are confused. Rather, you consider whether those statements are true. Moreover, you have good reasons to think and act in this way. What I am saying here is that you should extend this same courtesy to business. We are going to be making and evaluating claims about the ethical aspects of exchange activities. Insofar as you believe claims about abortion, ghosting, and grading can be true (or false), you should believe claims in business ethics can be true (or false).

I do not suppose that I have said anything nearly sufficient to convince the diehard skeptic about ethics. I have not proven that there are ethical facts or that ethical statements are true. Rather, I have given you some reasons to think that there is truth in ethics. Indeed, I hope to have alerted you to the fact that, in some cases at least, you already think this.

3. Proof

We are considering the suggestion that business ethics is not worth our time because in ethics, there are not facts, only opinions. We saw that the claim that business ethics is "all a matter of opinion" combines a metaphysical claim – there are no true statements in ethics – with an epistemological claim – we cannot prove the truth of statements in ethics. We considered the metaphysical claim in the previous section. Now we will consider the epistemological claim.

Like the suggestion that there is no truth about ethics, the suggestion that we can't get to the truth about ethics must be taken seriously. If nothing can ever be proven, you might think, then why waste our time on ethics? People will just be talking without getting anywhere. Also like the problem of truth in ethics, the problem of proof in ethics is not one that we can hope to resolve decisively here. Instead, what I want to do is to give you some reasons for thinking that we can prove the truth of some claims in ethics and to convince you that you already think that we can.

Before we get to the question of proofs, it is worth emphasizing that the question of whether ethical claims can be proven to be true is different from the question of whether ethical claims can be true. If an ethical statement – burning down your competitor's factory is wrong – is not true, then obviously it cannot be proven to be true. But just because a statement cannot be proven to be true, or cannot be proven true right now, doesn't mean it isn't true. For as long as our solar system has existed, the earth has revolved around the sun. But this wasn't proven to be true until Nicolaus Copernicus came along. So even if you end up thinking that ethical claims cannot be proven to be true, this need not lead you to revise your judgment that ethical claims can indeed be true. In what follows in this chapter, I will give some reasons for thinking that ethical claims can indeed be proven to be true.

3.1. Proofs and Arguments

First things first. Talk of proofs may call to mind mathematics, where a proof consists of a string of numbers and symbols. You typically don't find these sorts of things in ethics. But that does not mean that there are no proofs in ethics – or proofs in other fields, such as marketing, management, or communications. A proof just is *evidence sufficient to establish the truth of a claim.* What counts as evidence differs from field to field. What counts as evidence in mathematics is different from what counts as evidence in marketing, management, and law.

Aristotle, the ancient Greek philosopher, said that:

> It is the mark of an educated person to look for precision in each class of things just as far as the nature of the subject admits; it is evidently equally foolish to accept probable reasoning from a mathematician and to demand from a rhetorician scientific proofs.

Aristotle's point is that different kinds of claims require different kinds of justification. You will get one sort of justification in math and biology and another sort of justification in sociology and anthropology – and yes, business ethics. It would be a mistake to think that the only sort of reasoning that is real and solid is the kind that you find in math. The reasoning that you find in business ethics is still good reasoning; it is just different than the kind of reasoning that you find in math.

In philosophy, to which normative business ethics belongs, a proof takes the form of an *argument*. Arguments will typically contain several premises and a conclusion. The premises may consist of factual statements – for example, statements about the effects of a particular action – and value statements – for example, statements that a certain effect is good or bad. The point of the premises is to justify the conclusion. That is what they are there for.

We need to be careful here. To prove a claim is to provide an argument, which shows that the claim is true. So to say you have a proof is to say that you have an argument that is *successful*. But arguments can fail to prove their conclusions; they can be unsuccessful. To make things still more complicated, arguments might fail to prove their conclusions, in the sense of establishing for certain that they are true, but still provide evidence for their conclusions. To avoid biasing the discussion, then, it is best to talk of arguments rather than proofs. The question at hand is whether any arguments in business ethics provide good reasons to believe their conclusions.

Already this may address some worries about proofs in ethics. You might have thought that there are no proofs in ethics because you thought that arguments had to contain numbers or mathematical symbols. But a proof is just a successful argument, that is, an argument that provides evidence that is sufficient to establish the truth of a claim. We can have evidence that is sufficient to establish the truth of a claim even if we don't have numbers or symbols.

There is a lot that could be said about arguments. Entire classes are devoted to logic and critical reasoning. We cannot summarize a class's worth of material here, but we can say a bit more about what arguments are like and what makes them successful or unsuccessful.

3.2. *Types of Arguments*

Arguments can be usefully divided into two kinds: deductive and inductive. The main difference lies in the strength of the evidence that the premises are meant to provide for the conclusion. A deductive argument is an argument that attempts to guarantee the truth of its conclusion. An argument is *valid* if the truth of its premises guarantees the truth of its conclusion. If, in addition to being valid, the premises actually are true, then the argument is *sound.* By contrast, an inductive argument can at best provide strong evidence for its conclusion. A good inductive argument says that its conclusion is probably true but does not say that it is certainly true.

Here is an example of a deductive argument.

1. All public companies have shareholders.
2. Apple is a public company.
3. Therefore, Apple has shareholders.

In this argument (1) and (2) are premises, and (3) is the conclusion. This argument is valid. You can see this if you strip away the content of (1), (2), and (3). When we do this, we see that (1) says, "All P's are Q's"; (2) says, "A is a P"; and (3) concludes, "A is a Q." Surely, if all P's are Q's, and a thing is a P, then that thing is also a Q. If all tables have legs, then, if you are reading this at a table, then you are reading this at a thing with legs. This argument is also sound. That is because it is true that all public companies have shareholders and that

Apple is a public company. As a result, it is guaranteed to be true that Apple has shareholders.

Here is an example of an inductive argument.

1. Apple has the coolest packaging for its products; it also has the highest profit margins.
2. The first thing the new CEO did was to redesign the packaging that the firm's products came in.
3. All business students should take courses in graphic design if they want to be successful.
4. The attractiveness of packaging for a product fully determines whether it is a commercial success.

In this argument, (1), (2), and (3) are premises, and (4) is the conclusion. It doesn't make sense to call this argument "valid" or "invalid." Because a sound argument is one that is valid and has all true premises, it doesn't make sense to call this argument "sound" or "unsound" either. We reserve these labels for deductive arguments. Statements (1), (2), and (3) do, however, *provide evidence* for (4). For they provide concrete cases in which packaging matters to sales. However, (1), (2), and (3) do not guarantee the truth of (4). We can see this because we can think of counterexamples to (4). Many businesses thrive despite not having attractive packaging for their products, and some products struggle commercially despite having attractive packaging. In fact, since this argument provides only three cases where the attractiveness of a product's packaging is connected to its commercial success, it provides relatively weak evidence for the conclusion that having attractive packaging will lead to commercial success. This argument could be strengthened by identifying other cases in which attractive packaging leads to commercial success or by providing an explanation of this phenomenon.

3.3. How to Evaluate Arguments

When you read texts in business ethics or engage in arguments about business ethics topics, you are rarely going to see the arguments laid out in stepwise fashion, as they were laid out in the previous section. But it can be useful for you to try to lay them out in this fashion. This will help you to identify all the relevant pieces of the argument, including the various premises and the conclusion. Doing so provides you an opportunity to confirm that the argument does not smuggle in the conclusion as one of the premises – philosophers call that move "begging the question." It will also help you to identify which parts of the argument are strong and which are weak and so where to start your evaluation.

When evaluating arguments, above all, what you are trying to do is determine whether its premises are true and whether they provide support for the conclusion.

Whether a premise is true might be obvious, but it might not be. Establishing the truth of a premise might itself require additional facts or arguments. For the premises in an argument to provide support for the conclusion, they have to be related in the right way to the conclusion. This is perhaps easier to explain by example than in the abstract. Suppose I made the following argument:

1. Bill Gates is rich. (premise)
2. It is cold outside. (premise)
3. I am hungry. (conclusion)

You would say that I am confused. The premises are not related in the right way to the conclusion. They do not provide support for the conclusion.

When evaluating arguments, we should not only look at what is "good" about them – whether the premises are true and whether they support the conclusion – but also consider whether anything is "bad" about them. The process might be similar to buying a used car. You should be thinking about not only the good parts of the car but also its problems.

In this spirit, in the remainder of this section, I will identify a few of the ways that arguments go wrong. One was already mentioned. That is, you should consider whether there are any *counterexamples* to what is being claimed. A counterexample is a case that contradicts what is being claimed. The inductive argument mentioned earlier claims that "the attractiveness of the packaging for a product fully determines whether it is a commercial success." A search for a counterexample to this claim is a search for a product that is successful despite having unattractive packaging. If a counterexample can be found, then you know that the generalization that is being made is unjustified.

A second thing to keep in mind is whether any of the premises, or even the conclusion, in an argument *leads to a contradiction*, or otherwise has *absurd* results. This is perhaps especially true when evaluating the plausibility of moral claims. Suppose I said that people should never violate other people's rights. Rights are important, you might think, and so you might agree to this. But think this through more carefully. Think about all the rights that you have, all the ways that they might be violated, and most importantly, for what purposes your rights might be violated. Suppose you own a small cabin in the woods. You have a right to use this cabin, which means you can exclude others from using it. A person cannot just wander in from the woods and sleep in your bed. But suppose the person is not wandering in the woods but running from a bear, and the only place she can go to avoid being eaten is your cabin. If this person enters your cabin without your consent, however, she would be violating your rights. Should this person really not do so, on the grounds that it would violate your rights? Or should we modify the initial claim that people's rights should not be violated? (Of course, you might "bite the bullet" and claim that this person should not enter your cabin and should instead be devoured by the bear. But this is still a useful exercise. You are thinking through the full range of implications of the claims that are being made and asking whether they are acceptable.)

A third thing you should keep in mind when evaluating arguments is whether the *terms* in the arguments are *clear and precise*. An argument might appear to succeed only because it depends on an ambiguity – a double-meaning – in one of its terms. Suppose you said to me: "I want to be an accountant. Nothing is better than accounting." Suppose I replied: "But you will admit that being a philosopher is better than nothing." Suppose you agree to this. "Ah, ha!" I exclaim, "so you think that being a philosopher is better than being an accountant!" I explain: "You've said that philosophy is better than nothing, and nothing is better than accounting. Philosophy > Nothing > Accounting." You will feel, correctly, that some trick has been pulled on you. The way the trick works is by trading on an ambiguity in the word 'nothing'. When you say that "nothing is better than accounting," you are saying that *there is no job that is better than being an accountant*. When you say that "being a philosopher is better than nothing," you are saying that *being a philosopher is better than having no job at all*. These are clearly different things. There is a general point here. That is, you should be able to ask for, and receive, a precise definition of any term that is being used in an argument. If a clear definition isn't available, then that's a problem.

To take an example that's perhaps a bit closer to the subject matter at hand, suppose I claimed that employers should be able to take reasonable measures to ensure that their employees are not stealing from them. You might agree to this. So we are in agreement? Maybe, but maybe not. Much depends on what is meant by 'reasonable'. We might both agree that it is reasonable for employers to be able to search employees' bags when they leave company property. But we might disagree about whether it is reasonable for employers to install surveillance cameras in all areas of the workplace. The lesson is this. Even if terms are not ambiguous, they can be unclear, and this unclarity can mask disagreement. We must try to be as precise as possible in our use of language.

Finally, many arguments in business ethics make use of analogies. For example, some people argue that business is like a game. So, they say, the ethical code that is appropriate for business is similar to the ethical code that is appropriate for games or sports. "Hard bargaining" is permissible among competitors in business but not between friends splitting a dinner bill. To take another example – and a different analogy – some people argue that firms are like states. So, they say, if the citizens of a state should have a role in making the state's decisions, then the employees of a firm should have a role in making the firm's decisions. When evaluating these sorts of arguments, the question to ask yourself is, *how good is the analogy*? Is business *really* like a game? Is the firm *really* like a state? The better the analogy – the more alike (for example) firms and states are – the more likely it is that the conclusions we reach about states can also be applied to firms. The worse the analogy, the less likely it is that these conclusions can be imported from one context into another.

Let's remind ourselves what we're doing. We are considering the idea that we cannot prove anything in business ethics. We have said that a proof is simply *evidence sufficient to establish the truth of a claim*. In business ethics, proofs take the form of successful arguments. So we have said a bit about what arguments are and how to evaluate them. Just a bit: if you want to learn more, you should pick up a book or take a class on critical reasoning and informal logic. Insofar as you believe that successful arguments can be made for claims in business ethics, you should not be turned off from the study of business ethics by the skeptical claim that there are no proofs in business ethics.

3.4. Arguments in Business Ethics?

You might still be unsatisfied. You might say that of course we can make arguments for claims in *business*. And some of these arguments can even be sufficient to establish the truth of business claims. But you might remain skeptical that we can make successful arguments for claims in business *ethics*. To this point, you might note that the examples of arguments that we gave previously, which concluded that Apple has shareholders and that product packaging matters, are not claims about business *ethics* but about other aspects of the practice of business.

To an extent, the answer to this question can be found in the remainder of this book, where arguments for claims in business ethics are made and examined. To the extent that you find these arguments successful, then you will be persuaded that proofs in business ethics are possible. But you might want some reassurance going in, which I will now provide.

Consider again this claim, which is clearly a claim in business ethics.

1. Burning down your competitor's factory is wrong.

We argued in Section 2 that we have good reasons for thinking that claims like (1) can be true or false. In fact, I think that it is true, and I bet you do too. Our subject in Section 3 has been proof. Can claims like (1) be proven? Here is an attempt.

i. It is wrong to destroy other people's stuff without their consent. (ethical principle)
ii. When you burn something down, you destroy it. (fact)

iii. Your competitor did not give you permission to burn down her factory. (assumption)
iv. Burning down your competitor's factory is wrong. (conclusion)

Remember what we should look for when we evaluate arguments. We should look for premises that are true and that support the conclusion, which in this case is (iv).

Premise (ii) seems pretty clearly true. Reducing a building to ashes transforms the building in a way that destroys it. Premise (iii) is an assumption we are making for the purposes of argument. If you are wary of this, you might imagine that it is my factory we are talking about, and I have not given permission to anyone to burn it down. That leaves (i), the claim that it is wrong to destroy other people's stuff without their consent. That seems clearly true to me. Doesn't it seem true to you too? What would it mean to deny (i)? Would it mean that you would think it's fine if I piled up all of your possessions and lit them on fire? I doubt you would think that this would be fine. I think you would object. You would object by saying something very much like (i).

Do the premises provide support for the conclusion? It seems to me that they do. Minimally, the premises are "about" the conclusion. The conclusion says that burning down your competitor's factory is wrong, and the premises articulate moral principles and assert facts relating to burning something down. More specifically, the argument asserts a plausible moral principle – it is wrong to destroy other people's stuff without their consent – and adduces relevant facts to show that this principle would be violated by the burning down of your competitor's factory.

Beyond looking at what's "good" about the argument – whether its premises are true and provide support for the conclusion – we also need to look at what might be "bad" about it – whether it contains any of the kinds of errors we identified in Section 3.3. These are errors related to counterexamples, absurd conclusions, imprecise terminology, or bad analogies. The argument does not depend on an analogy, so there is no problem there. The argument's terms seem clear and precise. As far as counterexamples or absurd implications go – I don't see any. Do you?

If you find the contemplation of this example too far removed from your experience, you might return to the example of the unfair teacher – the teacher who assigns grades by drawing numbers out of a hat. We said that you are likely to think that this is unfair. You will regard your thought – this is unfair – as *true*. Now imagine, as before, that your instructor says: "Well, that is your view. My view is different. I think it is fair to assign grades this way." I suspect you will regard your instructor's claim as *false*. In Section 2, we gave reasons for thinking that this is a reasonable way to think about this. That is, it is reasonable to think that, when it comes to claims about ethics, it makes sense to speak of true claims and false claims.

But I think that you will do more than simply *assert* that what you think – that the instructor's way of assigning grades is unfair – is true. You will think that you can *prove* that it is true. There are a lot of ways that you might do this. You might note that the syllabus says that your grade will be determined by the quality of your assignments, and the syllabus represents a kind of promise that instructors make to students. When the instructor decides not to base students' grades on the quality of their assignments, but instead on numbers drawn out of a hat, the instructor breaks her promise to you. Or you might appeal to the purpose of grades. You might say that the purpose of assigning grades is to get students to work hard on their assignments. If grades are determined by numbers drawn out of a hat, then the purpose of assigning grades will not be realized. I'm sure that you can think of other ways to try to prove that this is unfair. What Section 3 of this chapter has been trying to do is to validate efforts like these. You already think that you can prove certain ethical claims to be true. Section 3 has given you some additional tools to help you do so.

We've done it! We have shown how to prove claims in business ethics. Of course, we have not proven very many claims, but we have done enough to get our task going. In this book we will be making and evaluating arguments, trying to establish where the truth lies when it comes to business ethics. This chapter has tried to prove that this sort of thing is possible.

3.5. A Couple of Loose Ends

You may still be skeptical. That is fine. As I said, the best way to show that things can be proven in business ethics is by proving those things or at least earnestly trying to prove them through deliberation and debate. That is what this book prepares you to do.

Let me close with two notes of caution. These notes are meant to provide you some comfort when you are deep in thought about business ethics, or deep in debate with others of good faith, and you begin to think that perhaps the truth cannot be found out after all.

First, it is important to keep in mind the distinction between proving a claim – producing an argument that provides evidence sufficient to establish that claim – and convincing someone to believe it. You can convince someone to believe something without producing sufficient evidence to establish it. And you can produce evidence sufficient to establish the truth of a claim and not get everyone to believe you. To see that this is true, we need to look no further than the members of the flat earth society. This is a group of individuals dedicated to the defense and promulgation of the view that the earth is flat. These individuals are wrong. The earth is a sphere. So these individuals believe that the earth is flat despite not having anything like a proof that it is flat. (They probably think that they have good reasons to believe that the earth is flat, but they are wrong to think this.) In fact, we have proof that the earth is a sphere, which flat-earthers refuse to accept.

Just as the existence of the flat earth society should not lead us to doubt that we have proof that the earth is a sphere, so the existence of people who do not believe – on the basis of the argument given earlier – that burning down your competitor's factory is wrong should not lead us to doubt that we have proof that it is wrong to burn down your competitor's factory. It is one thing to prove a claim and another to get someone to accept your proof. People can be bad reasoners, and they may not accept your proof, even if it is a good one. In this book, we are interested primarily in assessing the merits of arguments, not thinking about what actually persuades people.

Second, we don't generally talk about the easy stuff here. This is intentional. It would be a waste of time to fill a book on business ethics with things that are obviously true – things like "don't burn down your competitor's factory," or "don't defraud investors," or "don't subject underperforming employees to corporal punishment." (Of course, it is not obvious why these actions are wrong and what makes people do these things – that may require philosophical or psychological analysis.) We address hard questions – questions like these: Do corporations have an obligation to try to solve social problems? Should employers be able to make demands on how employees spend time outside of work? When should firms divest from severely ethically compromised business environments? The fact that we address only the hard questions may make you think that problems in business ethics cannot be solved and that we cannot prove one or the other side of the debate. Because the problems are hard, you will find reasonable people of good faith on both, or all, sides of the debate.

But the fact that we can prove things when it comes to the easy cases – involving the morality of burning down your competitor's factory or an instructor's assigning grades by drawing numbers out of a hat – should persuade you that we can prove things when it comes to the hard cases too. But since these cases are hard, it will be harder to arrive at answers. This is perfectly normal and even expected. It is easy for a mechanic to "figure out" the cause of a flat tire – just look for the hole. It may be harder for her to figure out the cause of a pinging in the engine. But she should believe that an answer can be found if she uses all of her skills and expertise. That is the attitude with which you should approach the hard questions that we will be discussing in business ethics.

As this last example shows, there is nothing unique about business ethics, or ethics in general, in this respect. There are a lot of problems in the world that are hard. The solutions to these problems are not obvious and require a lot of careful thought. The right approach is not to throw up your hands in despair or, more skeptically, to believe that there are no right answers to be found. It is instead to roll up your sleeves and do your best to discover the answers. Mechanics do this, but so do plumbers, carpenters, accountants, medical researchers, chemists, and many others. I am suggesting that we adopt this same attitude when it comes to problems in business ethics.

This is not to say, of course, that you will be able to solve all of the problems of business ethics when you are done reading this book. Some problems are very hard indeed, and solutions may be hard to come by. But you have reason to believe that if you understand the problems and approach them with the right tools, you will be able to go some way toward solving them. This is a good thing, because we will confront ethical issues in business whether we want to or not.

4. Chapter Summary

We started this chapter talking about facts and opinions. We considered the skeptical challenge to ethics that says that ethics is all a matter of opinion. When you unpack this claim, you see that one of two things could be meant. One is the metaphysical claim that there is no truth in ethics. The second is the epistemological claim that we cannot prove things in ethics. We noted that we could not establish decisively either that ethical claims are true or that they can be proven to be true. But we noted that many of us already think that they are true and can be proven to be true – we would certainly say as much if an instructor tried to assign grades by drawing numbers out of a hat – and we gave some reasons for thinking that this view is reasonable. This clears the way for thinking that it is reasonable to believe that claims about business ethics can be true and can be proven to be true. More precisely, it is reasonable to believe that we can make good arguments for the truth of statements in business ethics.

You may have noticed that, while we began by talking about facts and opinions, we quickly moved away from this language and never returned to it. This is intentional. Talk of facts and opinions conceals and blurs the distinction between metaphysics – in this case, what can be true – and epistemology – in this case, what can be proven to be true. This leads to confusion. When a person is saying that ethical claims are opinions, are they saying that there are no ethical truths or that no ethical truths can be proven so? To avoid this conclusion, we have spoken of statements or claims and have asked whether they can be true. We have *further* asked what proof – in the sense of what arguments or evidence – can be given for them. This is how we will speak in the remainder of this book. We will not be asking whether business ethics belongs to the realm or facts or opinions. Instead, we will be asking whether specific claims that are made about the ethics of business are true or false. We will further ask what proof, arguments, or evidence can be given for these claims. Thinking and speaking in this way help to avoid confusion and clarify what is really at stake.

5. Study Questions

1. The word 'opinion' can have two meanings. What are they?
2. Error theorists disagree with both prescriptivists and emotivists about the nature of ethical statements. Explain the disagreement.
3. What evidence do we have that we treat ethical claims as capable of being true in our own lives? Do you think ethical claims can be true? If so, which ones do you think are true?
4. What is a proof? In business ethics, we do not normally speak of proofs. What (more neutral) language do we use instead?
5. What's the main difference between deductive and inductive arguments?
6. What is validity, and what is soundness?
7. One way that an argument can go wrong is that it can lead to absurd results. What is an example of such an argument?
8. Another way that an argument can go wrong is that its terminology may be vague or imprecise. What is an example of such an argument?
9. What evidence do we have that we treat ethical claims as capable of being proven – or at least argued for – in our own lives? Do you think that some ethical claims can be proven to be true or false? If so, which ones?
10. Some people think that you can't prove claims in business ethics because you can't get universal agreement about those claims. Why is this confused?

Additional Readings

Joyce, R. (2020). Moral anti-realism. In E. N. Zalta (Ed.), *The Stanford encyclopedia of philosophy*. https://plato.stanford.edu/archives/fall2020/entries/moral-anti-realism/

Lyons, J., & Ward, B. (2017). *The new critical thinking: An empirically informed introduction*. New York: Routledge.

Mackie, J. (1977). *Ethics: Inventing right and wrong*. New York: Penguin Books.

Manley, D. (2019). *Reason better: An interdisciplinary guide to critical thinking*. Toronto, ON: Tophat Monocle.

McCoy, B. (1983). The parable of the Sadhu. *Harvard Business Review, 61*(5), 103–108.

Rachels, J., & Rachels, S. (2019). *The elements of moral philosophy*. New York: McGraw-Hill Education.

Sandbu, M. (2012). The business of ethics: Reasoning about right and wrong. In his *Just business: Arguments in business ethics* (pp. 1–14). New York: Pearson.

Shafer-Landau, R. (2003). *Whatever happened to good and evil?* New York: Oxford University Press.

Timmons, M., & Shoemaker, D. W. (2014). Introduction. In their *Knowledge, nature, and norms: An introduction to philosophy* (2nd ed., pp. 1–18). Belmont, CA: Wadsworth.

Vaughn, L. (2019). Evaluating moral arguments. In his *Doing ethics: Moral reasoning, theory, and contemporary issues* (5th ed., pp. 41–64). New York: W.W. Norton.

3 Ethics: Theory and Method

In the previous chapter, we considered reasons for being skeptical about the whole enterprise of ethics and gave reasons for thinking that this skepticism is unfounded. You already make ethical claims and try to justify them. It is reasonable for you to continue doing so and in fact to extend that practice to the business world.

While we all make and argue for ethical claims every day, it is worth trying to refine our ideas about ethics before wading too deep into specific issues in business. That is the purpose of this chapter. Its goal is to introduce some relevant ethical theories and consider some of their strengths and weaknesses. This will help you to recognize the ethically relevant aspects of situations and to decide what the right thing is to do in these situations.

1. The Relevance of Ethical Theory

Business ethics is a branch of applied ethics. Other branches of applied ethics are environmental ethics and medical ethics. If we understand business ethics this way, then it might seem as if the right thing to do is to figure out what the correct ethical theory is and then apply it to business. According to this idea – and to preview our discussion just a bit – we should figure out whether consequentialism or deontology (or some other theory) is correct and then see what it says about business. Consequentialism tells us to maximize the good. If this is the right ethical theory, it might seem, then we should maximize the good in business.

This is a problematic approach for two reasons. First, philosophers disagree about which ethical theory is correct. If you are thinking that first you will figure out which ethical theory is correct, and then you will "do" business ethics, then it will take a long time for you to get around to doing business ethics. You may never get around to doing it, because you will spend all of your time trying to figure out which ethical theory is correct. This is not to say that there is no answer to the question of which ethical theory is correct. Based on our discussion in the previous chapter, you may reasonably think that there is an answer, even if we do not now know it.

Second, doing business ethics does not require, in a lot of cases, figuring out which ethical theory is correct. What ethical theories like consequentialism and

DOI: 10.4324/9781351016872-3

deontology seek to provide us is not primarily a list of actions that are right or wrong but an account of *what makes* an action right or wrong. Different theories can agree *that* an action is wrong even if they disagree about *why* the action is wrong. I might say that LeBron James is the best basketball player ever, and you might agree, but we might have different reasons for this. I might say that James is the best player because he has scored more points in the playoffs than any other player. You might say that he is the best player because he has the highest career value over replacement player (VORP). We agree that James is the best basketball player, but we disagree about why he is the best. It is certainly worth our time to try to discover what makes someone the best basketball player ever. But as far as who is the best, there is no disagreement between us.

What I am suggesting is that doing business ethics is a lot like figuring out who the best basketball player is. In the basketball case, we need to attend to metrics of greatness like number of points scored in the playoffs and VORP. In business ethics, we need to attend to the morally relevant features of situations. This is what the ethical theories we will consider point out. But we don't always need to know which of these metrics (in basketball) or features (in business ethics) is the most important. For in many cases they will point to the same basketball player as being the best or the same action or policy in business as being the ethically correct one.

To be sure, if we use different metrics for determining who the greatest basketball player is, then we might arrive at different answers as to who the greatest player is. If I choose VORP and you choose most NBA championships won, then I will think James is the greatest player ever and you will think Bill Russell is the greatest player ever. To resolve our disagreement, we will have to debate about what matters most in basketball. We will have to critically assess the metrics we are using, or perhaps we will bring in new metrics. The same is true in business ethics. If we assign different degrees of importance to different features of situations, then we might arrive at different answers to the question of what the right thing to do is. Then further debate and discussion are required. We will have to critically assess the features we have appealed to and perhaps identify new features.

The point is this. In business ethics we cannot ignore disagreements between ethical theories. Sometimes it will lead to disagreements about what actions and policies are correct in business. But we don't need to be paralyzed by disagreement between ethical theories either. Sometimes it won't lead to disagreement about what to do in business.

2. Ethical Theories

In this section I will present the main elements of four ethical theories: consequentialism (including its most prominent version, utilitarianism), deontology, virtue ethics, and Buddhist ethics. I choose these theories for two main reasons. First, they are historically important. Each has been the object of sustained philosophical attention. This means that many people think that each of these theories is worthy of careful study. This means, in turn, that we should pay attention to these theories. Second, and relatedly, the fact that these are the most important theories means that a lot of current debate and discussion about business ethics are conducted using the language of these theories. This is especially so in the scholarly literature, which we will be discussing. So if we want to get a better grip on current debate and discussion, then we need to understand the fundamental elements of these theories.

Let me make explicit a point that is implicit in the preceding paragraph. There are many fascinating and important ethical traditions that we are *not* discussing. These include Confucianism, contractarianism, contractualism, divine command theory, existentialism, egoism, feminist ethics (which in fact comprises a group of related views such as care ethics, radical feminism, and ecofeminism), natural law theory, stoicism, ubuntu, and more. Many of the world's religions, not just Buddhism, contain sophisticated ethical systems. You can find detailed ethical prescriptions in Christianity, Judaism, Islam, Hinduism, Jainism, and Sikhism. You wouldn't learn about all of these theories even if you took a whole course on ethics. There is simply too much territory to cover. In this book, where our primary focus is business ethics, we can only cover a very small amount of this territory.

2.1. Consequentialism

We begin with consequentialism. The 19th-century British philosopher J. S. Mill is most closely associated with this view, though it was given its first recognizable statement by his 18th-century predecessor, Jeremy Bentham. Consequentialism offers us a way to determine whether an action is right or wrong. It has three main elements: (1) Only consequences matter. (2) Everyone's good matters equally. (3) Maximize the net good. I will explain each of these elements.

Suppose a salesperson lies to a customer about the features of a car. When you evaluate the salesperson's behavior, there are several things that you could be evaluating. You could be evaluating his motive. The agent's motive is why he does what he does. Perhaps he is lying in order to make the sale and, more generally, to advance his own interests. Alternatively, when you evaluate a person's behavior, you could be evaluating the type of act that he is performing. You might look to see whether the action is on a list of forbidden or required actions, such as the Ten Commandments. Finally, you could be evaluating the consequences of that behavior. This is what consequentialists do and what (1) says. When evaluating the ethics of a salesperson's lying to his customer about the features of a product, consequentialists say that we should look at the *consequences* of that lie. In particular, we should look at the amount of "goodness" that it produces.

Consequentialists owe us an account of goodness. They need to say what makes a consequence good. There are many possible answers to this question. You might say that the good is a mental state, such as happiness or pleasure. This is the answer that Mill and Bentham gave. It is a view called "hedonism." If you are a hedonist and you accept the other three elements of consequentialism, then you are a *utilitarian*. Utilitarianism is a version of consequentialism. All utilitarians are consequentialists, but not all consequentialists are utilitarians. You are a consequentialist who is not a utilitarian if you endorse a different theory of the good.

For example, as an alternative, you might understand the good in terms of preference satisfaction. That is, you might say that an action is good to the extent that it gets people what they want. Often people want things that make them happy. So there will be a lot of overlap between hedonism, which says that the only good is happiness, and preference satisfaction–based theories of the good. But the overlap will not be complete. You might prefer for something to happen that would cause you unhappiness or pain. Finally, some philosophers understand the good in terms of an "objective list." They put certain things on the list such as justice, beauty, knowledge, virtue, achievement, and pleasure and say that a consequence is good to the extent that it contains one or more of these items. Now you might be confused by the inclusion of achievement, which sounds quite a bit like preference satisfaction, and pleasure on this list. But it is important to realize that, for objective list theorists, these aren't the only goods. They are two among many goods on the list.

Returning to the example, we said that consequentialists will evaluate the salesperson's lie by looking at the goodness of the consequences of the lie. But consequences for whom? This is where claim (2) comes in. Consequentialists believe that, when evaluating actions, you need to take into account the consequences *for everyone*. This includes, in our example, the customer, the customer's family and friends, the salesperson, and more. Moreover, according to the consequentialist, the consequences for everyone must be given equal weight in our analysis. You can't give extra weight to good consequences experienced by you or your family or friends, or discount the significance of good consequences experienced by people you don't know or don't like.

This is an important point and frequently misunderstood. Sometimes you will hear things like this: "From the point of view of the salesperson, consequentialism says that lying is permissible, because it produces good consequences for him. But from the perspective of the customer, consequentialism says that lying is impermissible, because it produces bad consequences for him." But consequentialism does not recognize individual perspectives in this way. Rather, there is a single perspective – the perspective of God or the universe – from which actions must be evaluated. An action is right or wrong *for everyone*, taking into account all of the consequences *for everyone*.

The final piece of the puzzle is (3). This tells us how much goodness we should be looking for when we evaluate actions. Consequentialism tells us that goodness should be *maximized*. We have to be careful here. The point is not simply to produce as much goodness as possible. We also need to be mindful of the badness that is produced by an action. For example, if we are hedonists, we need to be concerned about both happiness and unhappiness. So it might be more accurate to say that consequentialism tells us that the right action is the one that maximizes the *net* good, where the net good is understood as the difference between the good and bad consequences that are produced. When evaluating the morality of the salesperson's action, we need to add up all of its good and bad consequences. The point is not just to see whether the result is positive or negative. The point is to compare the net good of the action – in our case, the salesperson's lie – to the consequences of all of the other actions that he might have performed in that situation. Consequentialism tells us that the action is right if and only if, compared to all other possible actions, it produces the most net good.

2.2. Deontology

Intuitively, consequentialism has a lot going for it. What could be wrong with promoting good consequences, for everyone equally, and as much as you can? It turns out, quite a lot. A classic objection to consequentialist ethical theories involves imagining a scenario in which you could bring about a very good result by doing something bad.

Suppose that a terrorist has planted a bomb somewhere in a busy café. The bomb will go off unless you can defuse it in time. The terrorist says that he will not tell you where the bomb is, but you think that you might be able to get the information out of him by torturing him. Is it permissible for you to torture the terrorist? A consequentialist would probably say 'yes'. To be sure, torturing a terrorist produces a bad result – it causes the terrorist great pain. But it is likely to produce good results for many others – it will save their lives. Since more net good (it seems) is produced by torturing the terrorist than not torturing him, consequentialism tells us to torture the terrorist. But you might think that there are some things that we should not do, no matter how good the consequences. Torturing people might be one of those things. The ends, you might say, do not justify the means.

In fact, we don't have to envision remote scenarios involving terrorists and torture to feel the force of this point. The lying salesperson might have a chance to bring about a great good for himself and his family by making a sale based on false information. Perhaps making this sale will help the salesperson to reach his sales goals for the month, which will earn him a large bonus he can use to help provide for his family. And perhaps the person who buys the product based on the salesperson's false claims will not be too badly harmed in the process. A consequentialist might say that, in a situation like this, the salesperson should lie. But you might think that this is wrong. Even if the consequences of lying are good, you might say, this does not mean it's permissible to lie.

(Some consequentialists try to accommodate these and other cases by "going rule." That is, instead of saying that the right action is the one that, out of all those available to you, produces the best consequences [this is "act consequentialism"], they say that the right action is the one that conforms to the rule that, if accepted by society, would have better consequences than any other possible rule [this is "rule consequentialism"]. Lying to make a sale might have better consequences than any other possible action in an unusual situation, but a rule that allowed salespeople to lie when it was to their advantage would probably have worse consequences than a rule that required salespeople to tell the truth always. A danger for rule consequentialism is that it threatens to collapse into act consequentialism, if the rules are fine-grained enough.)

If you are persuaded that there are some things that you just shouldn't do, even if the consequences are good, you might be a deontologist. Deontologists believe that morality consists in a set of rules that you should follow, even if doing so has bad consequences. (Many versions of deontology say that morality consists in a set of rules that you should follow *whatever* the consequences of your doing so are. But there are some "threshold deontologists" who think that you should follow the rules unless your following them would produce catastrophic consequences.) The idea that morality consists in a set of rules that you should follow will probably be familiar to you. It may have been the first way you were taught to think about morality, especially if you were taught about morality in the context of religion. The Ten Commandments, for example, is a deontological ethical system. It is a set of rules that you are required to follow with no suggestion that you can get out of following them if doing so in a particular case would have bad results.

The most famous deontologist is the 18th-century German philosopher Immanuel Kant. According to Kant, there is just one basic rule of morality. He called it the categorical imperative. This is not just a name but a description of the rule. It is imperative, because it is a command. Morality presents itself as something that you are required to follow. (Of course, people can ignore a command like "don't lie," but this does not make it any less of a command.) It is categorical, because it applies to you no matter what your desires are. You can't "get out of" morality by saying that you don't want to be moral or have no desires that are satisfied by being moral.

Kant formulated the basic rule of morality – the categorical imperative – in two different ways. According to the first formulation – the "universal law" formulation – people should only act on maxims that they can will as universal laws. This may seem confusing at first, but Kant is really just telling us: "Think about what you propose to do. This is the maxim of your action. Then ask yourself: can I will it to be the case that everyone acts as I do? That is, could this be a law for everyone?" If the answer is 'no', then what you propose to do is impermissible. That is, it is morally wrong. If the answer is 'yes', then what you propose to do is permissible. Sometimes people think Kant is saying something like: "Imagine if everyone did what you propose to do – do you think that would have good consequences?" But Kant is not saying this. This would turn him into a consequentialist (of a sort). For Kant, the question is not whether "universalizing" what you propose to do would have good consequences. The question is whether it is *possible* for you to will it as a standard of behavior for everyone.

In our example, the salesperson needs to ask himself: "Can I will it to be the case that everyone lies to a customer in order to make a sale?" Kant would say that the answer to this question is 'no'. The purpose of the salesperson's lie is to deceive his customer. In a world in which all salespeople lied whenever it helped them to make a sale, no one would believe salespeople anymore, and deception would be impossible. A simple way of understanding the universal law formulation of the categorical imperative is this. Don't make an exception of yourself. If you think other people shouldn't act in a certain way, then you shouldn't act in that way.

We said that Kant gives two formulations of the categorical imperative. According to the second formulation – the "humanity" formulation – you must treat all people never merely as means; rather, you must always treat people as ends in themselves. As in the case of the first formulation, Kant's choice of language can make the meaning of this formulation seem hard to grasp. But also in this case, Kant is trying to express a thought that, translated into more accessible terms, is quite powerful. When Kant says that we should not treat people "merely as means," he is saying that we should not *use*, *exploit*, or *manipulate* people. To take a literal example: if it looks like I am going to be hit by a limb falling from a large tree, then I shouldn't pull you on top of me to shield me from the blow. That does not mean that we can never get something of value from other people. If so, Kantian ethics would prohibit all business activity. But our transactions should be voluntary, which is to say that they should not involve force or fraud on either side. When Kant says that we should treat others as "ends in themselves," Kant is saying that we should *respect* people. We should, for example, allow them to make up their own minds about what to do, as opposed to trying to make their choices for them. If your parents tried to pick your major or career for you, you might say that they aren't respecting you. Your parents might have told you what you could do when you were a child, but now that you are an adult, you can decide for yourself. Respect requires not only allowing people to decide for themselves what to do but helping them to do it. Your parents respect you not only by allowing you to become an accounting major, if that is your choice, but by helping you to become an accountant. This help could take various forms, from encouragement to financial assistance.

While deontological theories can contain surprising complexities, we have said enough to understand the main lines of deontological ethics with a focus on Kant's system. Deontology is in some sense the most familiar ethical view – it says that ethics requires following a set of rules, of the sort that you find in many religions. An important takeaway from Kant's deontology is that acting ethically means not making an exception for yourself. It also means not using or manipulating people, but instead respecting them and their agency. These ideas seem intuitively powerful to a lot of people and animate much contemporary debate in business ethics.

2.3. Virtue Ethics

Consequentialism and deontology are ethical systems that are concerned primarily with action. On these theories, ethics consists of doing the right thing. Virtue ethics is different. It is concerned primarily with character. According to virtue ethics, we should focus mainly on becoming the right sorts of persons, and doing the right thing will take care of itself. The most famous proponent of virtue ethics is Aristotle, the Greek philosopher who lived in the 4th century BC. Contemporary discussions still draw heavily on his work, so that is where our focus will be.

When you think about ethics, you might be thinking about constraints on your behavior that you have to observe, even if you don't want to observe them. "I'd like to spend this $20 on a movie for myself, but I guess I really should give it to charity." But for Aristotle, ethics is all about living well. The virtues are traits of character that help us to live well. Since everyone wants, or should want, to live well, then everyone wants, or should want, to be ethical.

In one way, Aristotle had a familiar answer to the question of what it means to live well or to have a good life. It means to be happy. But for Aristotle the happiness of "living well" or "having a good life" is not simply the tickle of joy we feel when we get a good grade on a test or when our team wins a big game. It is the happiness of *flourishing as a person*. Aristotle called this idea "eudaimonia."

What must a life be like for it to be a good life, which is to say a flourishing one? For Aristotle, this is a perfectly general problem. We can just as well ask what a car has to be like to be a good car, or what a knife has to be like to be a good knife. Aristotle answered this question in terms of a thing's *function*. The function of a knife is to cut, so a good knife will be one that cuts well. The virtues of a knife, in turn, are the features of the knife that allow it to cut well. These are, among other things, having a sharp blade and a comfortable handle. Like cars and knives, Aristotle thought that human beings also have functions. Our function is rational activity, not just of the theoretical sort, but of a practical sort too. So a human being has a good life – a happy or flourishing life – to the extent that they carry out their rational activity well. To do this they need certain traits or virtues.

Aristotle identifies a multitude of virtues, including courage, generosity, temperance, proper pride, truthfulness, friendliness, and justice. He describes the virtues as states of character that are "means" between "extremes" of deficiency and excess. There is a character trait – let's call it C – that is courage, if it is had in the proper amount. If you do not have enough C, then you have cowardice. If you have too much C, then you have foolhardiness. The courageous or brave soldier faces the enemy with her squad. She neither runs from danger nor charges headlong into battle by herself. There is a character trait – let's call it T – that is generosity, if it is had in the proper amount. People who have too little T are misers (like Ebeneezer Scrooge). People with too much T are profligate (the guy buying the whole bar drinks). And so on for the rest of the virtues. This idea is referred to as the "golden mean."

If we want to be happy, Aristotle thinks, we need to be virtuous. There is good and bad news here. The bad news is that no one is born with the virtues. There are no lucky few who just come into the world with the virtues imprinted upon them. The good news is that everyone can acquire them. According to Aristotle, you can acquire them in pretty much the same way that you acquire any skill, which is through practice. If we want to acquire the virtue of courage, we need to practice doing courageous things. It may take courage for you to speak in class. You can acquire this trait, however. You can get yourself to be the kind of person who does speak in class. But the only way you are going to do this is by actually speaking in class. If you want to become a generous person – that is, acquire the trait of generosity – you can only do this through acts of generosity.

There are a lot of pieces in Aristotle's ethical system, and over time some have proved more attractive than others. Many people find Aristotle's talk of functions confusing or perhaps just confused. They say that cars and knives have functions. They might even agree that certain sorts of people have functions, if by "function" we just mean *job*. The job of a professor is to teach, and the job of a chef is to cook. But they deny that human beings *in general* have functions.

But many people are attracted to the idea that virtues are an important part of ethics. The Catholic Church identifies prudence, justice, courage, and temperance as the four central or cardinal virtues. The Bushido code for Samurai in Japan requires the practice of eight virtues: righteousness, courage, benevolence, respect, honesty, honor, loyalty, and self-control. Benjamin Franklin claimed to live by a set of 13 virtues, including temperance, silence, order, resolution, frugality, industry, sincerity, justice, moderation, cleanliness, tranquility, chastity, and humility. (Skeptics about the universality of ethics should notice that there is a lot of overlap among these lists.) Appeals to virtues are common in many contemporary discussions of business ethics.

Many people are also attracted to the golden mean or the idea that virtue requires finding a middle path between extreme behaviors. "Moderation in all things is best," as the familiar saying goes. This idea can be found, for example, in Buddhist ethics, a view to which we now turn.

2.4. Buddhist Ethics

Aristotle's virtue ethics is all about living well. So is Buddhist ethics. Aristotle says that we have to live our lives in a certain way, and if we do, then we will achieve eudaimonia, which is happiness or flourishing. Similarly, according to Buddhist ethics, if we live our lives in a certain way, then we will achieve nirvana, which can be understood as a kind of peace or contentment.

Siddhartha Gautama, also known as the Buddha, was an important religious and philosophical figure who lived in India around 2500 years ago. For the Buddha the key question was how to achieve nirvana in this life. He began with the Four Noble Truths. The first Truth is that human lives are filled with suffering, from birth to death. "Suffering" is a strong word. Is the Buddha saying that in each moment of our lives we are suffering intense pain, of the sort we suffer at the dentist when she pokes our gums? Not quite. He is saying that our lives, despite containing some moments of happiness, come up short, as it were, in a lot of ways. We are often not content or satisfied. What is the cause of this suffering? This is the second Truth. The cause of suffering is desire, and in particular, desires that go unfulfilled. Putting the first and second Truths together, we get this. Human life is filled with suffering, because human lives have many desires that go unfulfilled.

So if we are after nirvana – peace or contentment – then should we just try to satisfy all of our desires? Not according to the Buddha. You will never be able to satisfy all of your desires, because it is hard to get the world to conform to your will, and even when you do, the world will soon change in a way that causes your desires to go unfulfilled again. The Buddha calls this the doctrine of "impermanence." You might be able to see this phenomenon in other people or perhaps in yourself. You have a lot of wants, and no matter what you get, the number of wants you have doesn't diminish. The Buddha's solution is the third Truth: the way to avoid suffering is to free yourself from desires. Limit your efforts to get what you want. (I say 'limit' and not 'eliminate' because, as a human being, you cannot avoid desires for food, drink, and shelter – the basic necessities of life.) Instead of taking your wants as given and trying to satisfy them, try to reduce the number and intensity of your wants. Indeed, the Buddha thought that you should try to minimize the importance of yourself as a distinct, unchanging entity. This is the "non-self doctrine." The idea is that, the less you think about yourself as an object of enduring importance, the less you will worry about your desires or your future.

The next question is, how do we achieve the cessation of our desires and stop focusing on ourselves so much? The answer is given in the fourth Truth, which articulates a "Noble Eightfold Path." The fourth Truth says, in effect: follow this path in order to achieve nirvana. The eightfold path consists of (1) right view, (2) right intention, (3) right speech, (4) right action, (5) right livelihood, (6) right effort, (7) right mindfulness, and (8) right concentration. A stereotype of Buddhists is that they free themselves of all worldly possessions and practice extreme asceticism or self-denial. This may be true of some Buddhists, but it is not what the Buddha required of all of his followers. Yet at the same time the Buddha thinks it is a mistake to engage in too many worldly pleasures. The eightfold path is meant to identify a "middle ground" between these extremes.

Elements (1) and (2) are mostly about learning the precepts of Buddhism, including the Four Noble Truths, and resolving to follow them. Elements (6), (7), and (8) are about training one's mind to work in a certain way, especially through meditative practices. Elements (3), (4) and (5) – right speech, right action, and right livelihood – offer distinctly moral advice, of the sort we have found in many of the moral theories we have sketched so far. In "right speech," the Buddha tells us to avoid false, harsh, or idle speech, and instead strive to tell the truth in meaningful discourse. In "right action," the Buddha tells us to avoid killing or harming any living being, taking what does not belong to us (through stealing or fraud), and illegitimate sexual relations (e.g., adultery or sexual assault). This means, in "right livelihood," that we should avoid jobs in which we are required to kill or harm others. So Buddhists should avoid working in firms that produce meat, weapons, or drugs (the Buddha believes that drugs and other intoxicants are a source of harm). We should also avoid jobs in which we are required to defraud or exploit others. The requirements in right action and right livelihood are connected to the Buddha's direction in (2), "right intention," to cultivate compassion for our fellow creatures and act out of love toward them.

You might have thought, a few paragraphs ago, that the Buddha's teachings could not possibly be relevant to the study of business ethics. You might have said: "Trying to reduce our desires or our sense of ourselves as distinct entities might be fine for a meditative retreat on a mountaintop, but it isn't going to work in the business world. I need to get a job and get things done!" Hopefully by now you see the relevance of Buddhist ethics. The Buddha does not tell you to withdraw from the world to a mountaintop. His recommendations to speak the truth and not harm others are obviously relevant to the practice of business. He also has advice – whether or not you believe him – about what careers you should avoid. In fact, even a little thought reveals that Buddha's identification of unfulfilled desires as the cause of suffering is relevant to business. Firms need to create markets – that is, desires – for the products they create. What if these desires can't be met? As a consumer, should you give in to your desires for new products, or is it sometimes better to resist them? Buddhist ethics speaks to these and other familiar questions that attend business activity.

3. Searching for Common Ground

We have sketched the main elements of four important ethical theories, or rather kinds of ethical theories, since there are many versions of consequentialism, deontology, virtue ethics, and Buddhist ethics. Remember that the point of this exercise was not to lay out four types of ethical theory for you to choose among, with the idea that you will apply one of these theories to business situations. Rather, the point of this exercise is to begin to understand the morally relevant features of situations. This is what ethical theories do. They tell us *what matters* in evaluating people and actions.

You will have observed that the different ethical theories give different accounts of what matters in evaluating people and actions. This might make you nervous. You might ask: "Don't we first have to figure out what ethics requires *in general* before asking what ethics requires *in business*?" Here it is worth remembering that theories can offer different accounts of what makes an action right or wrong while identifying the same actions as right or wrong. In the same way, we said, we might have different ideas about what makes someone the best basketball player – that is, we might have different "basketball theories" – but we might both agree that LeBron James is the best player.

You might get the point already, but let me make just one last observation on this score. When explaining different ethical theories, writers often search out cases where one theory says that we should do one thing and another theory says that we should do a different thing. Perhaps consequentialists will say that you should torture the terrorist and deontologists will say you should not. But they do this simply to illustrate the differences between the theories. Their point is not that the theories tell people to do different things in *all* or even *most* cases. Indeed, they often have to use extreme or unrealistic examples to explain how the theories come apart. To be sure, this does not mean that different ethical theories never tell people to do different things. It just means that we shouldn't let these cases obscure the significant overlap among these theories.

In what follows I want to highlight areas of agreement among the ethical theories sketched in the previous section. Before doing so it is useful to take on board a distinction that many philosophers make, between fundamental norms and mid-level principles.

Fundamental norms are just that: fundamental. They are the "ground floor" in an ethical theory. The theories that we have just learned about can be understood as providing fundamental norms. Fundamental norms include the consequentialist claim that we should maximize the good and the deontological claim that we should act only on those maxims that we can will as universal laws. Mid-level principles – to continue with our spatial metaphor – can be found one step "up" from the ground-floor fundamental norms. They are justified by the fundamental norms but do not themselves justify the fundamental norms.

(This is not to say that no argument can be given for fundamental norms; it is just to say that fundamental norms are not justified, as mid-level principles are, by appeal to other norms.) Mid-level principles are typically more specific than fundamental norms: they tell us what sorts of behaviors might maximize the good or be the sorts that you could will as universal laws. But they don't have to be more specific. The eightfold path, which can be understood as a set of fundamental norms, contains specific recommendations.

What I want to do now is to identify a set of mid-level principles that I think would be supported by the fundamental norms of the ethical theories we have discussed and that are especially useful for thinking about the ethics of business activity. (For convenience, hereafter I will simply call them 'principles' and not 'mid-level principles'.) Two points here. First, I must confess: I do not try to prove *in detail* how each theory supports each of these principles in a point-by-point fashion. That seems like a worthy project, but it is not one we have time for. But I think – and I think you will agree, upon reflection – that these principles capture a lot of what is going on in these theories. If I am right, then despite the diversity of ethical theories, we will have established a common set of principles, which we can use in the discussions that occur in the following chapters. Second, I do not claim that the principles I identify are the only ones that could be extracted from the ethical theories we have discussed or even that they are the most obvious ones that could be extracted from these theories. My suggestion is that these principles are useful when it comes to thinking about business ethics.

I think you will also find that the principles I identify agree with commonsense. Once you see them, I believe that you will think: "It makes sense to say that these are the sorts of things we should be thinking about when we think about the ethics of business." Perhaps these are exactly the principles that you would come up with if you were asked to identify what sorts of things matter from a moral point of view when it comes to business.

4. A Set of Principles

If a consequentialist, a deontologist, a virtue theorist, and a Buddhist were asked to agree to a set of principles or guidelines for good business behavior, what might they come up with? In an attempt to answer that question, I offer the following seven principles.

4.1. Abide by Agreements

Business works by agreement. I agree to pay you for something now, and you agree to supply it at a later time. I agree to work for you, and you agree to pay me later. According to a popular theory of the firm, the firm is nothing more than a set of agreements, or a "nexus of contracts," among various parties, including employees, stockholders, suppliers, and the community. The firm agrees to pay taxes to the government, purchase supplies from other firms, and sell products to consumers. Business simply doesn't work unless these agreements are honored. So one of the principles of business ethics is this: abide by your agreements.

4.2. Avoid Deception

The duty to abide by your agreements is closely related to the duty to avoid deception. When you fail to keep your agreement, you fail to do something that you have said that you will do. You make a liar of yourself. But the duty to avoid deception extends beyond simply keeping your agreements. People enter into business agreements on the basis of information that parties provide to each other. The requirement to avoid deception means that you shouldn't "trick" people into doing business with you. You shouldn't get them to do business with you on the basis of false information. This means, minimally, that you should not lie to people. But you should also not deceive people – that is, create false impressions in them – in ways that fall short of outright lying.

4.3. Respect People

Respect is among the most potent ideals in ethics, though it is notoriously difficult to say what exactly respecting people requires or when a certain way of treating people disrespects them. The duty to respect people could be said to include the duties to keep your agreements and avoid deception. When you break agreements or otherwise deceive people, you disrespect them by using them as mere means to your end. But the duty to respect people seems to require more than this. Respecting people requires recognizing them as full moral agents with decision-making capacities of their own. You disrespect people when you treat them as children or, worse, as pets. This happens when you try to make their decisions for them or when you treat their preferences with casual disregard. In this way, the value of respect is bound up with the value of freedom or liberty.

4.4. Recognize Rights

We have talked about duties that people have toward each other. But recognizing rights is another important part of business ethics. Duties and rights are correlative. If I have a duty to you to tell the truth, then you have a right (or a claim) against me that I tell the truth. If I have a right to a piece of property, then you have a duty not to take that property from me. To say that business ethics is a matter of recognizing rights, of course, is not yet to say which rights people have. Some rights are determined by the duties that we identified in principles (1) and (2). But traditionally people are thought to have other rights as well, such as rights to privacy, safety, or property. In fact, there is disagreement about what rights people have. The principle requiring businesspeople to recognize rights is therefore not fully determinate. It tells you what to look out for – the rights that people have – but it does not tell you exactly what rights people have.

4.5. Do What Justice Requires

Problems of justice arise when the demand for goods exceeds their supply, and it has to be decided who gets what. Principles of justice are relevant for business ethics, because businesses and businesspeople are in competition for scarce goods. Those in command of scarce goods must decide how they should be distributed. That is, they have to decide who deserves what. Justice matters in cases small and large. An employer may need to decide which of his minimum-wage employees deserves a raise, and a CEO may need to decide where to direct a billion-dollar profit. Recognizing rights, especially rights to property, is an important part of justice in the context of business, but property rights may not exhaust what justice requires. While people feel strongly *that* justice is important, they have divergent ideas about *what* justice requires. This means that a principle directing businesspeople to act justly and produce just distributions of resources, like a principle directing them to recognize rights, is not fully determinate. As in the case of the rights principle, this does not mean that justice is unimportant after all. It just means that further analysis is needed to understand what it requires.

4.6. Minimize Harm

There are many ways business activity can harm others. Firms can harm society by polluting the air or water; employees can harm employers by quitting. It does not make sense to recognize a duty to do *no* harm in a business context. For example, given our current technology, we must accept some pollution as the price of producing anything. All but the most incompetent employee's leaving will cause an employer some pain and frustration. But we can recognize a duty to *minimize* harm. While an employee's quitting may cause her employer inevitable harm, she can minimize that harm by giving her employer fair warning of her departure. If a firm has two equally expensive ways of producing a product, it should choose the process that produces less pollution over the one that produces more pollution. This principle invites businesspeople to think about the harm that they do in their business activities and ask whether that harm is necessary or can be reduced without too much cost.

4.7. Promote Welfare

Just as there are many ways business activity can harm others, there are many ways that business activity can benefit others. Indeed, business activity typically aims at benefitting others. If you start a business, you probably think that you can make something that benefits people. You may provide further benefits by employing people and paying taxes. Thus, most business activity will meet the requirement to promote the good in a minimal way. But businesses and businesspeople can do a lot of good in other ways as well. Businesses can engage in philanthropic activities and reduce their pollution below legally required levels. Advertisers can provide consumers the information that they need to make wise choices; salespeople can encourage people to buy products that meet their needs and fit their budgets. A requirement to promote the good asks those engaged in business to think about how their activity already promotes welfare and whether there are other ways that it might do so.

4.8. The Principles in Focus

Let me highlight a few things about these principles. One is that some are more determinate than others. The duty to avoid deception is more determinate than the duty to respect people. That is, it is easier to see what counts as deceiving people than what counts as respecting them. We have a better sense of what it means to keep agreements than to recognize people's rights or to treat people justly – that is because there is disagreement about what rights people have and what justice requires. Would that it were not so! Then the job of a business ethicist would be easier. But we should not confuse determinacy with importance. That is, we should not conclude from the fact that some principles are less determinate than others that these (same) principles are less important than others. Besides, even the most determinate of the principles on the list aren't entirely determinate. What counts as deception in an advertisement might depend on whether the intended audience is a group of children or a group of adults.

A second thing to observe is that these principles pick out distinct but overlapping areas of ethics. You may have noticed this already. The duty to avoid deception can be understood as part of what is required to treat people with respect. But it is also true that deceiving people usually results in harming them. So the duty to minimize harm comes into play here as well. The duty to keep promises can be given a similar analysis. You might think that with enough analysis and patience we can reduce the seven principles down to two or three or perhaps even one. Perhaps it all boils down to respect for people or promoting the good. Perhaps. Or perhaps not. This is not our project. We are trying to equip ourselves with enough ethical awareness to recognize and try to resolve ethical dilemmas in business. We are better off equipping ourselves with too many principles than too few, even if our principles are partly overlapping. If we decide to focus on just the "basic" or "essential" principles, we risk leaving an important principle off our radar completely.

A third thing about these seven principles is that they articulate *pro tanto* duties. What this means is that these are things that you have good reason to do. They are not things that you are required to do, no matter what and, in particular, no matter what other reasons you have. So you have a duty to keep your agreements. But if keeping your agreements would cause massive harm in a certain case, then perhaps, all things considered, you should not keep them. We sometimes see this in cases of whistleblowing. Employees may agree to keep information about the firm secret. But if the firm is engaged in immoral or illegal conduct that may harm the public, then the employee might be justified, all things considered, in "blowing the whistle" on the company, that is, sharing information about the company's misdeeds with the public, in an effort to get the company to stop. The employee's duty to keep information about his firm secret does not vanish in this instance. It is simply outweighed by "factors on the other side," so to speak. This is the nature of a pro tanto duty. It provides a reason to engage in a certain behavior but not a decisive reason. It can be outweighed.

This brings us to a fourth observation about the seven principles. In fact, we have already made this observation and just need to highlight it. The principles can conflict. We saw that, in the case of whistleblowing, keeping your agreements can cause harm. If you want to minimize harm, you might need to break your agreements. Firms that generate large profits may be able to promote the good in their communities by donating generously to philanthropic causes. But this could be in tension with agreements and justice. You might think that firms promise investors any profits that they generate. Indeed, you might think that firms owe investors profits as a matter of justice. Should advertisers try to get customers to buy products that customers want or that are good for them? These examples can be multiplied. Business is ethically complicated, and different principles can pull us in different directions. This is not a cause for panic but an impetus for additional thought and reflection. You now have the concepts at your disposal to begin to see what must be seen when thinking ethically about business. It is up to you to deploy them to begin to understand what ethics requires in business.

5. How to Make Progress

Despite my uplifting rhetoric, you might feel worse now than before. I began by describing four distinct ethical theories. These theories provide different answers to the question of what matters in evaluating action and behavior. So you might have felt a bit lost. But, I said, proponents of these theories would agree on seven principles, telling us to keep promises, avoid deception, respect people, recognize rights, do what justice requires, minimize harm, and promote welfare. But I also said that none of the seven principles is fully determinate, and some (e.g., rights and justice) require a significant amount of specification. Moreover, I claimed, the principles are pro tanto and can pull us in different directions. In short, we've now got a set of principles that can guide our actions.

But these principles are not fully spelled out, and it is not clear how to combine them to figure out what is, in the end, the right thing to do. What now? How do we use what we have learned to help us make ethical choices in a business context? I have some good news and bad news.

5.1. The Good News

The good news is that we have a procedure we can use to make progress on ethical issues. That procedure is *reflective equilibrium*. This procedure relies on our considered moral judgments about both cases and principles and demands consistency between them.

Let us begin with your moral judgments. Consider the case of Merck and river blindness. As it was developing a drug to treat parasites in livestock, scientists at Merck realized that they might be able to develop a similar drug to treat the parasite in humans that causes river blindness, a debilitating and painful disease that eventually causes blindness. At its peak, this disease afflicted millions of people in some of the poorest parts of the world. But there was a problem. Developing a drug for humans requires an enormous amount of time and money, and the people afflicted with river blindness were almost all too poor to afford to buy any drug Merck might make. Merck faced a difficult decision. Should it develop the drug to treat river blindness or not? In fact, they decided to develop the drug – they called it Mectizan – and now distribute it for free, mostly at their own expense, throughout the developing world. This is just the barest sketch of the Merck case. (We will discuss it in more detail in Chapter 9.) You will want to know as much as possible about it before putting any weight on the moral response you have to it. Suppose that, once you know more, you judge that Merck did the right thing when it developed the drug for river blindness. This judgment – which philosophers call an 'intuition' – is important and should be taken seriously.

The next step is to think about what this intuition tells you. In particular, think about *why* you have the intuition that you do. Why do you think what Merck did was right? Here we are looking for principles that explain or justify our judgments. One reason we are doing this is that we want to be able to give some account of our judgments. Another reason is that we want to identify general principles that we can apply to cases where the result is not so clear – where, for example, people have different moral judgments about the case. A good starting place is the seven principles. So you might say that what Merck did was right because of principle seven – "promote welfare." By developing Mectizan, Merck improved many people's lives, so they did the right thing.

We are not done. A scientist does not make a single observation, use it to justify a principle, and then call it a day. She seeks out new observations to test her principle, seeing whether the principle does just as good a job accounting for the new observations as it does the original one. The same goes for ethics. You've got a moral judgment about a case that you have used to support a moral principle. You now need to test this principle against judgments generated by new cases. If the principle is correct, then it should yield judgments in new cases that are just as intuitively plausible as the judgment in the original case. If the judgments do not support the principle, or reveal some vagueness or other problem in it, then the principle requires alteration or specification.

We might try this in the case of principle seven. What does it mean for Walmart, as it considers whether to raise the starting wages of their entry-level workers? What does it mean for Mars, as it decides where to source its cocoa beans? What does it mean for Middletown Sprinkler Company, as it decides whether to sponsor a little league baseball team? In fact, we can already see that our principle seven requires specification if it is going to be useful for answering these questions. This is because *many* actions that companies perform promote welfare. If, for example, Walmart raises the wages of its entry-level workers, those workers will be better off. But if it sends that money to shareholders in higher dividends, shareholders will be better off. So perhaps we should understand principle seven to be saying "*maximize* welfare." In this case, it implies that Walmart should perform whatever action creates the most welfare. But is that really correct? Walmart is not a charity like the Red Cross or a food bank. Walmart is a business. It exists to sell products to people and make a profit. So, you might think, it shouldn't exploit its workers, but beyond this they don't need to pay them more than what the market will bear. If that's so, you might wonder what Merck was doing when it decided to devote millions of dollars to the development of a drug that wouldn't make them any money. Yet didn't Merck do something remarkable for which it deserves the highest praise?

We are getting ahead of ourselves. We are not trying to figure out whether Merck did the right thing in the Mectizan case. We are simply trying to show how the process works. You have a judgment about a case. You use this judgment to generate, or provide support for, a principle. You then test this principle against a new case. If your judgment in the new case aligns with the principle, great. If not, some adjustment is in order. Sometimes you will decide, based on the judgment you have about the new case, that the principle needs modification. Sometimes you will decide to keep the principle as is and abandon your judgment about the new case. Some of the cases that you consider will involve more than one principle. You may use your judgments in these cases to attempt to establish a rank-ordering among the principles. This process goes on. Your goal is to reach a kind of balance, a *reflective equilibrium* between your ethical principles and judgments about cases. In this state, the principles you support are consistent with the judgments about cases you have.

Why are we going for consistency? It is because of its connection to truth. If there is an inconsistency between the principles you accept and the judgments you have, then you are being irrational. Some part of what you believe – either your principles or your judgments – must be false. This is a perfectly general fact. If you believe several things, and some of the things you believe are inconsistent with other things you believe, then one of the things you believe is false. If you believe that 2 + 2 = 4 and 2 + 2 = 5, then one of the things you believe is false. If you believe that the earth is a sphere and that the earth is flat, then one of the things you believe is false. Minimally, for your set of beliefs to be true, it needs to be consistent. In the case of ethics, you need to adjust either your principles or your judgments about cases for your set of beliefs about ethics to have a chance of being true.

Reflective equilibrium might seem quite abstract and philosophical, but I guarantee you are familiar with the basic idea. I bet you have had the experience of arguing with a person about an ethical or political issue who says things like "Well, what about this case?" and "How about that case?" Perhaps you say that abortion is wrong, because it ends an innocent life. This person might say: "Well, what about eating animals, which also ends innocent lives?" Or perhaps you say that Barry Bonds shouldn't be in the Baseball Hall of Fame because he used a lot of steroids. This person might say: "Well, what about Andy Pettitte, who admitted to using human growth hormone to recover from an injury?" This person is a *whataboutist*. Many philosophers are like this.

You might find the whataboutist annoying. But he is getting at two important things. First, he is forcing you to think about the reasons for your judgments in particular cases. He is asking you to articulate *general principles* to justify the judgments that abortion is wrong and that Barry Bonds shouldn't be in the Hall of Fame. Second, and relatedly, he is demanding *consistency* between your general principles and your judgments in cases. Perhaps there are differences between abortion and killing nonhuman animals that explain your different judgments about them. The same with Bonds and Pettitte. The whataboutist may be confused or off base in drawing parallels between these cases. But he is pushing you in the right direction. He is forcing you to engage in exactly the kind of *reflective equilibrium* that is necessary for discovering the truth about ethics or indeed the truth about anything.

In sum, while we have a set of principles, which are under-specified and can pull us in different directions, there is good news. We have a procedure for making progress on ethical issues, namely, reflective equilibrium. As we consider issues in business ethics – questions about Merck and Mectizan, or how much Walmart pays its workers, or whether Middletown Sprinkler Company should sponsor a little league baseball team – we should consider not just the judgments that we have in these cases, but the general principles that justify these judgments, and we should work toward consistency between our principles and our judgments across the widest possible range of cases.

That's it for the good news. Now for the bad news.

5.2. The Bad News

The first piece of bad news is that reflective equilibrium is a process that takes time. I hinted at this earlier, when I said that we should work toward consistency between our principles and our judgments *across the widest possible range of cases*. You will find that the seven principles that we identified are relevant in a wide variety of situations in business. This is because ethical issues arise in all areas of business. There are ethical issues in marketing, sales, human resources, and much more. If this is not already clear to you now, it will be by the end of this book. This means that you will have a wealth of judgments about what is right and wrong in specific cases. Each of these cases provides a data point for you to take into account as you try to bring your judgments and your principles into alignment. You might think you have everything worked out by the end of our discussion of ethical issues between employers and employees. But our discussion of corporate social responsibility may cause you to rethink your commitments.

In fact, reflective equilibrium not only takes time, it probably never has a definite ending point. There are always new cases to consider, which may cause you to rethink the content of the principles you support or their relative importance, or which may cause you to revise judgments that you had about previous cases. Perhaps a new technology emerges that causes you to revise your ideas about the nature and limits of workplace privacy, or perhaps a new form of political advocacy is tried, which causes you to rethink your views about corporate political activity. As you proceed through this book, and indeed your life, you should always be gathering information, judging, testing, and revising. If you make an effort, you will make progress toward bringing your principles and judgments into alignment. You will refine your principles, confirm some judgments, and reject others. But you should not let your set of beliefs become ossified or hardened against new ideas and experiences. Reflective equilibrium prescribes a way of making progress but also tells us that we are never truly done.

The second piece of bad news is that reflective equilibrium, even if carried through to completion, does not guarantee the truth of one's set of beliefs. Remember that, when we engage in reflective equilibrium, we seek consistency between our principles and our judgments. Consistency is a necessary condition of truth. If your belief set contains inconsistent beliefs – for example, both '2 + 2 = 4' and '2 + 2 = 5' – then one of those beliefs must be false. But consistency is not a sufficient condition of truth. Just because all of the beliefs in a belief set are consistent with each other, does not guarantee that they are all true. This is easy enough to see. You might believe that '2 + 2 = 5' and '2 + 3 = 6'. Your beliefs are consistent with each other; they can both be true at the same time. But both are false. In fact, you could have beliefs in your belief set that are consistent with each other and that are mutually supporting, but that are false.

You might believe that 'the moon is made of Swiss cheese' and 'the surface of the moon has craters in it'. These beliefs are true and mutually supporting. The moon being made of Swiss cheese could explain why its surface has craters in it. The surface of Swiss cheese has craters of a sort in it. Yet one of these beliefs is false. The moon is not made of Swiss cheese.

What can be done about this? There is no magic bullet. That is, there is no simple formula for determining which, among multiple sets of true beliefs about business ethics, contains all true ones. But that is no reason for despair. There is a way to move forward. That is to *do more business ethics*. You might have a consistent belief set and your neighbor might have a consistent belief set, and these might contain different beliefs. Perhaps you think that employers should not be able to ask prospective employees whether they smoke, and your neighbor thinks that they should be able to. Perhaps you accept different principles, which justify these different judgments. But how comprehensive are your sets of beliefs? How many cases have you considered? In what ways have you tested your principles? By considering more cases, and subjecting your principles to more tests, you may yet arrive at agreement. We noted in the previous chapter that you probably think that there are ethical truths and that you can prove them through argument. When you disagree with your neighbor, and you both have consistent sets of beliefs, you have a chance to put this conviction to the test.

This is not to say that doing more business ethics – considering more cases, thinking more carefully about principles – is guaranteed to help you resolve all of your disagreements with your neighbor in the end. That is so even if both of you are being honest with yourselves, engaging in good reasoning practices, and trying to find out the truth. But doing more business ethics will still be useful for you. It will help you to clarify what *you* think the right thing is to do in business, and what principles are guiding your decisions. That is, doing more business ethics will help you find out something about yourself, and that is a very important thing to understand. Socrates said that an unexamined life is not worth living. This might be an exaggeration. But it strikes many people as true that your life goes better to the extent that you live deliberately, according to principles that you have reflected on and accepted, as opposed to simply reacting to whatever is in front of you. Engaging in reflective equilibrium allows you to do that and, in doing so, makes your life go better.

6. Chapter Summary

We covered a lot of ground. Our subject is business ethics, so our goal was to try to get a handle on what, in general, is ethical. To do this we considered four prominent ethical theories: consequentialism (of which utilitarianism is a version), deontology, virtue ethics, and Buddhist ethics. The point is not that you should choose the one you think is best or like the most and then apply it mechanically to issues in business. The point is simply to draw your attention to what people who have thought a lot about ethics think are ethically relevant features of situations. It is these features that you should pay attention to when you think about business.

We noted that, when philosophers present these theories, they tend to emphasize the ways that they come apart. While they do come apart in some cases, these theories have a lot in common too. We sketched a list of seven principles that, I suggested, proponents of all of these theories can support: abide by agreements, avoid deception, respect people, recognize rights, do what justice requires, minimize harm, and promote welfare. These principles provide a good foundation for thinking about ethical issues in business, but they need spelling out, and when they pull in different directions, we have to decide which has priority.

There are no easy solutions here. But there is a process that we can use to make progress, and that is reflective equilibrium. That is, we should make sure that there is an alignment between our judgments about particular cases and the principles that we draw upon to justify these judgments to ourselves and others. If there is an inconsistency between our judgments and our principles, or among our judgments or our principles, then something we believe must be false. We must either revise our judgments about particular cases, or modify or adjust the importance of our principles, until we achieve consistency. While consistency does not guarantee truth, it helps us to avoid falsity and can even help us to discover our own values.

7. Study Questions

1. What is the primary purpose of an ethical theory?
2. What are the three main elements of consequentialism?
3. Kant said that we should treat people as "ends" and not as "mere means." In plain language, what did he mean by this?
4. Aristotle understands the "good" of anything – even a human life – in terms of its function. Explain what Aristotle means by this.
5. Buddhist ethics requires that we have the "right intention." What is this intention, and how could it be translated into practice?
6. What is the difference between a fundamental norm and a mid-level principle in ethics?
7. We identified seven mid-level principles that could be used to evaluate business activity. Which ones do you find most compelling, and why?
8. We said that the seven principles are *under-specified* and articulate *pro tanto* duties. What do these (italicized) terms mean?
9. What is reflective equilibrium? Why is it helpful in avoiding false beliefs?
10. Why doesn't reflective equilibrium guarantee that we hold true beliefs?

Additional Readings

Aristotle. (1999/350 BC). *Nicomachean ethics*. T. Irwin (Trans. and Ed.). Indianapolis, IN: Hackett.

Arras, J. (2006). The way we reason now: Reflective equilibrium in bioethics. In B. Steinbock (Ed.), *The Oxford handbook of bioethics* (pp. 46–71). New York: Oxford University Press.

Beauchamp, T. L. (2003). The nature of applied ethics. *A companion to applied ethics* (pp. 1–16). Malden, MA: Blackwell Publishing.

Bowie, N. E. (2017). *Business ethics: A Kantian perspective* (2nd ed.). New York: Cambridge University Press.

Gowans, C. (2003). *Philosophy of the Buddha: An introduction*. New York: Routledge.

Kant, I. (1997/1785). *Groundwork of the metaphysics of morals*. M. Gregor (Trans.) & C. M. Korsgaard (Ed.). New York: Cambridge University Press.

McMahan, J. (2013). Moral intuition. In H. LaFollette & I. Persson (Eds.), *The Blackwell guide to ethical theory* (2nd ed., pp. 103–120). Malden, MA: Blackwell Publishing.

Mill, J. S. (1998/1863). *Utilitarianism*. R. Crisp (Ed.). New York: Oxford University Press.

Moore, G. (2017). *Virtue at work: Ethics for individuals, managers, and organizations*. New York: Oxford University Press.

Rachels, J., & Rachels, S. (2019). *The elements of moral philosophy*. New York: McGraw-Hill Education.

4 Political and Economic Systems

We have said that 'business' has two meanings. 'Business' can mean an activity, a voluntary exchange of goods and services. This is the meaning of 'business' we have in mind when we say that Abigail does business with Bob when she exchanges something that she owns – say, an amount of money – for something that Bob owns – say, a car. By 'business' we can also mean an entity that sells things, usually with the goal of making a profit. This is the meaning of 'business' we have in mind when we say that Bob's Beauties, a used car dealer, is a business.

Business does not occur in a vacuum. It occurs against a background of political, social, and economic institutions. In our example, Bob owns a business, and we can imagine Bob and Abigail freely bargaining over the price of the car until they settle on a mutually agreeable price. But things could have been arranged differently. Businesses could be owned by the public, not individuals, and prices could be set by government authorities, not through bargaining by private citizens. The purpose of this chapter is to help you learn more about the institutions in the background of business activity. We will focus on markets, property, and the welfare state.

We cannot say all that needs to be said about the nature and value of markets, property, and the welfare state here. These are subjects for other books. But we need to say something about them, because it is important to understand the institutional context for business activity. What ethical questions arise about business and who has to answer them depend on what sort of political and economic institutions are in place. No matter what systems are in place, however, there is going to be business activity. That is, there is going to be exchange and entities that offer goods and services for exchange. So in any political and economic system, there is a need for business ethics.

1. Capitalism Versus Socialism

For a long time in the 20th century, there appeared to be a great struggle between two kinds of political/economic system: one exemplified in the U.S. and the other exemplified in the Soviet Union.

DOI: 10.4324/9781351016872-4

Consider the political/economic system exemplified in the U.S. This system, it was said, featured three main elements: free markets, private ownership of the means of production, and a minimal welfare state. "Private ownership of the means of production" means that individuals – people like you and me – own the factories and other business organizations. "Free markets" means that individuals like you and me decide what to produce, how much of it to produce, and how much to sell it for. More generally, individuals determine the conditions under which an exchange of property is made. You can offer your stuff for sale at whatever price you want, and I am free to pay that price, or not, as I chose. "Minimal welfare state" means that people get some stuff (roads, sewers, and military protection) from the state funded by taxes, but mostly what people get is determined by what they produce themselves or what others voluntarily give them, either as gifts or in market exchanges. This system was called "capitalism" or perhaps "free-market capitalism."

Consider next the political/economic system exemplified in the Soviet Union. In this system, the three main elements were different. These were planned economies, in which the means of production were collectively owned, and that had robust welfare states. "Collective ownership of the means of production" means that society as a whole owns the factories and other business organizations. Individuals like you and me might work in a factory or other business, but we could not own them individually. They would be owned by you and me and everyone else *together*. "Planned economy" means that a committee of people gets together and decides what to produce, how much of it to produce, and what to sell it for. "Robust welfare state" means that people get a lot of stuff from the state funded by taxes – not just the roads, sewers, and military protection, but things like healthcare, a basic income, free or nearly free advanced education, subsidized travel on public transportation, and more. The name given to this system was "socialism."

(The Soviet Union can also be described as a communist country, but this label is complicated. 'Communist' is the name of the political party that controlled the Soviet Union, whose full name was the "Union of Soviet Socialist Republics." But Karl Marx, the 19th-century German philosopher, and one of the main intellectual proponents of communism, distinguished between this view and socialism. Marx thought that socialism is one [lower] post-capitalist economic system, and communism is another [higher] post-capitalist economic system. He was not clear, however, about how exactly communism differs from socialism. Marx seemed to think that in communism there would be no division of labor, no material scarcity [and hence no need for private property of any kind], and no strong state, but all of these would exist under socialism. To avoid the problematic implications of the term 'communism', we will use 'socialism' only.)

My descriptions of the U.S. and Soviet economies are caricatures or ideal types. They are exaggerated descriptions of economies that did not exist in exactly this form. In the U.S., not all productive organizations are privately owned. Governments provide many services – mail, utilities, and education – that could be provided by private businesses. Many exchanges, including the prices of goods (e.g., in the insurance industry), are highly regulated. In the Soviet Union, individuals were sometimes permitted to sell small amounts of goods that they produced through farming or hunting. The terms of these exchanges were determined by voluntary agreements between buyers and sellers. Finally, the U.S. has a significant welfare state, providing healthcare and income support to seniors and others.

What this should tell you is that an economy is not either "capitalist" or "socialist," but rather that it has more of what the U.S. has or more of what the Soviet Union had. That is, an economy might feature more or less private ownership of the means of production, more or less government regulation of markets, and a more or less robust welfare state.

In fact, things are more complicated than this. This is because views about (1) ownership of the means of production, (2) the role of markets versus planning, and (3) the nature of the welfare state can come apart. An essential part of socialism is that the means of production are socially owned, or owned by the people collectively. And it is typical for socialists to think that decisions about production should be made by planning – either by a central authority or by groups of individuals in a decentralized fashion. But some socialists – "market socialists" – advocate an economic system in which firms compete with each other in markets to provide goods to the public. A robust welfare state is also typical of socialist economies. But capitalist economies – that is, economies that feature private ownership of the means of production and free markets – can also have robust welfare states. The 20th-century American economist Milton Friedman – whom we will hear more about later – was a fierce advocate for both but also thought that there should be a social safety net in the form of a negative income tax. You can think that the social safety net should be minimal but think the government should play a significant role in economic affairs. You can see some of these differences in practice. Compared to Denmark, markets in the U.S. are more regulated, but the U.S. has a weaker social safety net.

What this should tell us is that it is a mistake to talk *in general* about the merits of capitalism versus the merits of socialism. Any political/economic system contains various elements, and a general discussion risks glossing over which elements the system contains. What we should be focusing on instead is the *specific features* of political and economic systems. In particular, we should be focusing on questions about (1) who should own the means of production, (2) when and how markets and planning should be used, and (3) how robust the welfare state should be.

I started this section by saying that *for a long time* there appeared to be a struggle between two kinds of political and economic systems: the capitalist system found in the U.S. and the communist system found in the former Soviet Union. This suggests that the struggle is over. In a sense, it is. The U.S.'s political and economic system is still around, but the Soviet Union no longer exists. The Soviet Union's collapse was due in part to failures of its political and economic system. No serious person wants to try to recreate exactly that system again. But in another sense the struggle goes on. This is because there is still debate about the ownership of the means of production, the proper role of markets and planning in the economy, and the nature of the welfare state. While the U.S.'s political and economic system is still around, there is no reason to think it is perfect. Lots of people – on every point of the political and economic spectrum – think it can be improved. Perhaps you do too.

In what follows you will be introduced to debates about property, markets, and the welfare state. This will put you in a better position to understand the nature of the institutions against which business activity is conducted and to evaluate those institutions. Like our discussion of ethical theories in the last chapter, here we are just scratching the surface. Those interested in a fuller discussion of property, markets, and the welfare state must pursue them outside of the pages of this book.

2. The Welfare State

What are the reasons for and against the welfare state? As a way of answering this question, I will present two theories of justice – John Rawls's justice as fairness and Robert Nozick's entitlement theory – and explain their implications for the welfare state. Both Rawls and Nozick were American philosophers who were active around the same time in the late 20th century. Indeed, they both worked at Harvard University and had offices down the hall from each other. We are focusing on these theories because they are the most significant contemporary theories of justice and because as a consequence they play an important role in contemporary discussions of business ethics.

2.1. Rawls's Justice as Fairness

When people get together to form a society, there have to be principles that structure or govern their interactions. It's like joining a club or university. The club or university has rules that you are expected to follow. For Rawls, a theory of justice provides the most fundamental of these governing principles for society. Rawls offers a "social contract" theory of justice. In a social contract theory, principles of justice are arrived at through a kind of agreement, or contract, among the people subject to the principles. So, for Rawls, the principles of justice for our society are principles that we choose, and they are just because we chose them. The idea is not, however, that we all get together in the same room and actually choose. Our choice is hypothetical, not actual. The principles of justice are ones that we would choose, if we had an opportunity to choose.

It is important for Rawls that the hypothetical choice is made under specific circumstances, what he calls the "original position." The point of the original position is to model people as *free and equal persons*. This guarantees, he says, that the principles that we choose are fair. Rawls says that we are free insofar as we think of ourselves as distinct individuals with goals and plans of our own. We can make demands of others (for example, that they leave us alone to pursue our goals), but we also must take responsibility for our actions (for example, we must live within our means). We are equal in that none of us is more important than others. Your needs are important, but they are no more objectively important than mine. Rawls realizes it can be hard to see ourselves as equal in this sense, so he builds into the original position a "veil of ignorance." Behind the veil we do not know our natural talents (whether we are good at math or reading) or social status (whether we come from a high- or low-status family). We don't even know our likes and dislikes. The goal of this is to ensure that, in choosing principles of justice, we do not choose principles that unduly favor ourselves.

Rawls says that, in the original position, we would choose two principles. The first principle regulates the distribution of basic rights and liberties and says that "each person has the same indefeasible claim to a fully adequate scheme of equal basic liberties, which scheme is compatible with the same scheme of liberties for all." According to Rawls, a "fully adequate scheme" of basic liberties includes the right to free speech and association, the right to vote and run for public office, and the right to hold private property – though not, Rawls says, a right to property in the means of production.

The second principle regulates the distribution of social and economic goods and says that "social and economic inequalities are to satisfy two conditions: (a) they are to be attached to offices and positions open to all under conditions of fair equality of opportunity; and (b) they are to the greatest benefit of the least advantaged members of society (the difference principle)."

The second principle is more complicated, and more relevant for our discussion, since it helps us to understand the robustness of the Rawlsian welfare state. Rawls's position is that all economic and social goods should be distributed equally unless an unequal distribution of them has the effect of making the worst-off people in society better off. Focusing on the first part of the claim, you might think that Rawls is offering an extreme form of egalitarianism – that he is saying that everyone should have equal shares of everything. But he is not. In fact, he thinks that distributing economic and social goods unequally *does* make the worst-off people in society better off. This is because we respond to incentives to promote our self-interest. If the salary you earn for your job were to be redistributed to all members of society equally, then you might not work very hard. But if you get to keep most of it, then you will. When you work hard, you will produce more, and society will benefit. Moreover, your higher salary can be taxed to support welfare programs. What the second principle says is that inequality-generating incentives – such as high salaries – are only permissible to the extent that they make the worst-off people in society better off. This is part (b) of Rawls's second principle of justice, known as the difference principle. Moreover, your high-paying job must have been "open to all under conditions of fair equality of opportunity." This is part (a) of the second principle.

There is a lot of scholarly debate about what exactly a society modeled on Rawlsian principles of justice would look like. But it seems clear that it would contain a fairly robust welfare state. Consider Rawls's claim that desirable jobs and positions must be open to all under conditions of fair equality of opportunity. For Rawls this means that people born equally talented and motivated must have the same opportunity to land the best jobs. Their life chances shouldn't be diminished by being born into an unsafe community with bad schools. A society modeled on Rawlsian principles will ensure that people have equally safe communities and equally good schools. Or consider the difference principle. It doesn't demand that everyone have equal shares of resources. But it does say that no one will have more than an equal share unless their doing so makes the worst-off in society better off. This creates a strong incentive to fund social programs that benefit the worst-off, such as programs of guaranteed healthcare, education, and pension payments. Indeed, Rawls thinks that a just society will have a "social minimum" or a standard of living that no one in society will fall below.

It is important to realize the limits of Rawls's theory. He offers his two principles of justice for the "basic structure of society." These are society's major political, social, and economic institutions such as its constitution, court system, and tax code. The point is that these systems as a whole must be in conformity with the two principles of justice. Rawls does not think that each individual institution within society has to be governed by the two principles. He does not think, for example, that businesses should distribute resources to their employees or other stakeholders according to the difference principle so that CEOs can make a lot of money only if this helps entry-level workers. Rawls would be concerned about inequalities between the poor and rich, but he would address this problem at the societal level – for example, through the tax code – and not through rules of firms.

2.2. *Nozick's Libertarianism*

Nozick thinks that many scholars who try to figure out what justice requires approach the issue the wrong way. They imagine that there is a big pile of resources somewhere, and a central authority of some kind has to decide how to distribute them. But this is not the case, Nozick says. While there are a lot of resources scattered about in society, they are mostly already owned by people, and people's ownership rights need to be respected. Nozick's belief in the fundamental importance of property rights informs his theory of justice and his rejection of competing theories.

Nozick's theory of justice – which he calls the "entitlement theory" – has three principles: (1) a principle that tells us how a piece of property can come to be owned, (2) a principle that regulates the transfer of owned property, and (3) a principle that tells us how to rectify things when people's property is stolen. One way that Nozick tries to explain and argue for his theory is by comparing it to alternative theories and showing why they are problematic.

Nozick says his theory is "historical," which makes it different from "current time-slice" theories. On a current time-slice theory, to decide if a certain distribution of resources is just, all you need to do is look at the distribution *right now*. An extreme form of egalitarianism on which justice requires that everyone has exactly the same amount of all resources is an example of a current time-slice theory. If everyone doesn't have exactly the same amount of all resources right now, then the distribution is unjust, according to this theory. By contrast, according to Nozick's historical theory, it matters how a distribution came about, not just what it's like right now. To discover whether a distribution of resources is just on Nozick's view, we need to know whether it was acquired justly, transferred justly, and whether any improper acquisitions or transfers were rectified justly.

Nozick also distinguishes his entitlement theory from "patterned" theories. A patterned theory of justice is a theory that says that people's shares of resources should be based on their possession of a specific criterion or set of criteria. "To each according to her need," is one patterned theory of justice. "To each according to what she deserves" is another. By contrast, according to Nozick, just distributions on his entitlement theory will not conform to any pattern exactly, because people will exercise their property rights in ways that cause patterns to be upset.

Nozick illustrates this point using an example involving Wilt Chamberlain, a famous basketball player from the 1970s. Let us update this example and use Jimmie Johnson, the famous NASCAR driver. Pick your favorite patterned theory of justice. Mine is desert. I think that justice requires giving each person what they deserve. Suppose that we (somehow) bring this world about. Next suppose that in this world Jimmie Johnson makes a deal with the owners of the Daytona International Speedway. He will race in the next Daytona 500, but everyone who enters the stadium will have to deposit $1.00 in a box that goes directly to Jimmie. The owners agree to this deal, because they think that people will pay to see Jimmie race. They are right. A capacity crowd of 167,785 attends, and each deposits $1.00 in the box for Jimmie. At the conclusion of the race, Jimmie now has an extra $167,785.

One point this example makes, Nozick says, is that when people exercise their property rights, patterns are upset. Before the Jimmie/Daytona deal, things were arranged exactly according to my favorite pattern. After the deal, they are not. If you want to preserve the pattern, you are going to have to stop people from doing these sorts of deals. Since people make these deals all the time, you are going to have to interfere in people's lives all the time. A second point this example makes, according to Nozick, is that you shouldn't. Jimmie and the Daytona Speedway owners do nothing unjust, he says, when they make the deal involving the $1.00 box. Jimmie owns his labor, and the Daytona owners own the track. Doing this deal is a legitimate exercise of their property rights.

We now have a better sense of what Nozick's theory is *not* – a set of current time-slice or patterned principles of justice – and why it is not these things. What about the content of Nozick's own theory – the principles of justice in acquisition, transfer, and rectification? Nozick doesn't try to provide fully worked-out versions of these principles, but he does say a few things about them that help us to understand their meaning and limitations.

A principle of justice in acquisition identifies the conditions under which you can come to own something that was previously unowned. Here Nozick embraces the 17th-century English philosopher John Locke's idea that an acquisition is just only if there is "enough and as good" left for others. You might think that this condition is rarely met. Every time you take something out of public circulation, as it were, and make it your own, you leave less for others. But Nozick interprets the "enough and as good" condition to mean that your coming to own something can't make anyone worse off. And Nozick thinks this condition is often met. A farmer who claims a piece of land for her own will grow crops that other people will be eager to buy. An oil company that claims a piece of ground as its own will draw oil from it that will power people's cars. And so on. Instead of making other people worse off, Nozick thinks that people's coming to own things actually makes others better off.

A principle of justice in transfer tells us the conditions under which a thing – assuming it is justly owned – is justly transferred from one owner to another. Nozick says that transfers that happen through fraud or force are unjust. So are transfers that have the effect of granting a person monopoly rights over an essential resource, such as water or power.

Nozick says the least about the principle of justice in rectification, but a little thought shows how important this principle is. History is rife with theft of property and labor. In many countries, including the U.S., the fruits of slave labor are still in abundant supply. A principle of justice in rectification is needed to tell us how to set matters right.

While there is much in Nozick's theory that is still vague at this point, we can see some clear implications for the existence of the welfare state. Nozick gives a starring role to property rights. While there are some limitations on how you can acquire something, and how much of it you can acquire, once it's yours, your right to it is absolute. You can do with it pretty much anything you want, and provided you don't violate others' rights, no one can take it from you. At the same time, this means that no one is obligated to give you any of their property. If you are down on your luck, people might decide to help you for charitable reasons, but they will not be required to do so.

Nozick's emphasis on property rights leads him to think that only a "minimal state" can be justified. This is a state that is concerned only to protect people's rights to life and property, and not to provide any sort of social benefits, including roads, sewers, basic education, pensions for senior citizens, and much else. To provide these sorts of benefits, the state would have to tax its citizens, and Nozick thinks taxation is not just a violation of property rights, but a form of forced labor. When you are taxed, the state takes some of your money. Since you labored to earn that money, this is like forcing you to labor for the state for free. Since we don't think that the state (or anyone) should force you to labor for free, we must object to taxation. Of course, there would be no problem if you decided to give a portion of your earnings to the state. But taxation is mandatory. Since a welfare state of any kind requires taxes, Nozick's minimal state is not any sort of welfare state at all.

2.3. Debating Rawls, Nozick, and More

We have now reviewed two theories of justice – Rawls's and Nozick's – and considered their implications for the welfare state. Rawls and Nozick offer very different visions of justice and the state. You might be wondering: who is right?

This is a question that cannot be answered here. But the method that we described for solving ethical problems in the previous chapter – the method of *reflective equilibrium* – will be a useful tool as you entertain this question. Indeed, Rawls is one of the main writers who popularized this method of ethical problem solving. You should evaluate each theory's principles and the judgments that these principles yield in particular cases and ask whether the principles and judgments are consistent with each other and whether they are independently plausible.

Perhaps you think that Nozick is correct that property rights are absolute, or nearly so, and that taxation is like forced labor. But think about the full implications of this idea. It seems to imply that the state is not justified in taxing people to provide roads and sewers. Do you believe that? If not, then you might need to revise your view that property rights are absolute. Or perhaps you think that Rawls is right that people should have fair equality of opportunity for scarce positions. But think about the full implications of this idea. It would require, among other things, ensuring that everyone attended schools of equal quality to ensure that no one had an advantage over anyone else in the competition for prestigious jobs. Do you believe that? If not, then you might need to revise your view that justice requires fair equality of opportunity for scarce positions.

To be clear, determining the right view about the welfare state is not simply a matter of determining whether Rawls or Nozick is right about justice. There are many other theories of justice out there, and you will have some ideas of your own. But we have done something valuable here. We have familiarized ourselves with two theories of justice that are important in their own right and that are frequently mined by scholars for insights relevant to business ethics.

More generally, we have begun to think explicitly about the kinds of social support that is or should be available to people in a just society. This is important because it will affect our views about what ethics requires of businesses. What obligations businesses have to their workers, or to society at large, will depend to some extent on what society is like and, in particular, what people's lives are like outside of the firm. In a society with a weak welfare state, businesses may have more extensive ethical obligations. More people may need help, and businesses may be in a good position to provide help. There also may be more vulnerable people, and businesses will need to take care not to exploit them. In a society with a robust welfare state, businesses' obligations may be less extensive. There may be fewer people who need help and who are at risk of exploitation.

3. Private Versus Social Ownership of the Means of Production

Our goal in this chapter is to consider the institutional background against which business activity occurs. First we considered the welfare state, focusing on the theories of justice of Rawls and Nozick. Now we consider private property.

Our question is not whether any property can be owned. In certain communist societies, there was very little private property. People didn't own their cars or kitchen appliances. These days it is hard to find anyone who thinks this is a good way to live, and we will not consider it. Our subject is private property in the means of production. By "means of production" I mean businesses, factories, machines, and offices – the sorts of things that *produce* goods and services. Our question is whether these sorts of things can be owned by individuals, as capitalism maintains, or whether they should be owned collectively, by the public, as socialism maintains.

Now you might say that if you allow individuals to have private property in things like cars and kitchen appliances, then you *have* to allow individuals to own the means of production. This is because people can use these things to produce and sell goods. You can use your car to make money as an Uber driver and your kitchen appliances to make money as a caterer. Socialists know this. They say that you are allowed to use your possessions to make things for yourself, but not to sell to others. Capitalists, of course, deny this. We will examine what can be said in defense of each view.

3.1. For Private Ownership

Let us begin with arguments for private ownership of the means of production. While the question of whether people can own property in the means of production can come apart from the question of whether people can own any property at all – that is, you can consistently say that people cannot own the means of production but can own other property – some would argue that the reasons that it is good for people to be able to own any property also imply that it is good for people to be able to own property in the means of production.

One reason that is sometimes given for why people should be able to own property (in general) is that it promotes freedom. You have certain things that you want to do with your life, certain things you want to accomplish. For almost all of these things, you are going to need some property. Maybe you want to drive across the country. For that you need a car. Maybe you want to write a novel. For that you need a computer or at least a pen and paper. If you did not own these things, then perhaps you could borrow or rent them. But this would make accomplishing your goals dependent on the whims of others. You are more likely to accomplish your goals, in the way you want to accomplish them, if you own these things, for this would give you control over them.

A similar freedom-based story can be told about the value of private ownership in the means of production. In addition to driving across the country or writing a novel, you might want to start a business. Perhaps you want to work for yourself as a lawyer, accountant, or home inspector. In a society that permits you to own thc mcans of production, you are able to do these things. You are able to be a sole proprietor. In a society that does not allow the means of production to be privately owned, you cannot do this. You could find work as a lawyer, accountant, or home inspector for a socially owned firm, and you might exercise joint control over this firm with your co-workers. But this would not be the same as being your own boss in a firm that you alone own.

Milton Friedman gave a slightly different freedom-based argument for private ownership of the means of production. The previous argument appeals to personal freedom. You are better able to accomplish your goals if you can own things, including a business. Friedman appeals to political freedom to defend private ownership of businesses. The state already has considerable power over us, Friedman observes. It would make things worse, he says, for the state to have control over the means of production also. Then the state would be in a position to wield total control over our lives. If we could trust the state to act wisely and listen to us, then this would not be a problem. In fact, for reasons discussed later, it might be better. But Friedman thinks we cannot trust the state or indeed anyone with that much power. As the old saying goes, "power corrupts, and absolute power corrupts absolutely." Because we cannot trust the state, Friedman says, it is better for the state not to have control over the means of production. It is better for the means of production – the factories and other businesses – to be owned by private individuals, even if you are not one of them.

A second reason that is sometimes given for why people should be able to own private property is it promotes welfare. Perhaps the main way private ownership promotes welfare is that people tend to take better care of the things that they own, and invest more in them, as opposed to the things that are held in common. You might see evidence of this in your own life. Perhaps you occasionally drop a cigarette out your car window onto a public street, but you probably don't do this in the kitchen of your apartment. You might invest your time and energy into making your garden look beautiful, but you probably don't spend a lot of time beautifying a public park.

A similar welfare-based story can be told about the value of private ownership in the means of production. According to this story, people take better care of businesses if they are their own than if those businesses are socially owned. A business may have machines, or it may involve complicated formulas. You will take better care of these machines and will work to maintain those formulas if they are yours than if they are public property. Moreover, you will invest more in the machines and formulas if they are yours than if they are public property. You will invest time trying to make your machine better or make your business processes work more efficiently. You will not have the same incentives if these things are not yours, and the fruits of your labor are shared with others. Ultimately your private investment benefits society as a whole. When your machines and formulas keep working or get better, we all benefit. This is because, insofar as you stay in business, you are producing things that society wants.

3.2. *For Public Ownership*

We have considered freedom-based and welfare-based arguments for private ownership of the means of production, that is, the right for an individual to own a business. Now we will consider arguments for public ownership of the means of production, that is, the view that all businesses should be publicly owned. Interestingly, the same two considerations – freedom and welfare – play an important role in these arguments.

We said that private ownership of the means of production might be thought to promote freedom because it gives individuals one more freedom, namely the freedom to own businesses by themselves. Socialists are not impressed with this freedom. (By 'socialist' in this section I will mean someone who thinks that the means of production should be publicly owned.) Starting a business is often both expensive and risky. Most individuals do not try to start them. So the freedom to be a sole proprietor is not worth much to the average person. Moreover, the costs to freedom of allowing businesses to be privately owned, socialists say, are quite steep. This is so in two ways.

First, when businesses are privately owned, employees will lack freedom at work. This is because ownership implies control. The owner of a business controls what goes on in the business. The owner of the business sets the rules, and the employees of the business follow the rules. Perhaps you have experienced this yourself. Your boss tells you what to do and you do it. If your boss is not the owner, then she is told what to do by her boss. The ultimate boss – the person who is not told what to do but tells others what to do – is the owner. The decisions that get made at work can be really important. They can include decisions about raises, hiring and firing, and relocation. When firms are privately owned, decisions get made that affect employees in serious ways, and employees have no control over them.

Two caveats here. One, your boss – suppose it's the business owner – can invite your input into the decision-making process. But you cannot claim a right to input; it is up to the owner to decide what role you will play. Second, the owner of a business does not acquire the right to order you around just by virtue of her ownership of the business. But it does give her a right to control your access to the business, and if you want to get access to the business – say, to do the work you need to do in order to earn a paycheck – then she will have power over you.

Another way that private ownership of the means of production can diminish freedom, according to socialists, is that it can damage political freedom. History shows that owners of the means of production are able to amass huge quantities of wealth. They are then able to use that wealth to get their way politically. One way this happens is through campaign contributions and lobbying. Liberals worry about the influence of people like Charles and David Koch, who donate millions of dollars to conservative causes. Conservatives worry about people like Tom Steyer and George Soros, who donate millions to liberal causes. Business owners can influence the political process in another more subtle way. They can get politicians to enact, or not enact, certain laws by saying what they will do if those laws are enacted or not enacted. When the state of Indiana passed a law that seemed to permit employers to discriminate against LGBT people on grounds of religious liberty, the CEOs of powerful companies like Salesforce.com and Angie's List protested, threatening to curtail their operations in the state if the law were not revised. The law quickly *was* revised. Now you might approve of this result, or you might not. What socialists object to is *how* it was achieved. It was achieved by complaints from very rich people, who were made rich by their ownership of businesses.

Socialists think that both freedom at work and political freedom are compromised by private ownership of the means of production. They think that social ownership of the means of production – ownership of businesses by the public as a whole – remedies both problems.

Consider freedom at work. When the means of production are privately owned, most people at work will simply carry out decisions that others make. When the means of production are publicly owned, this will not be the case. Everyone will have a role to play in making decisions. Just as "we" control what happens to us politically in a democracy, so "we" control what happens to us economically under socialism. Does this mean that you personally will have a say in everything that goes on in the company for which you work, or even that you will get to veto decisions you don't like? No, in the same way that you don't have a say in or veto power over everything that goes on in your town, state, or country. Some decisions will be made by your representatives, and some will be made by experts. Different versions of socialism will give different answers to the question of how much control, and what sort of control, individuals will have in the economy. But you have much more say over the process of production when its means are socially owned than when its means are privately owned.

Consider political freedom. The problem with private ownership of the means of production, socialists say, is that this concentrates wealth in the hands of a small group of people, some of whom will use it to exercise disproportionate political power. If the means of production are publicly owned, then there is no problem. The same people who control the political process also control the means of production. In both cases, those people are us. Socialists are under no illusion that all people in society will be able to exercise exactly equal political power. Some people, through superior charisma or intelligence, will always be able to get others to follow them. But socialists are keen to see one source of unequal political power – control of the means of production – diminished or eliminated.

What about Friedman's argument that giving the state control over the means of production gives the state too much power, which might be used for oppression and domination? Some socialists will agree with this. But they will say that this shows only that control over the means of production should not be concentrated in the hands of a government elite (as it was in the Soviet Union) but instead should be dispersed more widely among the people.

So far we have considered freedom-based arguments for social ownership of the means of production. What about welfare? The welfare-based argument for private ownership of the means of production is that people take better care of, and invest more in, things that they own – including businesses – than things that are collectively owned. Socialists think that this ignores even stronger welfare considerations for public ownership of the means of production. We said that social control of the means of production promotes freedom – when the people own businesses, they control what happens in them. But this same control, socialists say, translates into greater welfare for more people in society. The public can use its control over the workplace to enhance its own well-being.

This can happen in at least two ways. One is by controlling how the revenue that businesses generate is allocated. If a single person is in control of a business, then she can keep all of the profits that the firm generates for herself. If all of the people who work at the business are in control of it, then they can distribute the firm's revenues in a more equal fashion. In many societies in which the means of production are privately owned – and that is most societies – there is enormous inequality. Some live in unimaginable luxury while others barely scrape by. How firms distribute their resources is a significant driver of this inequality. If this process were brought under public control, socialists claim, there would be less inequality and, even more important, less poverty.

A second way that public control over the means of production can increase welfare, according to socialists, is by changing the conditions of work. A business owner will have certain ideas about how she wants the work process to be structured: what sorts of things you will do, how you will do them, under what conditions you will do them, when you will do them (e.g., how long your working day is), and so on. The business owner cannot make things too unpleasant for you. If she does, you will leave. But she makes the decisions. If means of production are socially owned, then you will help to make these decisions. You will not be in the position of a supplicant to a lord or ruler. Instead, you will be a joint owner, able to craft a workplace that is better suited to your needs and wants. This is not to say, of course, that you will be able to get everything you want. It is a joint decision, and you may be overridden. But you will have more ability to get what you want.

A defender of private ownership of the means of production might reply to these points that how much people are paid at work and what the labor process is like are less under the control of the business owner than you might think. How much she can pay and how long she makes people work are determined in part by market forces. Public ownership may not change this very much. This reply is not decisive, but it makes a reasonable point. To better understand it, we need to turn to the final piece of the background of business: the market.

4. Markets Versus Planning

In both capitalist and socialist societies, stuff – goods and services – needs to be produced. The debate about markets versus planning is primarily a debate about how society is going to produce stuff. To produce stuff, resources are required. So this is a debate about the mechanism through which society should allocate its productive resources.

One answer to the question of how we are going to decide what stuff to produce, or how society's resources will be allocated, is *planning*. On this view, a group of people get together and decide what stuff to produce, how much of it to produce, what the price of the stuff is going to be, and where to send it. They give the orders, and producers execute them. Some socialists advocate central planning, where all decisions are made by a central group, and others prefer a decentralized approach, where decisions are made by small groups dispersed throughout society.

A second answer to the question of how we are going to decide what stuff to produce and how we are going to allocate resources is *the market*. This answer says that there is no official "we" who decides what to produce, how much of it to produce, what price to sell it for, and where to sell it. Rather, these sorts of decisions are made by individuals. They make decisions by responding to signals sent by prices. You may decide to produce something if you can sell it for a lot more than it costs you to make. I may decide to make something different than you or make the same thing as you. In a market economy, competition among producers is not just permitted but encouraged.

Spoiler alert! Most people now think that economies that are mostly planned are infeasible. (This explains the rise of market socialism, which features public ownership of the means of production and the use of markets to allocate productive resources.) Almost all modern economies feature a heavy dose of markets to allocate productive resources. Yet almost all economies feature some amount of planning, and there is debate about how much planning is optimal. Let us now review the strengths and weaknesses of planning and markets.

4.1. For Planning

Suppose you own a pizza place and you want to feed your customers. How will you manage your resources, including your workers, to accomplish this? Very generally, you will tell your workers what to do. You will tell worker 1 to make the dough, worker 2 to make the sauce, worker 3 to shred the cheese, worker 4 to slice the pepperoni, and so on. You will need to coordinate their actions. Worker 2 shouldn't make more sauce than is needed for the doughs that worker 1 makes. Worker 4 shouldn't slice more pepperoni than customers will order. Through precise direction and coordination, you can produce just enough pizzas to feed your customers.

What defenders of economic planning propose to do is take this style of economic production from inside the business and extend it to the economy as a whole. You – the pizza place owner – would not think it's a good idea to let your workers decide on their own how much dough and sauce to make, how much cheese to shred, and how much pepperoni to slice. You might end up with too much of some and not enough of the other. For the same reason, planners say, it wouldn't be a good idea for production decisions to be made by isolated individuals in the economy. There needs to be some person or group coordinating the process of production for society as a whole.

Defenders of economic planning see it as rational and efficient, and markets as wasteful and chaotic. To understand the charge of wastefulness, consider the videotape format war of the 1980s. These days, people stream movies at home over the internet. But in the 1980s and 1990s, they watched movies at home on VCRs, which played tapes. The first tape format introduced was the "Betamax," created by the electronics giant Sony. A short time later, a different format came out, the "VHS," manufactured by JVC. It was expensive for movie and television studios to produce content in both formats. So they had to make a choice: VHS or Betamax. A competitive "war" ensued between JVC and Sony. Eventually many other electronics companies joined the fray. Competition was fierce, for a lot was at stake. You can look at it this way. For the losers, all of the work that its scientists, engineers, designers, marketers, and lawyers did to make and sell their tape format would be wasted. Eventually JVC won. The VHS format became the dominant format for VCR tapes. Even though it won, this battle cost JVC too, in fees for marketers and lawyers, among others.

This is not an isolated case. Almost the exact same "format war" was repeated in the mid-2000s with the Blu-ray Disc and HD DVD. (The Blu-ray won.) Indeed, this sort of thing happens all over the economy in every sector and industry. Firms compete with each other to provide almost exactly the same thing to consumers, vying to get their attention through flashy ads and marketing campaigns, protecting their property with teams of expensive lawyers, and inevitably some lose. How much less wasteful it would have been, the advocate of economic planning says, for this competition never to have happened. Instead of JVC and Sony competing with each other to produce and sell different, but almost equally good, formats of tape for the VCR, we should have decided upfront on a preferred format and then focused all of our collective efforts on producing that format. We could have produced a lot more of what people needed and wanted at a lower price, with no wasted effort.

The charge that markets are chaotic also draws on the idea that markets are competitive. People need and want things, and in a market economy, there is no plan for getting them those things. There is just a void, which producers may (or may not) fill. Marx developed a particular version of the "chaos" argument against markets in his writings. As modern economic systems began to take shape in the 19th century, when Marx was doing his most influential work, there were periods of great productivity and prosperity followed by periods of woeful idleness and poverty. First booms, then busts. Marx thought this wasn't an accidental feature of the times, but an inescapable feature of capitalism and, in particular, of markets. To survive in a competitive market, firms need to be as productive as possible. They build more factories and hire more workers, producing as much stuff as they can. Inevitably, firms collectively produce too much stuff. Prices fall, and the rate of profit drops. Some firms go out of business, and their workers are fired. With so many unemployed workers, demand for goods falls, and the remaining firms begin to struggle too. Eventually the economy stabilizes – but not before fortunes are lost and people suffer. Then the whole process repeats itself. Many contemporary Marxians see echoes of the "chaos" objection to markets in the financial crisis of 2007–2009.

The story we have told about economic planning is theoretically attractive. And as noted, all modern economies feature some planning. But for a variety of reasons, planning has not proved successful as the dominant mode of economic organization.

4.2. For Markets

Some people argue that, if you think that the means of production can be privately owned, you have to think that markets should be used to allocate productive resources. To say that markets should be used to allocate productive resources, the argument goes, is just to say that people should be allowed to exchange the resources they own – their land, machines, and labor – with the resources other people own – their land, machines, and labor. But part of what it means to own something is to be able to trade it with someone else, for something that they own.

Suppose I own a piece of land. This is a productive resource. Crops can be grown on it. I discover that people really like raspberries, and my land is perfect for growing them. So I decide to grow raspberries. Then I sell them to people like you who like raspberries.

The scenario I have described is the use of a market to allocate productive resources. There is no authority telling me to grow raspberries. I just grow them in response to perceived demand. But – some people argue – the scenario I have described is *also* a legitimate exercise of private property rights in productive resources. In fact, they would say, if I'm not allowed to grow raspberries on my land and sell them, then it's not the case that I own my land. Ownership implies control. Their point is that once you accept that people have property rights in productive resources, you have to accept that productive resources should be allocated, or put to use, through markets and not through planning.

In addition to a rights-based defense of markets, some argue that markets are superior to planning for reasons of *freedom*. Remember that, in a market economy, there is no authority that decides what will be produced, how much of it will be produced, and so on. These decisions are made by individuals. This means that, in a market economy, individuals have more freedom when it comes to making decisions about production. This can translate into more freedom when it comes to making decisions about consumption. If you have a desire for a good or service, and make this fact known, a producer may decide to satisfy your desire. There is no need for a governmental authority or a production council to approve the creation of a product that satisfies your desire.

Most socialists would reject both of these arguments, of course. With respect to the rights-based defense, they would say that people don't have private property rights in the means of production. These are to be socially owned or owned by the people. With respect to the freedom-based defense, they would argue that this ignores the freedom of those who do not own productive resources or who cannot afford the goods and services that the market produces.

More important than the rights- and freedom-based defense of markets, however, is the welfare-based defense. According to defenders of markets, markets "deliver the goods" in a way that planned economies do not. We can see some evidence for this in differences between living standards in market-based and planned economies. In 1989, at the time of its collapse, per capita income in the Soviet Union, a planned economy, was $9211, compared to $21,082 in the U.S., $19,600 in Canada, and $14,300 in the U.K., all market economies. China is an example of a country that once had an economy with a high degree of planning, and is now a market-based economy, and this has resulted in tremendous economic growth. China started to introduce substantial market-based reforms in the late 1970s. In 1980, its GDP per capita was less than $500. By 2016, it had risen to $15,700.

Economists explain the efficiency of markets in terms of the first fundamental theorem of welfare economics. According to this theorem, market outcomes are efficient in the sense of Pareto-optimal. This means that no one can be made better off without at least one person being made worse off. The details of the proof of the first fundamental theorem of welfare economics are complex and need not concern us here. But the intuitive idea is simple. People trade because they see some advantage in it. If you leave them alone, they will trade with each other until they cannot make themselves better off. This theorem is sometimes seen as a version of the "invisible hand" hypothesis of Adam Smith, the 18th-century Scottish philosopher and economist. Smith thought that if people are free to produce and consume what they want, and trade as they see fit, then society as a whole will benefit. In pursuing their self-interest, market participants are guided "as if by an invisible hand" to promote the public interest. (There is also a second fundamental theorem of welfare economics. This says that any efficient or Pareto-optimal distribution of holdings can be a market outcome. The implication of this theorem is that you can change people's initial holdings – to make it more equal, for example – and if you allow the market to work, a Pareto-optimal outcome will be reached.)

Why are market economies more efficient than planned economies? One reason is that it gives people *incentives* to try to satisfy other people's needs and wants. If you can satisfy someone else's needs and wants, then you can make money. I can make money by growing raspberries in my field and selling them to you. Here again competition plays a crucial role, by intensifying this incentive. If you and I both grow raspberries, then consumers have a choice: my raspberries or yours. This gives me an incentive not just to grow raspberries, but to grow raspberries that are in some way better than yours. That is, market competition leads to *innovation*. I may look for ways of creating tastier raspberries, or cheaper raspberries, or raspberries that hold up better in the shipping process, and so on. Consumers are ultimate beneficiaries of this innovation.

These types of incentives are lacking – or at least dulled – in a planned economy. There is no advantage to me in making my raspberries tastier, cheaper, or sturdier, because there is no one whom I am competing against. This is related to a concept you hear often in business circles, namely, *market discipline*. If I make a bad or expensive raspberry, the market – consumers – will punish me by shopping elsewhere. Of course, in a planned economy, there can still be discipline. The planners can provide it. If they have consumers' best interest at heart, they will. Perhaps they will install new management at the farm. But they may not. I may be able to convince the planners that I am doing the best that can be done. Maybe I will bribe them to look the other way. Consumers are the ones who suffer.

Consider again the videotape format war. Defenders of planned economies see this as a story of waste and loss. Firms compete with each other, one loses, and all their work is wasted. Defenders of market economies see this as a story of innovation and improvement. They say that the whole reason that people spent so much time and effort trying to discover a way to play movies at home is because they saw some advantage in it, and they knew that their product had to be better than its competition to be successful in the market. Without the market, there would be no VHS *or* Betamax. The loss that comes from market competition is a necessary part of this innovation.

Another reason that market economies are more efficient than planned economies has to do with *information*. In a planned economy, the planners need information. They need to know what people want, what raw materials exist, what sort of technology exists, what sort of labor is available, and more. They need to give instructions to hundreds of thousands if not millions of people simultaneously, and they need to update these instructions constantly as preferences, resources, and technology change. This is known as the *calculation problem*, and according to the 20th-century Austrian economist F. A. Hayek, it was practically unsolvable in a society of any significant size. There is no way for even well-meaning and thoughtful economic planners to figure out how to allocate productive resources in society to meet people's needs and wants. Or more precisely, markets do this better than planning.

How does the market do this? The answer is through individuals' choices, motivated by self-interest, and coordinated through prices. People want things (like raspberries), and this gives me an incentive to produce them. Whether I do produce them depends, among other things, on whether I can make money doing so. That in turn depends on how much people are willing to pay for raspberries. If the price is high, and the cost to me of producing raspberries is low, then I will produce them. But if the price is low and the cost to me of producing them is high, then I will not. Prices provide information. They tell me where my scarce resources (my land and labor) are effectively deployed. They are constantly updating. If people start to prefer blueberries over raspberries, the price of raspberries will fall, and I may deploy my resources accordingly. All of this goes not just for me of course, but for every producer in society, and for society as a whole. Hayek's view – which is now the received wisdom – is that prices, and the choices individuals make in response to them, do a better job of allocating scarce productive resources than the deliberate decisions of economic planners.

For reasons of incentives and information, markets seem to be able to satisfy our needs and wants better than planning. But it is not the case that modern economies are entirely unplanned. Most modern economies are "mixed." Markets are used to allocate most resources, but governments also direct economic resources to certain uses. Governments fund scientific research, build parks, stockpile weapons, provide education, maintain roads and sewers, and much more. Productive resources are allocated to these functions not through market mechanisms but by deliberate decisions of government authorities. Many governments also engage in planning of a less intrusive kind, by offering subsidies to increase the production of some goods and levying taxes to decrease the production of others.

Why is this? If markets are so great, why not leave all decisions about what is produced, how much to charge for it, and who gets it to private individuals? Part of the answer is found in the case we made for planning. To this we can add the simple fact that markets sometimes fail. Left alone, they don't always produce the mix of goods that people most want.

One major way that markets fail is that they don't produce enough public goods. The goods we identified as those that governments usually pay for – scientific research, parks, defense, etc. – are public. In economic terms, a public good is a good that is both non-excludable and non-rivalrous. That means that, once the good is produced, you can't stop someone from enjoying it (non-excludability), and their enjoying it doesn't leave less for others (non-rivalry). It is because public goods have these features that the market doesn't produce enough of them on its own. Individuals are tempted to free ride off of the contributions of others and not pay their fair share, lowering demand. If your country has a strong national defense, then you will benefit from it, whether or not you pay. This is clearly not the case with private goods like shoes. If you don't pay, you'll go barefoot. A second major way that markets fail is that they produce too many of certain private goods, in particular, goods with negative externalities. A negative externality is an uncompensated cost of an activity that is imposed on a person not engaging in the activity. Pollution is the classic negative externality. The production and consumption of many goods generate pollution – of air, water, and land. If the prices of these goods do not include the cost of the pollution, then they will be overproduced. If the operator of a coal-fired power station is able to emit all the pollution she wants, as opposed to installing expensive smokestack scrubbers, she can charge a lower price for her power, and people will consume more. This won't reflect how much people actually want her power, once its true costs are factored in.

For these reasons, despite the advantages of markets, no one is prepared to rely on them exclusively to decide how to allocate productive resources. There is still a lively debate about what allocation decisions should be made by states and what ones should be left to market forces.

5. Chapter Summary

In this chapter we learned more about the institutions against which business activity takes place. One sometimes hears talk of a debate between "capitalists" and "socialists." But putting things this way masks debate about three separate things: how robust the welfare state should be, whether productive property should be privately or socially owned, and whether productive resources should be allocated by planning or through markets. These institutions can be combined in different ways, so it is important to consider them independently. In this chapter we considered justifications for a more or less robust welfare state, private or social ownership of the means of production, and markets or planning to allocate productive resources.

We began with the welfare state, considering the theories of justice of both Rawls and Nozick. These philosophers offer very different accounts of what justice requires in terms of a social safety net. Nozick thinks it should be minimal; Rawls thinks the state should do more for people. What you think about these theories, and the welfare state more generally, will depend in part on what you think about property rights, for social programs will require a significant tax base. So it made sense at this point to turn our attention to property rights, and in particular, property rights in the means of production (i.e., the entities that produce goods and services). We saw how considerations of freedom and welfare can support both private and public ownership. We concluded our discussion with the question of how productive resources should be allocated, considering arguments for planning and for markets. Most people now believe that economies that are mostly planned are inefficient and that markets should be used to allocate many productive resources. At the same time, most modern economies use planning to allocate some resources.

The society in which you are reading this will have a certain arrangement of political and economic institutions. What you have learned in this chapter will help you to understand the reasons for this arrangement and may also give you some ideas about how this arrangement can be improved. That's important already. But understanding and being able to critically evaluate political and economic institutions is also vital for understanding issues in business ethics. To take but a few examples: your views about the welfare state may inform your views about business's obligations to society; your views about ownership may inform your views about whether employees should play a role in managerial decision-making; and your views about the value of markets may inform your views about the nature and value of corporate political activity. We will return to the themes introduced in this chapter many times over the remainder of this book.

6. Study Questions

1. Debates between "capitalism" and "socialism" can sometimes obscure what three elements of a political/economic system? Why is it important to evaluate these elements separately?
2. John Rawls thinks that social inequalities should be arranged to the greatest benefit of the least advantaged. What does this mean, and why might arranging inequalities this way justify allowing people to keep a lot, but not all, of what they earn at their jobs?
3. Robert Nozick says maintaining a "patterned" theory of justice is incompatible with allowing people to exercise their property rights. Explain this.
4. Why does Nozick think taxation is like forced labor? Do you agree?
5. If we value freedom, should the means of production be privately or publicly owned? Explain your answer.
6. If we value welfare, should the means of production be privately or publicly owned? Explain your answer.
7. Defenders of economic planning say that markets are wasteful. What do they mean by this?
8. Defenders of market economies say that recent economic history provides good evidence that markets make us better off. What are they talking about?
9. One reason that market economies are thought to be more efficient than planned economies is that markets lead to more innovation. Why might this be?
10. What does it mean to say that most modern economies are "mixed"? Do you think the economy in which you live has the right mix of privately and publicly owned enterprises?

Additional Readings

Arnold, S. (n.d.). Socialism. *The Internet Encyclopedia of Philosophy*. https://iep.utm.edu/socialis/

Brennan, J., & Arneson, R. (2022). *Debating capitalism*. New York: Oxford University Press.

Cohen, G. A. (2009). *Why not socialism?* Princeton, NJ: Princeton University Press.

Friedman, M. (2002/1962). *Capitalism and freedom* (40th anniversary ed.). Chicago, IL: University of Chicago Press.

Gaus, G. F. (2010). The idea and ideal of capitalism. In G. G. Brenkert & T. L. Beauchamp (Eds.), *The Oxford handbook of business ethics* (pp. 73–99). New York: Oxford University Press.

Hayek, F. A. (1945). The use of knowledge in society. *American Economic Review, 35*(4), 519–530.

Nozick, R. (1974). *Anarchy, state, and utopia*. New York: Basic Books.

Rawls, J. (1971). *A theory of justice*. Cambridge, MA: Harvard University Press.

Schmidtz, D., & Goodin, R. E. (1998). *Social welfare and individual responsibility*. New York: Cambridge University Press.

Wolff, J. (2002). *Why read Marx today?* New York: Oxford University Press.

5 What Can Be Sold?

In the last chapter we considered the virtues of different political and economic systems, focusing on the extent of the social safety net, the ownership of property, and the value of markets. In this chapter we dig deeper into markets and ask what can be sold in them.

You can buy many things, including shoes, pencils, computers, and tarot card readings. But some things you cannot buy, including human organs, children, landmines, and drop-side cribs. What's the difference? What is it about a product that makes it permissible or impermissible to sell?

Exchange is central to business. To "do business" with someone is to exchange one thing of value for something else of value. A business is an entity that offers goods and services for sale. So the question of what goods and services should be sold in markets is a foundational question in business ethics.

The decision about whether an item can be sold or not is often made, like the decision about what economic system to have, by the state. But in some cases – for example, when products are new and the state hasn't yet had a chance to contemplate whether it should be sold – individual businesspeople will have to make this decision.

In this chapter we explore the question of what can be sold by considering some reasons for thinking that certain things should *not* be sold. We consider functionality, safety, and what we will call "fitness." That is, we ask: does it work? Is it safe? Is it fit for sale, in the sense of being an appropriate object to be exchanged for money? It is possible that there are other reasons for thinking that certain things should not be for sale. But these are the reasons that come up most often in contemporary debates, so this is where we will focus our attention.

1. Does It Work?

Some retailers offer goods for sale that don't seem to "work," on an intuitive understanding of what it means to work. They do not perform the function for which they are ostensibly designed. Do retailers do anything wrong when they offer such products for sale? To see what we are talking about, it will be helpful to have an example in mind.

DOI: 10.4324/9781351016872-5

The company Copper Fit offers a variety of compression braces for people's calves, knees, elbows, hands, and backs. In many ways these are ordinary compression braces, of the sort you would find in any sporting goods store. Compression offers verifiable health benefits. It provides support for sore muscles, it improves circulation, and it reduces inflammation. What's different about the braces from Copper Fit is that they are lined with copper. Copper is a scientifically proven antimicrobial agent, so Copper Fit's products are less prone to growth of molds, fungi, and viruses. But Copper Fit's advertising does not emphasize this fact. Instead, it highlights the performance benefits of their braces. In one video, Copper Fit says that their braces are made of a special "therapeutic fabric, blended with copper, to aid in faster recovery and performance, and guaranteed relief of muscle aches and pains." They hired Brett Favre and Jerry Rice, two former NFL players, as spokespeople. "I perform best with Copper Fit," Favre says. "Where was this when I was playing in the NFL?," Rice asks.

In fact, there is no scientific evidence that copper improves performance. Based on everything we know, a compression brace with copper offers the exact same performance benefits as a compression brace without copper. The most that can be said is that Copper Fit's products are slightly cleaner than ordinary compression braces.

The makers of Copper Fit are aware that there is no scientific evidence that copper has any performance benefits. So they are careful not to claim that it is the copper in their braces *specifically* that has this effect. They note that their products offer health benefits and have copper in them, and both of these claims are true. They allow their customers to infer, without justification, that copper provides a performance benefit.

Is there anything wrong with what Copper Fit is doing? Before answering this, note that Copper Fit is not alone in selling products that we have reason to believe don't "work," in the sense we are talking about. Drug stores are full of homeopathic treatments for common ailments. You can buy ignatia amara to treat anxiety, arnica to treat pain, apis mellifica to reduce swelling, and ginkgo biloba to boost cognitive function. (All of these substances are derived from plants, with the exception of apis mellifica, which is a liquid that is made by crushing bees.) But there is no scientific evidence that any of these substances work as indicated. Indeed, there is considerable evidence that they don't work. You can pay a tarot card reader to learn about your past, present, and future. You can pay a psychic or medium to talk to the dead. You can buy liquids to detoxify your body. Like copper and homeopathy, there is no evidence that any of this works, in the sense under consideration.

One thing you might say is that it is no problem for retailers to sell products that don't work as long as they don't promise, or otherwise mislead people into thinking, that they do work. In the next chapter we will consider the obligations of retailers when it comes to truth and deception in advertising. But let us suppose for now that Copper Fit is doing nothing wrong on this score. Then is there nothing wrong with the sale of these (and many other) items?

Here it is useful to recall the discussion in the previous chapter about the value of markets. Why should people be allowed to offer goods for sale in a market to other people? One reason appeals to rights. To own something is to have a bundle of rights regarding that thing. One of these rights is a right to transfer it to someone else. So we might say that Copper Fit has a right to transfer their compression braces to consumers (for consumers' money), and consumers have a right to transfer some of their money to Copper Fit (for Copper Fit's braces). Another justification of market exchange appeals to freedom. People have an interest in shaping their lives according to their own plans. These plans may include selling or buying copper-lined compression braces. This might seem like a small or insignificant freedom, but it might be meaningful for those who choose to exercise it. It may be important to you to have the option to buy a copper-lined compression brace, even if it is no better than a brace without copper. If we focus on rights and freedom, then, we might be convinced that people should be allowed to sell and buy products that don't work. It respects people's rights and enhances their freedom.

Arguably the more important justification of the market, however, derives from its effects on welfare. People are better off – their wants are satisfied to a greater extent – in market economies than in planned economies. But we might wonder whether people's wants are truly satisfied by purchasing products that don't work. Suppose you purchase a trumpet because you want to learn how to play. But when you get the trumpet home, you discover that it doesn't work, because isn't a real trumpet, but just a sculpture of one. In this case, your desire has not been satisfied. The same might be said of Copper Fit products. You might believe these products work, but your belief is unjustified. So, if we focus on welfare, we might conclude that products that can't be proven to work shouldn't be sold.

We might think that there is a role here for government intervention. Governments are and ought to be concerned with their citizens' welfare. The government prevents us from doing things that cause harm to other people. You cannot kill other people or take their property, among other things. The government also prevents you from harming yourself in certain ways. In some jurisdictions, you are not allowed to ride in a car without wearing a seatbelt, drive a motorcycle without wearing a helmet, or set off certain kinds of fireworks. These restrictions might conceivably have some basis in a concern for harm to others. Perhaps if you are killed in a motorcycle accident, your family and friends will be sad, and that is a sort of harm to them. But for the most part, their basis is in harm to you. Restrictions that are justified by reference to the welfare of the person who is being restricted are instances of *paternalism*. You might think that, for paternalistic reasons, the government should ban the sale of products that don't work. To be sure, when someone buys something that doesn't work, they don't always put their health or life at risk. But they waste their money, and this is a kind of harm.

A key question in this debate is, who decides? There seem to be two options. One is to let private individuals decide. This idea is known as *consumer sovereignty*. You might want to call it "producer and consumer sovereignty," but the party who ultimately decides whether a product will be sold is the consumer. A seller can offer a good for sale, but unless a consumer decides to buy it, the good will not be sold. The other option is to allow the state to forbid the sale of products that do not work. Perhaps there should be some agency that tests products for effectiveness, and if the products cannot be shown to work, then they shouldn't be offered for sale.

Here it is worth mentioning a fact that we have treaded lightly over so far. I have noted that there is no evidence that copper works as a performance enhancer. There is also no evidence that energy healing, homeopathic treatments, or tarot card readings work. In fact, the evidence points in the other direction. But can we be certain that these products don't work? No, we cannot. If we are being honest, we need to say that there is some chance, however small, that copper-lined compression braces reduce pain and inflammation more than copper-free braces. Perhaps psychic mediums really are talking to dead people and tarot card readers are seeing our futures. When we cannot be absolutely sure, who should get the final say? People sometimes make bad choices for themselves. Can governments do better? This question is probably best answered on a case-by-case basis.

2. Is It Safe?

In the previous section we considered whether it should be permissible for firms to sell products that don't work. We might think that they shouldn't, on the grounds that these products don't do any good for those who buy them. In this section we consider products that don't just fail to benefit people but may actively harm them.

2.1. Deciding to Sell

In 2005, Phusion Projects, a Chicago-based company founded by recent college graduates, introduced a drink called "Four Loko." In its 2005 formula, the drink contained four main ingredients: alcohol, caffeine, guarana, and taurine. Four Loko was sold in a 24 oz bottle and had an alcohol content of up to 12%, depending on state regulations. With its sweet taste (flavors included blue raspberry, sour grape, and fruit punch) and colorful labels, Phusion Projects hoped its drink would catch on with young people. It did. Indeed, it became enormously popular among college students, with dangerous results. The sweetness of Four Loko masked its high alcohol content, and the stimulation of the caffeine and guarana made it difficult for people to perceive how intoxicated they were. The drink was blamed for many cases of alcohol poisoning and, as a result, was banned from several college campuses.

As news of Four Loko's effects spread, the Food and Drug Administration (FDA) in the U.S. took an interest in the drink and in caffeinated alcoholic beverages more generally. They warned their manufacturers, including Phusion Projects, that caffeine was being investigated as an "unsafe food additive" in alcoholic beverages and that legal action could follow. In response, in 2010, Phusion Projects decided to reformulate Four Loko. It continues to have a sweet taste, but the caffeine, guarana, and taurine have been removed. The alcohol content is now more clearly visible on the can.

Four Loko was a dangerous product in 2005. It is now less dangerous. Is it still too dangerous? More generally, when is a product too dangerous to be sold?

We might begin by noting that there are in fact many things that everyone accepts should be available for sale that can cause serious injury and death, including cars, knives, golf clubs, axes, chainsaws, bleach, ammonia, and cigarettes. So the question "is this product too dangerous to be sold?" cannot be answered simply by considering whether the product can cause serious harm or death. Other factors must be in play. One is whether the product is dangerous in a way that surprises users. It is perfectly obvious that if I use a knife carelessly I can do serious harm to myself. But it is not so obvious that if I drink a Four Loko I will be extremely intoxicated. Another factor is how valuable the product is, and what the alternatives to it are like. Knives, chainsaws, and bleach (etc.) perform essential functions, and it is not clear what we might use in their place. Four Loko is not an essential product. It is something that people consume for enjoyment, but could easily do without.

One answer to the question "when is a product too unsafe to be sold?" is "never." Four Loko is dangerous, it might be admitted. But there is no problem with that, you might think. Manufacturers just need to disclose what the dangers are. Consumers can then make their own choices about whether to purchase the product. Call this the "contract view" of product safety.

An alternative to the contract view of product safety is the "due care" view. According to this view, manufacturers should exercise a substantial degree of caution when designing and manufacturing products so that those products do not pose an unreasonable risk of injury to consumers. When manufacturers fail to exercise this degree of care, they are said to be negligent. This is the regulatory standard that governments in the U.S., Canada, and Europe use to determine whether products are too dangerous to be sold. The due care view requires manufacturers to think ahead about the various ways that their products can be used or reasonably misused by consumers and try to design them in such a way that reasonable (not necessarily correct) use of it cannot cause injury. Instead of simply disclosing dangerous surprises, this view directs manufacturers to eliminate them.

With respect to Four Loko, an adherent of the contract view would say that Phusion Projects has only an obligation to disclose pertinent information about the drink. Minimally, it would need to disclose the ingredients in Four Loko. Perhaps more expansively, it might need to give consumers some idea of how those ingredients in combination are likely to affect them. An adherent of the due care view would say that this does not go far enough. On this view, it is not enough for Phusion Projects simply to disclose Four Loko's dangers; it must take steps to eliminate them. Phusion Projects would need to think about how their product is likely to be used by consumers. This includes both recommended use and reasonable misuse. Consumers are likely to drink Four Loko in excess, given the way its stimulants mask its intoxicating effects. Then, Phusion Projects would need to take steps to eliminate the dangers. Arguably this is what it did when it removed the caffeine from Four Loko. It changed the drink so that it no longer posed an unreasonable risk of harm to consumers.

Perhaps a better question to ask than "when is a product too unsafe to be sold?" is "who decides when a product is too unsafe to be sold?" As in the case of products that don't work, some argue that consumers should be sovereign. Consumers should be able to purchase products that are unsafe – or more precisely, products that others call unsafe – if they want. All manufacturers need to do is not deceive or mislead consumers about how safe those products are.

To others this view is insufficiently protective of people's welfare, which is one of the key justifications for markets. Even if manufacturers make available information about a product's dangers, that is no guarantee that consumers will access this information, still less that they will understand and act on it. Why give consumers the chance to harm themselves or others?

Consider drop-side cribs. Cribs have high sides to keep infants from falling out. But this makes it difficult for caregivers – especially short ones – to reach in and pick them up. In a drop-side crib, one side drops down to enable easier access to infants. Unfortunately, this creates a danger. If the crib is not assembled correctly, or if its hardware is damaged, sometimes the moveable side of the crib will detach from the frame, trapping the infant between the mattress and frame. Between 2001 and 2010, 32 infants died by suffocation in drop-side cribs; hundreds more were injured. The contract view of product safety says, "make the dangers of drop-side cribs known, and let caregivers decide whether to purchase them." But perhaps caregivers shouldn't have this option. There are plenty of other crib designs available, and it is not that hard for short people to pick up infants in cribs with non-moveable sides. Plus, inevitably some people will not see the warnings and place their children at risk unintentionally.

A second answer to the question of "who decides whether a product is too dangerous to be sold" is the government. Most nations have governmental agencies whose job it is to decide whether products are too dangerous to be sold. In the U.S., at the federal level this agency is the Consumer Product Safety Commission (CPSC). In Canada, it is the Ministry of Health. In 2010 the CPSC decided that drop-side cribs were too dangerous and banned them. Canada followed suit in 2016.

If the main problem with leaving it up to consumers whether to purchase dangerous products is that it is insufficiently protective of people's welfare, the main problem with allowing governments to decide which products are too dangerous is that it is insufficiently respectful of people's freedom – another key justification of market exchange.

The case of fireworks is illustrative. In the U.S., rules about fireworks vary widely from state to state. Some states permit the sale of almost all kinds of fireworks; some states permit the sale of only certain kinds of fireworks or limit their sale to certain times of year; one state – Massachusetts – bans all fireworks. (The fireworks we are talking about are "consumer fireworks." The sale of the "display fireworks" you see on television is restricted to licensed professionals.) Imagine you live in Massachusetts. Why, you might think, does your government prevent you from enjoying the sights and sounds of fireworks, especially around important holidays like the 4th of July? You can't even light a simple sparkler! The government of Massachusetts might observe that every year several people nationwide are killed by fireworks (in fact, about the same number as were killed in drop-side cribs, before they were banned) and hundreds more are seriously injured. In response, you might observe that no activity in life is riskless, and consumers should be able to decide for themselves whether the risk of injury from fireworks is worth the visual and auditory reward.

The debate here is not simply between welfare, on the one hand, and freedom, on the other. It is messier than this. When the government prohibits a product from being sold on grounds of safety, it may limit the freedom of some people to purchase the product (e.g., caregivers), but it may enhance the freedom of those who might be harmed by it (e.g., infants). People who complain about government restrictions on the sale of products like fireworks on the basis of freedom – they are being denied the freedom to choose – may also express their complaint in terms of welfare – the government is wrongly supposing that, for them, the harms of using fireworks outweigh their benefits. We can only conclude at this point that the question of when a product is too dangerous to be sold is complex. What we have in hand now is not an answer to this question, but a grasp of the concepts that are essential for answering it. The answers we arrive at will vary from case to case and product to product.

2.2. Paying for Injuries

So far we have been considering whether and when products are too unsafe to be sold. A related question is what to do when products harm people. One thing we might do is prohibit their sale in the future. But what about the injuries they have already caused? Who should pay for them? At its heart, this is an ethical question. But since people who are injured often seek redress in courts of law, it is tied up with legal issues. In particular, it is tied up with an area of law called "tort law," which deals with harms to people and property. Our discussion will focus on ethics but will also make reference to several legal cases in the U.S., which is where our examples are drawn from.

Consider the Johns Manville Corporation and asbestos. Asbestos is a naturally occurring fibrous mineral that is resistant to heat, water, electricity, and corrosion. While it has been in use for thousands of years (it was weaved into the burial shrouds of Egyptian pharaohs), it came into widespread use only in the late 19th century. In the U.S., one of the most prominent asbestos producers was the Johns Company – later Johns Manville – which operated huge asbestos mines and manufactured a variety of asbestos-containing products. Due to its insulating properties, asbestos was a popular additive in construction materials, including cement, shingles, floor tiles, and insulation. If you grew up in a house built during the mid-20th century, it probably contains asbestos. Left alone, asbestos is not harmful. The problem is when asbestos is disturbed or manipulated, as it often is in the construction process. Then small fibers are released into the air and can become lodged in people's lungs, causing asbestosis, a chronic lung disease, or mesothelioma, a type of cancer. These facts were not known when asbestos products were becoming widely used. But eventually it became clear that asbestos was dangerous, and then its use was largely discontinued. Many countries have banned asbestos. In other countries, its use is highly regulated.

If we had it to do all over again, we probably wouldn't have allowed asbestos to be so widely used. Perhaps we would not have let it be used at all. But asbestos was used, and people got hurt. Should these people be compensated for their injuries – for their hospital bills, their lost opportunities to work, their pain and suffering? If so, who should compensate them?

When the first lawsuits connected to injuries from products emerged, courts said that people could collect damages only if there was a contract between them (the consumers) and the manufacturer. If there was no contract, then the consumer could not collect, even if he was injured by the manufacturer's product. This contract-based view – referred to by legal scholars as "the doctrine of privity" – was challenged in the case of *Macpherson v. Buick Motor Company* in 1916. Macpherson was injured when one of the wheels on his Buick cracked, causing his car to crash. Macpherson sued Buick for damages. Buick objected on the grounds that Macpherson purchased his vehicle from a car dealership, not Buick itself. So there was no contract between Macpherson and Buick. If Macpherson wanted to sue someone, Buick argued, he should sue the dealership. The judge disagreed. He claimed that Macpherson could sue Buick for damages, even though he hadn't purchased the vehicle from Buick, because Buick didn't exercise due care in manufacturing the vehicle. Buick could have discovered the weakness of the wheel through testing, but it did not test. In other words, Buick was negligent.

Macpherson v. Buick Motor Company helped to establish a "negligence standard" for product liability. This case is important because it gave manufacturers an extra incentive to consider the welfare of consumers when they design and produce their products. Manufacturers' legal responsibility doesn't end when they sell their products to retailers. They retain responsibility for their products even when they reach consumers' hands. This means that manufacturers need to think about how their products will be used – both correctly and reasonably incorrectly – and try to design them in such a way that they do not cause harm. Of course, manufacturers will not be the only parties thinking about the harm their products may cause. Retailers will think through these issues before purchasing the products from manufacturers, because they too can be sued for selling unreasonably risky products.

What does this mean for the people who were harmed by the asbestos products that Johns Manville manufactured? There was typically no contract or agreement between the construction workers who were harmed by asbestos products and companies like Johns Manville. But post-*Macpherson*, the lack of a contract was no defense. Injured parties could sue for damages if they proved that the manufacturer was negligent, that is, if it failed to exercise due care in designing and manufacturing the product. It is not clear, however, that Johns Manville was negligent. Buick was negligent because the problem with its wheels could have been discovered through simple testing, but Buick didn't test. That was not the case with asbestos. No one knew that asbestos was dangerous when it first began to be widely used. Indeed, Johns Manville argued, no one *could have* known. The best science at the time didn't reveal any problem with asbestos. So Johns Manville said they weren't negligent. Because they weren't negligent, they further said, it wasn't their fault in a morally significant sense that people got injured, and it would be wrong to hold them financially responsible.

It is possible that Johns Manville knew more about the dangers of asbestos than they let on. But a decision in another court case made this issue moot. In the 1963 case *Greenman v. Yuba Power Products*, a court decided that people who were injured by products did not have to establish that manufacturers were negligent – that they failed to exercise due care in the design and manufacture of the product – in order to collect damages. This case helped to establish the doctrine of "strict liability" in the U.S. According to this doctrine, manufacturers can be made to pay for injuries their products caused even if they exercised all due care in manufacturing them, and even if the problems with their products were not realistically discoverable at the time of sale. At this point, you might be able to guess what courts thought about Johns Manville's defense in the asbestos cases. Courts rejected it. They said that it didn't matter whether the dangers of asbestos were known, or even if they could be known, when the products were sold. All that matters is that asbestos injured people, and Johns Manville produced it. So Johns Manville had to pay. It paid a lot. Under the weight of countless lawsuits, Johns Manville declared bankruptcy in the early 1980s. When it emerged, it established a $2.5 billion trust to compensate the tens of thousands of people injured by its asbestos products.

We now have a good sense of the responsibilities that U.S. law assigns to businesses when their products harm consumers. Businesses can be made to pay for the harms their products cause, even if they exercised due care in producing them. But what the law says is not necessarily what is morally right. The legal doctrine of strict liability has been criticized from a moral point of view.

Consider again Johns Manville's claim that it shouldn't be made to pay for the injuries that construction workers who used its products suffered. They said that these injuries weren't its fault, and so it's unfair to hold the company financially responsible. Johns Manville has a point. Suppose your friend asks you to feed her dog Ozzie while she's away. Unbeknownst to you, Ozzie has developed a severe allergy to his usual food. You feed Ozzie, and he dies. In a sense, you killed Ozzie. You fed Ozzie food that killed him. But it's not your fault that Ozzie died. You didn't know that Ozzie had developed a severe allergy to his food, and you had no reason to suspect that he did. Fault requires a "guilty mind" (in legal terminology, a *mens rea*), and you don't have one. You didn't intend to kill Ozzie; you weren't even negligent. So, it seems, you shouldn't be held responsible for Ozzie's death or made to pay for it. Your situation, we might think, is like Johns Manville's. Johns Manville was providing what it had every reason to believe was a safe and valuable product to the public. Years later, its products were proven to have seriously injured people. But Johns Manville didn't know any of this. If it is unfair to hold you responsible for Ozzie's death, why is it fair to hold Johns Manville responsible for the injuries and deaths suffered by those who handled its asbestos-containing products?

It might be said in reply that it isn't fair to Johns Manville. But it isn't fair to the people who were injured that they were injured. It would be even more unfair if the injured people had to bear the full costs of their injuries. So considerations of fairness cannot tell us how to resolve the problem. There will be unfairness whether companies like Johns Manville are made to pay for the injuries that their products cause or whether they are not made to pay.

Some defend strict liability on the grounds that it gives companies strong incentives to make their products safe. The negligence standard, we said, gives companies an incentive to exercise due care when making their products. Strict liability goes beyond the negligence standard in requiring companies to pay for injuries even when these injuries aren't their fault. It is not clear, however, how this might work. Is there some level of attention to detail beyond "due care" that companies are supposed to exercise? "Extreme care"? In fact, there is evidence that strict liability is not about getting companies to care more about product safety than they already do. In the asbestos case, Johns Manville was made to pay for injuries that no amount of caring would have allowed them to discover.

There is another incentive-related problem with strict liability for firms. If a firm is worried about being sued for a product, it may decide not to sell it. This can be bad for consumers, if the product is better than what is currently available in the market. This is an especially pressing problem for pharmaceuticals. No drug is risk-free. Some people might be willing to take the risks of injury to gain the benefits the drug offers, but a firm worried about lawsuits may decide not to give people the choice. A concern about safety may dampen innovation and the benefits it brings.

There is also the question of incentives on the other side of the transaction, that is, the incentives of the consumer. Some argue that strict liability decreases consumers' incentives to be careful when they are using products. If producers are held strictly liable, then consumers know that they won't have to pay the costs of their injuries; they can get producers to pay. It is hard to assess the truth of this claim, however. Winning a lawsuit is a time-consuming and potentially expensive process with no guarantee of success. Payouts are typically quite small, on the order of a few thousand dollars. It is unlikely that many consumers are willing to put their health and even their lives on the line for the mere possibility that they (or their heirs!) will receive compensation for harms they suffer.

In the end, the debate about liability for products may be a debate about distributive justice. Products cause harm, and these harms have costs. How should these costs be distributed? One answer is that consumers should bear them. We might conceive of these harms as a sort of bad luck on a par with contracting a disease, tripping and breaking a bone, or getting struck by lightning. We ask people to bear the costs of these harms, so maybe we should ask them to bear the harms they suffer from products too. Another answer is that producers should bear the costs. Firms are typically wealthier than consumers. It is usually easier for a firm to pay for the cost of an injury that a consumer suffers than for a consumer to pay this cost. But there may be a role for the government to play too. In fact, people don't have to bear the full costs of many injuries they face. Governments provide social safety nets in the form of free or reduced-price healthcare, especially for the elderly and poor. Governments sometimes bail out important firms that get into financial trouble. We might think that governments should play a more active role when it comes to product safety, not just evaluating *ex ante* products for riskiness, but compensating *ex post* those who are injured, and providing support to firms who non-negligently produce risky products. This is a difficult question to which there are no easy answers.

3. Is It Fit for Sale?

You can buy a puppy. You cannot buy a human embryo. If your kidneys fail, you can receive a donated kidney. You cannot buy a kidney. You can engage in consensual sex with another person, but in most places you cannot engage in sex for money. There is no question that these things "work" and are "safe," but to many they seem "inappropriate" or "unfit" for sale. We need a term to identify such things. Let us call them "contested goods." In this section we will consider the reasons for and against buying and selling – or markets in – contested goods.

Let us begin with an example. Kidneys perform an essential function in your body. Their main job is to filter out waste products in your bloodstream, which are then excreted as urine. Kidneys also help regulate the amount of water, vitamins, and minerals in your body and aid in the production of red blood cells. It is possible for people whose kidneys stop working to continue to live with the help of dialysis machines. Dialysis doesn't perform all of the functions of kidneys, however, so people who use them must also follow special diets and take certain drugs. In addition to its imperfections, dialysis is also inconvenient. Each treatment takes about 4 hours and must be repeated three times per week. The lifespan of people on dialysis is 5 to 10 years.

The best cure for kidney failure is a kidney transplant. Currently, the only way to get a kidney is through donation, from either a living or recently deceased donor. Unfortunately, kidneys are in short supply. To receive one, most people have to get on a waiting list, and waits average around 3 to 5 years. In the U.S., more than 100,000 people are on the waiting list for a kidney. According to the U.S. government, 13 people die each day waiting for a transplant, and another 10 become too sick to receive one. Governments try to incentivize people to donate, but with limited success.

Is there a simple solution to this problem? People have two kidneys, but they can live quite well with one. People who have just one kidney – for example, because they have donated a kidney to someone or because they have had one removed due to injury or disease – experience no ill health effects and have normal lifespans. Why not allow people to sell their kidneys? This would save potentially thousands of lives and spare many people the hassle and expense of dialysis. The demand for kidneys would be high, so you could make a lot of money by selling your kidney. Yet almost everywhere in the world it is illegal for people to sell their kidneys. Kidneys are contested goods. Why is this?

Sometimes arguments against markets in kidneys and other contested goods are put in terms of "commodification." Markets in kidneys would have the effect of "commodifying" kidneys, and such things should not be "commodified," critics say. But this is simply a statement of a position, not an argument for it. To "commodify" something is just to make it available for sale. What we are asking is why things like kidneys should not be made available for sale.

3.1. Expressing the Wrong Value

One worry people have about markets in contested goods is an expressive one. It begins with the idea that buying and selling a thing is an expressive act, a form of communication. When you buy or sell something, you express a certain attitude about the thing or make a certain statement about it. According to some writers, if you were to buy or sell a kidney (or sex or a human embryo), you would be expressing the wrong attitude about it. In particular, you would be saying that kidneys have only instrumental value, not non-instrumental value. To prevent expression of this wrong attitude, there shouldn't be markets in kidneys; that is, they shouldn't be bought and sold.

To say that a thing has instrumental value is to say that it has value *for* something else. Money is the paradigmatic instrumental good. It is valuable because of what it can get you, which is pretty much anything (that is for sale). To say that a thing has non-instrumental value – sometimes called "intrinsic" value – is to say that it has value *in itself*. Philosophers debate about what things have non-instrumental value, but leading candidates include pleasure and happiness. We want these things for themselves, not because of what they can get us.

When you purchase something, you indicate that it has instrumental value for you. You get something out of it. That is why you purchase it. But some things have non-instrumental value. According to the expressivist objection, if you were to purchase one of these things, you would be expressing the wrong idea about them. You would be expressing the idea that they are useful for you, when in fact they have value in their own right.

Now you might think that this is exactly the right thing to say about kidneys. Kidneys are valuable, you might say, because of the function they perform in our bodies. There is nothing valuable about kidneys in themselves. But defenders of the expressivist objection see a deeper problem. The problem is that people need at least one kidney to live, so a market in kidneys is tantamount to a market in human lives. This means, they say, that if you were to purchase a kidney, you would be expressing the idea that human life is instrumentally valuable, or valuable because of what it gets you. But human life is non-instrumentally valuable, or valuable for its own sake.

Markets in other contested goods provide even clearer targets for the expressivist objection. Suppose there were a market in human embryos. In the course of fertility treatments for a couple trying to procreate, typically many fertilized eggs are created, only some of which are implanted in the woman. The rest are donated or thrown away. But suppose you could buy and sell them. If you bought one, according to this objection, you would be expressing the idea that children are instrumentally valuable. You are buying one to satisfy your desires, perhaps for help around the house or for companionship. This would express the idea that children have the same sort of value as other things you buy to satisfy your desires, like clothes and shoes. But, the proponent of the expressivist objection says, children do not have the same sort of value as clothes and shoes. Children are non-instrumentally valuable; clothes and shoes are merely instrumentally valuable.

Sometimes the worry about markets in contested goods is put in terms of respect. There are ways you can behave that express disrespect for things. Many people would say that burning the flag of one's country expresses disrespect for one's country. Defacing a statue or gravestone conveys disrespect to the person memorialized by the statue or gravestone. The reason these actions express disrespect is that they communicate that the things in question lack value. It is permissible to burn a log, but impermissible, according to many people, to burn a flag. According to this argument, buying and selling kidneys and children similarly express disrespect for those things. When you buy or sell kidneys and children, you treat them as things to be used up and thrown away, not cared for and preserved. Because your actions don't recognize the true value of these things, they are disrespectful.

What should we make of the expressivist objection to selling kidneys, embryos, and other contested goods? This objection says that, when you purchase a thing, you express the idea that it has instrumental value. That much seems true. But it goes on to say that, in doing so, you also express the idea that the thing *lacks* non-instrumental value. Some question this claim.

First, they note that it is possible to value something instrumentally as well as non-instrumentally. You can value a piece of art instrumentally, because you want to impress your friends with it. But you might also value the art non-instrumentally, because you think it is beautiful. You might value the knowledge you get in college instrumentally, because it helps you get a good job. But you might also value that knowledge non-instrumentally, because you think it is simply good to know things. Second, they say that, while purchasing an item communicates that you value the item instrumentally, it does not say anything about whether you value it non-instrumentally. Your purchase does not convey that you *don't* value the item non-instrumentally; it is silent on this issue. Putting these points together, we arrive at the conclusion that it is possible to value things that you purchase both instrumentally and non-instrumentally. This includes art and knowledge, but also pets and trees.

What about the idea that buying or selling certain things conveys disrespect for those things? Respect is a slippery notion, so you might be unsure. But it is noteworthy that the examples of disrespect we considered – burning flags, defacing statues or gravestones – involve destruction or damage. In purchasing a kidney or an embryo, you are not damaging these things. Indeed, you hope to receive them in good shape, minimally because you have a use for them, and perhaps because you care about them for their own sakes. So it is not at all clear that buying or selling an item express disrespect for it. In some cases, they may do the opposite.

Expressivist objections to markets are important, but they aren't the only possible objections to such markets. The other main concern about them is consequentialist. That is, people have argued that markets in contested goods will not have the good consequences that people think they will have or that such markets will have other bad consequences.

3.2. Consequences: Good and Bad

We will begin by considering the claim that markets in contested goods will not have the good consequences that they are promised to have. Then we will consider the claim that they will have other bad consequences.

3.2.1. *Will the Promised Good Consequences Materialize?*

The waiting list for kidneys is long. In the U.S. alone, several thousand people die each year waiting for one. Why not allow people to sell their "spare" kidney? People who think there should be markets in kidneys argue that the main benefit of allowing people to sell their kidneys is an increase in the supply of kidneys.

This claim seems plausible at first glance. If you want people to make you shoes, or build a road, or teach philosophy, you will probably have to pay them. You could ask people to do these things for free, and a few might, but most wouldn't. The supply would be very low. But if you offered to pay people for doing these things, you would get a significant increase in their supply. Why not suppose the same is true of kidneys? If you ask people to give up their kidneys for free, you would get some kidneys, but if you paid people for them, you would get a lot more. As with many questions in business ethics, things are more complicated than they appear.

In the 1970s, the British social scientist Richard Titmuss argued that the British system of procuring blood – which relied exclusively on donated blood – was superior to the U.S. system – which relied on both donated and purchased blood. He thought that if you paid people for blood, it would incentivize people to donate blood who shouldn't be donating, like people who had communicable diseases. They would try to hide their illnesses and collect the money. So a blood supply that was based exclusively on donations was a higher-quality blood supply. You might think that what holds for blood holds for kidneys. That is, you might think that a kidney supply built up exclusively through donations will be of higher quality than a kidney supply built up through a combination of donations and purchases.

This argument might be correct, but it might also miss the point. People die on the waiting list for kidneys. Would it satisfy them to know that, right now, the quality of our overall supply of kidneys is very high, and if we paid people for kidneys, the quality of the overall supply might be lower? They might reply: "I don't care about the quality of the overall supply. I just want a working kidney. I would prefer a slightly lower-quality kidney than to be dead." Plus, there are ways to test people's kidneys to see if they are working. We could just perform those tests before transferring the kidney.

But Titmuss had another argument in favor of the British system for blood. Not only would paying people for their blood reduce the quality of the blood supply, he said, it would reduce its quantity as well. If you offered to pay some people for their blood, you would get not only worse blood, but less blood. To understand how, let us introduce a distinction, between intrinsic and extrinsic motivation. You are intrinsically motivated to perform some action (or task, or job, or activity) if you get some pleasure or satisfaction out of the action itself. You want to perform the action for its own sake. You are extrinsically motivated to perform some action if you get some external reward, or avoid some external punishment, for performing the action. You want to perform the action because of something else it gets you or enables you to avoid getting. You might be intrinsically motivated to play basketball because you love the game. You love scoring points, playing tough defense, and sprinting up and down the court. Or you might be extrinsically motivated to play basketball because of the rewards it gets you. Maybe you earn the respect of your peers or admiring stares from fans. If you are a professional, you might play for money. You can be both intrinsically and extrinsically motivated to perform an action. You can play basketball for love and for money.

It is clear that paying people for blood increases their extrinsic motivation to donate blood. They can now do it for money. (Of course, it is not really "donating" blood if you are doing it for money, but we'll let this linguistic infelicity slide.) Other things equal, this should increase the supply of blood. But other things are not equal. The problem, Titmuss said, is that paying for blood decreases people's intrinsic motivation to donate blood. People will get less pleasure or satisfaction out of giving blood and will be less inclined to do it for its own sake. This is sometimes described as a "crowding out" effect. Extrinsic motivation crowds out intrinsic motivation. This claim might strike you as odd at first, but a little reflection shows how it might happen. Suppose you regularly donate blood because you enjoy helping others and you think it's the right thing to do. Now you see that some people are getting paid to donate blood. You might think: "Why should I do for free what others are getting paid to do? That would make me a sucker." If you think like this, you might stop donating.

The question we are really interested in, of course, is not how paying people for a good changes the nature of their motivations to supply that good. The question is what this means for the total quantity of the good supplied. Titmuss thought that permitting purchases of blood in the U.K. would drive down the total supply of blood. The decrease in donations resulting from a decrease in people's intrinsic motivation to give would be greater than the increase in donations resulting from an increase in people's extrinsic motivation to give. If something similar is true for kidneys, then the decrease in donations resulting from a decrease in people's intrinsic motivation to give would also be greater than the increase in donations resulting from an increase in people's extrinsic motivation to give. Paying people for kidneys might induce some people to donate who otherwise would not have, but it would induce a greater number not to donate who otherwise would have.

So far this is just a suggestion or hypothesis. Should we accept it? Obviously Titmuss did not mean his hypothesis to apply to all goods that you might want to buy. No one is suggesting that offering to pay people for shoes or roads will reduce the total quantity supplied of these goods. Titmuss thought there was something special about blood. The donor shares a part of her body with another person, in a way that is necessary for that person to live. Perhaps kidneys, and perhaps other contested goods, are like blood in this way.

There is reason to be skeptical of Titmuss's argument. Consider first the claim that increasing extrinsic motivation decreases intrinsic motivation. This has been confirmed in many experimental studies. But to say that increasing extrinsic motivation decreases intrinsic motivation is not to say that increasing extrinsic motivation decreases *overall* motivation. Even if intrinsic motivation is decreased by the introduction of extrinsic rewards, overall motivation might be increased, if the rewards are large enough. If you are given money for getting good grades, you might be less intrinsically motivated to study, but you still might study harder, if you are given enough money. Markets in blood or kidneys might reduce people's intrinsic motivation to donate, but they might increase their overall motivation to donate, if the prices for these goods are very high.

Consider the market for blood plasma. Plasma is a yellowish liquid that makes up the majority of your blood. (Blood is given its red color by red blood cells.) It is given to burn victims and people who are in shock, helping to save their lives. Plasma is also used by drug companies to make drugs that treat bleeding and immune deficiency disorders. Because of its uses, hospitals and drug companies want plasma. The U.S. has plenty of it. It has so much plasma that it exports it to other countries. One of the major buyers of U.S. plasma is Canada. Canada has a serious deficit of plasma and gets up to 70% of its plasma from the U.S. What explains the U.S.'s excess of plasma and Canada's deficit? One plausible answer is that the U.S. allows people to be paid for donating plasma, while in most places in Canada, it is illegal to pay people for their plasma. In most places in Canada the only way a hospital or drug company can get plasma is if people donate it. People in the U.S. also donate plasma, but they can sell it as well. It may be the case that, in countries like the U.S. in which people are paid to donate plasma, fewer people donate for intrinsic reasons, that is, because they want to help people and they think it's the right thing to do. But clearly many more people overall donate in the U.S.

In fact, we don't even need to try to infer what might happen if there were a market in kidneys from the market in blood plasma. Earlier I noted that it is illegal to sell your kidney *almost* everywhere in the world. There is one place in the world in which it is legal to sell your kidney. This is Iran, and Iran has virtually eliminated its waiting list for kidney transplants. This provides strong evidence that markets in kidneys would increase their supply and help to save people's lives. So should we start allowing people to sell their kidneys? Not so fast. Many people argue that we should not do this, because of the bad consequences that will result.

We'll get to these consequences in a moment. First, let me sum up what we have said so far. The standard story is that allowing people to sell a good will increase its supply. We have reason to suppose this is true in most cases. But Titmuss's explanation of how and why people give blood is an intriguing one. Even if we don't in the end accept it, it teaches us to be alert to the possibility that the standard story may not always be true, especially when it comes to contested goods.

3.2.2. Will There Be Any Bad Consequences?

Markets in different contested goods will have different consequences, including different bad consequences. A market in kidneys will have different consequences than a market in sex. But consequence-based objections to markets in contested goods tend to have a common theme, and that is where we will focus our attention. The main concern about such markets is that they are exploitative. The worry is that the rich and powerful will force the poor and vulnerable into transactions that benefit the rich disproportionately, and benefit the poor hardly at all, or make them worse off. We need to prohibit such markets, the argument goes, to prevent this exploitation.

To evaluate this objection, let's begin by thinking about what exploitation is. There are many different theories of exploitation in the scholarly literature, but most agree on the basic outline of the concept. One person Q exploits another person P when Q extracts an excessive benefit from P in circumstances in which P cannot reasonably refuse Q's offer. Suppose you (P) are taking an exam, and your pencil breaks. You need a new pencil, and fast. If you don't finish the exam, you will fail the class, and you will have to repeat it, at a cost of thousands of dollars. Pencils are cheap, costing only about $.25 each. But you don't have one. As luck would have it, the person next to you (Q) in the examination room has several spares. She offers to sell you one, but for $40. You are outraged by the high price, but it seems to be your best option. You don't see anyone else with a spare pencil, and you don't have time to run to the store to get one (even if the instructor would let you). So you pay. Q exploits you in this case because she is able to extract an excessive benefit from you – a profit of $39.75 – in circumstances in which you don't have a decent alternative to accepting Q's offer.

People worry that this sort of exploitation will happen in a market for kidneys (and other contested goods). It is conceivable that some people who are relatively well off will decide to sell a kidney to finance an extravagant purchase, like a second car or a boat. But in many if not most cases, the people doing the selling will be desperately poor. They may be under a crushing debt; they may face eviction and life on the streets; they may have no other way to provide food for themselves and their families. A kidney is not something that you can get back or replace, like a car or boat. Once it's removed from your body, it's gone. The surgery itself, like all surgeries, is risky. Selling a kidney is an act of desperation and will be engaged in only by desperate people.

People who sell their kidneys will be vulnerable, and vulnerable people are ripe for exploitation. But a vulnerable person who engages in a transaction isn't necessarily exploited. Suppose in the previous example that Q offered to sell you the pencil for $.25, which is exactly what she paid for it. You accept the offer. You are vulnerable, and you engage in a transaction, but you aren't exploited. For exploitation to happen, you must be vulnerable *and* someone has to take advantage of you, in the sense of getting a lot more from the exchange than they should get. Q exploits you when she sells you the pencil for $40, not when she sells you it for $.25.

To determine whether people who sell their kidneys are actually being exploited, we would have to know not just whether they are vulnerable, but whether they receive enough money for their kidneys. Then we need to know what counts as "enough." We make the judgment that Q extracts too much money from P in the pencil case because we know the market price of a pencil, and P pays more than a hundred times that price. If we use this standard, then we would say that people who sell their kidneys are exploited just in case they get paid a lot less than the market price for kidneys, that is, the price that is set by the forces of supply and demand. Against this, you might think that, when it comes to kidneys, the fair price and the market price are different.

Some argue that, even if exploitation occurs in kidney markets, it is a kind of exploitation we should be willing to allow, because it is mutually beneficial. Kidney markets are obviously beneficial for the buyers. They get new kidneys. But it is also beneficial, some say, for the sellers. They get a sum of money, which they value more than their kidneys. Why assume that the seller values the money more than their kidney? Because they decided to sell. If they did not value the money more than their kidney, they would not have sold. If you were to prevent people from selling their kidneys, then you would prevent people from being exploited, but you would also prevent them from improving their lives. (We will return to this argument in Chapter 11 when we discuss overseas sweatshops.)

Others deny that the kind of exploitation that we see in kidney markets is mutually beneficial. They claim that it is harmful exploitation. Obviously the transaction is still beneficial for the recipient of the kidney. But, these others say, the party who sells their kidney is worse off after the exchange than before it. Yes, they receive a sum of money for selling their kidney, and this may provide some temporary improvement in their life. But they often spend this money quickly and are back in the same spot they were prior to the sale, but now with one fewer kidney. It is true, we said, that you can live a normal life with only one kidney, but it decreases your margin for error.

You might wonder why someone would agree to sell their kidney if it made them worse off. One reason is that people do not always know what is best for them. Prohibiting people from selling their kidneys may prevent people from doing something that they will later regret. It is also possible that if there are markets in kidneys, then some will be coerced by others into selling them. Prohibiting all kidney sales may protect the vulnerable from harm in this way too.

The possibility that some people will be forced by others to sell their kidneys may seem farfetched, but the market in another contested good – sex – should make you take it seriously. Some people are sex workers by choice. They are able to command relatively high prices for their work and can perform it in a relatively safe environment. But many people are forced to have sex for money. According to a report by the International Labor Organization, approximately 4 million adults and 1 million children worldwide were victims of commercial sexual exploitation in 2016. There can be no doubt that children do not and cannot consent to sex. But if there are markets in sex, then it is sadly predictable that children will be forced by unscrupulous others to have sex for money. Similarly, it is predictable that if there are markets in kidneys, then some people will be forced by others to sell their kidneys.

It might be thought that this criticism is unfair to the defender of markets in kidneys and sex. No one thinks that people should be forced to sell their kidneys or have sex. But the solution is not, they say, to eliminate all kidney sales, but to eliminate forced kidney sales. People should be given adequate information about the costs and benefits of selling a kidney, so they don't make the decision in ignorance. Perhaps they should be interviewed by public health workers to ensure that they are not being forced to sell. If we are worried that aggressive salespeople will try to induce impressionable people to part with their kidneys to make their sales quotas, we might decide that the government should be the only buyer of kidneys and pay a predetermined price.

This gets at a larger issue, and that is regulation. Even those who think that there should be markets in kidneys do not think that there should be totally free markets in kidneys. The markets would need to be tightly regulated to prevent the sort of injustices and abuses we just described. Opponents of such markets deny that any regulation could be tight enough and claim that we would do better – we would prevent more injustice and abuse – by banning them altogether.

Suppose kidney markets are banned, as they are now. Does this mean that no kidneys will be sold and all the harms we have been talking about will not occur? Unfortunately, no. When there is demand for a good, like kidneys or sex, there will be a market in this good. If the markets are prohibited by law, then these will be black markets. There is a thriving black market for kidneys in places like India, China, and Pakistan. There are sex workers in every country in the world, even though in many countries, selling sex is illegal. These markets will have all of the bad consequences that we have been describing, but others as well, since hiding one's activities from the authorities has costs. Just witness the enormous collateral damage from the illegal drugs trade. So the choice when it comes to markets in kidneys – and other contested goods like sex, embryos, and plasma – is not a choice between free markets and no markets. It is a choice between free markets, various kinds of regulated markets, and black markets. We have not tried to determine whether there should be a market in kidneys or any other contested goods, and if so, what they should be like. These questions are enormously complex. What we've done is identify the considerations that any responsible solution to this problem must address.

4. Chapter Summary

Selling is essential to business. In this chapter we considered what types of goods should be for sale. We focused on reasons commonly given for excluding things from markets. We considered functionality, safety, and fitness.

With respect to functionality, we asked: does it work? Products like Copper Fit compression braces products don't work in the sense that they appear to. Should such things be for sale? If autonomy is our primary concern, we might say 'yes'. We might think that people should have the freedom to sell and buy what they want, as long as they don't deceive each other about what is being sold. If welfare is our primary concern, we might say 'no'. Because these goods don't do what they seem to, they cannot benefit those who buy them in the right way. A further issue is who gets to decide. Should we allow consumers to make choices, which we have every reason to suppose are suboptimal, given their preferences, or should the government prevent consumers from making these choices?

With respect to safety, our question was, when is a good too unsafe to be sold? In this case also consumer sovereignty is a key issue. Emphasizing autonomy, you might think that consumers should be allowed to purchase dangerous products, as long as sellers disclose their risks. Or you might think that the government should more tightly regulate what can be sold, given that consumers will predictably fail to understand how dangerous certain goods are. We also considered who should pay for injuries that products cause. We traced the development of product liability law in the U.S. from privity of contract, through the negligence standard, and finally to strict liability. As we saw in the asbestos case, firms can now be required to pay for injuries that their products cause, even if they exercised due care in developing them. This raises difficult ethical issues of fairness and distributive justice.

With respect to fitness, we asked, when is a good or service the wrong type of thing to be sold? Some believe that, when people buy contested goods like kidneys, they express the wrong values about those goods, in particular, that they are only instrumentally valuable. Others think this reads too much into people's choices. Other concerns about markets in contested goods are consequentialist. The conventional wisdom is that if you offer to pay people for goods, you will increase the supply of those goods. Some claim that this wisdom does not apply in the case of some goods, because increasing extrinsic motivation to supply the good may decrease intrinsic motivation to supply it. Another worry about these markets is that they will be rife with exploitation. Even if this is true – and it may not be – we might not want to block people from engaging in trades that can improve their lives. Much depends on whether markets in kidneys and other contested goods can be effectively regulated or whether the only way to prevent people from being seriously harmed is to ban them entirely.

5. Study Questions

1. You can buy products that we have no reason to think "work" in the sense that they are intended to. Give an example of one such product and explain how it fits this description.
2. What is paternalism? What is consumer sovereignty? How are these concepts relevant in debates about what goods and services should be for sale?
3. In your view, should retailers be allowed to sell copper-lined compression braces? What about homeopathic remedies? Tarot card readings?
4. Most countries have government agencies that prohibit the sale of goods that don't meet certain safety standards. Is this a good idea? Explain your answer.
5. What do you think about the Four Loko case? Was the 2005 formulation of the drink too dangerous to be sold? Is the 2010 formulation too dangerous?
6. The U.S. has had different approaches over the years to the issue of who pays for the injuries that products cause over the years. These are the contract view, the negligence standard, and strict liability. What are the differences among these views? Which do you think is best?

7. What is one objection to the doctrine of strict liability? What might someone who supports this view say in response?
8. Titmuss thought that if you allowed people to sell blood, you would end up with a smaller total quantity of blood of worse quality. Why did he think this? Was he right?
9. Some people think that markets in kidneys should be prohibited because they are exploitative. Explain this claim. What, if anything, can be said against it?
10. Do you think that people should be allowed to sell their kidneys? Explain your answer.

Additional Readings

Anderson, E. (1993). *Value in ethics and economics*. Cambridge, MA: Harvard University Press.

Bengali, S., & Mostaghim, R. (2017, October 15). 'Kidney for sale': Iran has a legal market for the organs, but the system doesn't always work. *Los Angeles Times*. www.latimes.com/world/middleeast/la-fg-iran-kidney-20171015-story.html

Brennan, J., & Jaworski, P. M. (2016). *Markets without limits: Moral virtues and commercial interests*. New York: Routledge.

Calhoun, C., & Hiller, H. (1988). Coping with insidious injuries: The case of Johns-Manville Corporation and asbestos exposure. *Social Problems*, *35*(2), 162–181.

Hasnas, J. (2010). The mirage of product safety. In G. G. Brenkert & T. L. Beauchamp (Eds.), *The Oxford handbook of business ethics* (pp. 677–697). New York: Oxford University Press.

Kesmodel, D. (2009, August 3). Buzz kill? Critics target alcohol-caffeine drinks. *Wall Street Journal*. www.wsj.com/articles/SB10001424052970203674704574328322293679870

Macdonald, C., & Gavura, S. (2016). Alternative medicine and the ethics of commerce. *Bioethics*, *30*(2), 77–84.

Satz, D. (2010). *Why some things should not be for sale: The moral limits of markets*. New York: Oxford University Press.

Valdman, M. (2009). A theory of wrongful exploitation. *Philosophers' Imprint*, *9*(6), 1–14. http://hdl.handle.net/2027/spo.3521354.0009.006

Velasquez, M. (2012). The ethics of consumer production and marketing. In his *Business ethics: Concepts and cases* (7th ed., pp. 303–343). New York: Pearson.

6 How Can It Be Sold?

In the last chapter we asked what can be sold. We asked questions about functionality, safety, and fitness. In this chapter we consider how things can be sold. Once a product is made, what means can sellers use to get people to buy it? We are talking about the ethics of marketing.

The American Marketing Association defines marketing broadly as "the activity, set of institutions, and processes for creating, communicating, delivering, and exchanging offerings that have value for customers, clients, partners, and society at large." Marketing starts with the creation of the product and includes everything up to its exchange or sale to a buyer. The set of activities that comprise marketing is sometimes described as the "four p's": product, price, place, and promotion. Marketers help to design products (product), guide decisions about how they will be distributed and to whom (place), and facilitate their sale through pricing decisions (price) and advertisements (promotion). Ethical issues attend each of these activities.

We discussed ethical issues relating to products in the previous chapter and will not retrace our steps. The subset of marketing activities that are the most ethically fraught are those connected with promotion, especially advertisements. That is where we will focus most of our attention. We will also have something to say about price, as this is a growing area of concern.

We do not in this chapter devote separate attention to the ethics of sales. One reason is simply that our space is limited. Another is that the ethics of sales is largely continuous with the ethics of advertising. Salespeople can be understood as the "last advertisers." They try to complete the sale of the product to consumers. As a result, many of the same issues – issues of deception, persuasion, and vulnerability – that come up in our discussions of advertising come up in sales.

1. What's Good About Advertising?

Chuck Norris is a martial arts champion, television and movie star, and best-selling author. Late in his career, he became the pitchman for Total Gym, an in-home weightlifting system. In short segments, Norris, sometimes together

DOI: 10.4324/9781351016872-6

with Christy Brinkley, former model and actress, explains how the Total Gym is designed and what it can do. He models the exercises that people can do on the Total Gym and explains their value.

The programs that Chuck Norris hosts are infomercials – informative commercials or advertisements – for Total Gym products. It is no secret why these programs are on television. Total Gym hopes that they persuade you to buy one of its weightlifting systems. But why should we let Total Gym advertise its products? What can be said in favor of these advertisements?

1.1. The Main Benefit

In Chapter 4, we noted that one good thing about markets is that they tend to make people better off, at least compared to the alternatives. According to the first fundamental theorem of welfare economics, competitive markets generate efficient, in the sense of Pareto-optimal, outcomes. Intuitively, if you leave people alone to trade as they see fit, they will trade until they cannot make themselves better off through additional trades. For this to happen, however, certain background conditions must be in place. One of these conditions is perfect information (others include the frictionless movement of factors of production and an absence of market power). This makes sense. For people to be able to make themselves better off through trading, they must understand what they are giving up and what they are getting, and what alternatives are available.

Advertising promotes this end. Advertisements provide information and, in doing so, help markets function more efficiently. In his infomercials, Chuck Norris provides us information about the features and uses of the Total Gym. After viewing them, we are in a better position to decide whether it would enhance our welfare to own a Total Gym compared to the alternatives – joining a fitness center, hiring a personal trainer, or keeping our money and just doing push-ups in our living rooms. The same goes for other advertisements. You want to buy a car that is safe. In its advertisements, Volvo informs you that its cars are safe, having received the highest possible rating from the government. You want to buy a car that is reliable. Toyota informs you in its advertisements that its cars are the most reliable according to an independent auditor. Advertisements give you information you can use to satisfy your preferences and, in doing so, increase your welfare.

There is a complication. No amount of advertising can provide perfect information. New information is constantly being produced, and there is a limit to what the human mind can absorb. Moreover, an increase in information does not necessarily lead to an increase in market efficiency. This is due to another economic theorem: the theorem of the second best. In a market rife with imperfections, eliminating one imperfection can sometimes lead to a worse, in the sense of less efficient, result. Think of it this way. If no fitness companies advertise, and consumers make their own decisions based on their own research, this might be better in terms of efficiency than if one firm advertises, and consumers are unduly swayed by that firm's advertisements. This complication aside, if we think about advertising on an individual basis, it can clearly be beneficial. Without Chuck Norris, you would not know all the things the Total Gym can do or even that there is such a thing as a Total Gym.

In addition to its positive effects on welfare, advertising is valuable for the promotion of autonomy. The autonomous person is self-governing. She makes decisions for herself, as opposed to allowing others to make decisions for her. She lives according to her own plans and does what she wants. This includes her choices as a consumer. To live according to your plans, or to do what you want, you need information. You seek to drive a safe or reliable car. You want to buy organic, fair trade, or GMO-free foods. You want to buy products made in the U.S. Advertising is one source of this information.

To be sure, when people live according to their plans, and do what they want, this often increases their welfare. You seek chocolate ice cream because you like the taste; it gives you a pleasurable feeling to eat it. But this is not a guarantee, and not even something we always aim at. Sometimes we choose to do things – for example, buy organic foods or things made in the U.S. – because we think they are the right things to do, not because they will make us happy. Even if it were demonstrated that someone – your mother or father or best friend – consistently made choices for you that made you happier than the choices you made for yourself, there would be value in making those choices yourself. In any event, there is a conceptual distinction to be made between living life, including making consumer choices, because those choices are part of our life plans (autonomy) and because those choices make us happy (welfare). By providing information, advertising promotes both values.

1.2. Other Benefits

In addition to its positive effects on consumers' autonomy and welfare, advertising has several other benefits. First, advertisers subsidize movies, television shows, radio broadcasts, and internet content. These all cost money to create. Sometimes consumers cover their full costs. This is the case with subscription-based services like HBO and Netflix. But sometimes they do not. In these cases, the remainder is paid by businesses like Total Gym, which purchase airtime to show advertisements. Without advertising, we would have fewer movies, television shows, radio broadcasts, and internet programs than we do. Insofar as these programs have artistic or entertainment value, advertising is instrumentally valuable in helping to create them.

In addition to helping to create programs that have artistic and entertainment value, advertisements themselves can have artistic and entertainment value.

Some people enjoy watching sporting events like the Superbowl just so they can be amused or delighted by the advertisements that are shown. The famous 19th-century French painter Henri de Toulouse-Lautrec produced a wide range of drawings, prints, and paintings, but the works for which he is perhaps best known are his posters for the Moulin Rouge, a cabaret in Paris. Our world is made richer not just by the art and entertainment that advertisers sponsor, but at least in some cases by advertisements themselves.

A third benefit of advertising is found in its connection to production and innovation. Economies are powered by consumption. Some produce because others consume. Advertising encourages people to consume and, in doing so, requires people to produce. This production has value because it is a source of jobs and income for workers. It can also lead to innovation, because producers can make money by coming up with better ways to make things or by inventing new things.

Fourth, advertising and promotion itself is a source of jobs and income. Before anyone will buy your product, they must know that it exists. So it is vital that companies get the word out. It must not simply inform the public (as your professor might inform you of the latest research in business ethics) but do so in an interesting and exciting way (as your professor might not), to "break through the noise." According to one estimate, $223.7 billion was spent on advertising in 2018 in the U.S. alone. This provides work for hundreds of thousands of people.

Having understood the value of advertising, now let us consider its limits. What makes an advertisement bad? What sorts of advertisements should be prohibited? When answering these questions, we should keep in mind the main benefit of advertising in a market economy, which is to provide information to consumers that helps them make wise choices. At the same time, our analyses needn't be exclusively focused on this purpose. We can evaluate advertisements in terms of how they treat people, not just in terms of the outcomes they help to bring about.

2. Deception

If good advertising provides the truth about products to prospective consumers, then you might think bad advertising contains false claims. There is something to this. In the 1980s the children's food company Beech-Nut advertised as "100% apple juice" a drink that contained little or no juice. The drink it sold was a mixture of beet sugar, cane sugar syrup, corn syrup, and other flavorings. For its actions, Beech-Nut paid a $2 million fine and two of its executives went to prison. There is nothing wrong with selling drinks that contain a mixture of sugar and water. Most sodas and sports drinks are like this. The problem was that Beech-Nut made a false statement about what was in its drink. It said that its drink contained 100% apple juice when it contained close to 0%.

There are some advertisements, however, that contain false statements that do not seem so bad. The energy drink company Red Bull uses the slogan "Red Bull gives you wings." No matter how many Red Bulls you drink, you will not grow wings. In the 2000s, Old Spice sold shower and aftershave products with the tagline, "If your grandfather hadn't worn it, you wouldn't exist." This too is false. Those products weren't around when your grandfather had his kids. But while Red Bull's and Old Spice's slogans are false, they probably don't fool you. Why not? We might say that they aren't warranted as true, so their falsity does not deceive. These cases are different than the Beech-Nut case. When a children's food company advertises a drink as 100% juice, this purports to be a true statement. Since Beech-Nut's statement was in fact false, their advertisement was deceptive and deserved to be condemned.

Another arena in which we sometimes see false statements that do not deceive is sales, and in particular, bargaining over the price of "big ticket" items, like houses or cars. I am selling my car, and you would like to buy it. I would like a high price and you would like a low price. You make me an offer of $10,000, and I say: "I can't let it go for less than $12,000." I am not telling you the truth. I would let it go for $11,000. But you are not deceived. We bargain some more and eventually I agree to sell it to you for $11,000. Why didn't you accept my claim that I wouldn't sell my car for less than $12,000 – why did you try to continue to obtain a lower price? Because in a sales negotiation over a big-ticket item, the claims the parties make about how much they are willing to sell an item for, or how much they are willing to pay, are not warranted as true. No reasonable person takes them at face value.

The lesson of these examples is that the key issue is not falsity but deception. False statements can deceive when they are offered as truths. When they deceive, they are impermissible. When they do not, as in the Red Bull and Old Spice cases, they are not deceptive and may be permissible.

What is deception? It is easy to point to clear cases of deception like Beech-Nut's, but much harder to define the boundary of this concept precisely. According to the Federal Trade Commission (FTC), the governmental authority in the U.S. that regulates advertising, "a representation, omission, or practice is deceptive if it is likely to mislead consumers acting reasonably under the circumstances and is material to consumers – that is, it would likely affect the consumer's conduct or decisions with regard to a product or service." Several aspects of this definition are worth observing.

The first is that there is no mention of lying in the FTC's definition. A lie is conventionally defined as a false statement that is intended to deceive. As seen, false statements may deceive, but they may not. And deception can occur without falsity. In the movie *The Empire Strikes Back*, Luke Skywalker tells a small green creature that he is looking for a Jedi Master. The green creature says, "Yoda! You seek Yoda! Take you to him I will." As a result, Luke comes to think the small green creature is not Yoda. But the small green creature *is* Yoda. Yoda has deceived Luke without lying to him.

A second aspect of the FTC's definition is that intention is unimportant. Some ethicists believe that to deceive someone is to *intentionally* cause them to believe something false. If you say or do something that causes people to have false beliefs without intending them to have false beliefs, you have merely misled them. The FTC doesn't recognize a distinction between deceiving and misleading. From a practical point of view, we can see why. It is bad if advertising causes consumers to have incorrect beliefs. This calls for remedy, whether these beliefs were caused intentionally or unintentionally.

A third notable feature of the FTC's statement is its inclusion of omissions as possibly deceptive. A series of statements can create a false impression in consumers' minds about the features of a product if an additional statement – a disclaimer – is not also included. Consider Nutrisystem's advertisements for its weight loss program. These typically feature "before" and "after" photos of people who have lost weight. In one case, Nutrisystem promoted the 41-pound weight loss of Jillian Barberi, a television host. What Nutrisystem failed to disclose was that, in her "before" photo, Barberi was pregnant, and in the "after" photo, in addition to joining the Nutrisystem program, she had given birth and hired a personal trainer. The FTC decided that advertisements such as these gave the false impression that losing 40, 50, or 60 pounds using the Nutrisystem program was typical, when in fact it was not. To remedy this, the FTC asked Nutrisystem to add a "results not typical" disclaimer to some of its advertisements.

A fourth aspect of the FTC's definition is the "acting reasonably" qualification. Red Bull says that its products will give you wings. This is an example of "puffery" or exaggerated, over-the-top praise. Yet it is possible that some person will believe it. This person may decide to start drinking a lot of Red Bull in an effort to grow wings. But they never do. Does this advertisement run afoul of the FTC's definition? No, because the person who believes that drinking Red Bull will give them actual wings is not acting reasonably. No reasonable person takes puffery at face value. (Red Bull had to pay a $13 million settlement for deceptive advertising in the U.S. But this is because it said that consuming its drinks would improve people's attention and mental performance, claims that it could not substantiate.) Things are not always so simple. There can be disagreements about what reasonableness requires. We may understand reasonableness in terms of the abilities of the actual average person. Or we might understand it as a normative standard, one that the average person can fall short of or exceed. Moreover, what counts as reasonable depends on which people we are talking about. Advertisements aimed at teenagers must be held to different standards than advertisements aimed at adults.

In light of a proper understanding of the FTC's definition of deception, consider again Copper Fit's advertisements for its compression braces, discussed in the previous chapter. Copper Fit says that their braces are made of a special "therapeutic fabric, blended with copper, to aid in faster recovery and performance, and guaranteed relief of muscle aches and pains." In its advertisements, the former NFL quarterback Brett Favre says, "I perform best with Copper Fit." Based on everything we know, however, a compression brace lined with copper offers the exact same performance benefits as a similar brace without copper. Are Copper Fit's advertisements deceptive? The FTC says that we need to consider what these advertisements actually cause reasonable people to believe. If reasonable people come to believe on the basis of these advertisements that copper offers performance benefits, then they qualify as deceptive. It does not matter that Copper Fit does not technically lie or make false statements in them. It also does not matter whether they intend to deceive anyone. Among the statements and testimonials in their advertisements, Copper Fit's failure to state that there is no scientific evidence that copper has any performance benefit may qualify as deceptive.

We have been focused so far on what deception is and when it is wrong. A deceptive advertisement is one that causes reasonable consumers to have relevant false beliefs about a product. False claims can deceive, but they may not, if they aren't warranted as true. Deception can occur through commission or omission. When asking whether an advertisement deceives, the relevant standard is not whether anyone is deceived, but whether the reasonable consumer is deceived.

A further issue is *why* deception is wrong. Here we might refer to the main benefit of advertising, which is to give consumers information that they can use to make wise choices, choices that promote their autonomy and enhance their welfare. When consumers are deceived, they may make purchases that don't reflect their values and make them worse off. Suppose you want to purchase cooking pans made in the U.S., because you want to support U.S. workers. A company advertises its pans as made in the U.S. and you purchase them on this basis. Then you discover that the advertising is false. The pans are made in France. This is bad both for your autonomy and for your well-being. You made a choice that you did mean to, and you are unhappy as a result.

Instead of looking at things from the perspective of the consumers, we can look at things from the perspective of advertisers. We might think that advertisers who deceive consumers are disrespecting them. In the language of Kantian deontology, they are using consumers as mere means to their (advertisers') ends. Instead of offering information to consumers that they can use to make up their own minds about whether to purchase the product, they manipulate them into making choices that they don't really want to make. This criticism applies not just to advertisers who intentionally deceive but to those who do so by accident. Advertisers should take care that their communications do not give consumers the wrong impression about the features of their products.

A third concern about deceptive advertising comes into focus when we look at things from the perspective of society. As a general matter, it is good if we can trust what others tell us to be true. The world is a complicated place, and we can't do everything ourselves. You may ask a stranger for directions; you may ask a mechanic what's wrong with your car; you may ask a doctor whether you need an expensive procedure. In each of these cases, we depend on others to provide us with accurate information. If we cannot trust others to tell us the truth, our lives go worse. We have to find out more things ourselves. We will enter into fewer exchanges with others, and when we do, we will try to protect ourselves against possible deception. This will be both inconvenient and costly. For all these reasons, when we provide information to others, we should aim to provide accurate information and not create false impressions. The same goes for advertisers, who collectively provide enormous amounts of information to the public. In doing so, we help to create a better world.

3. Persuasion

Advertising does not merely inform. It attempts to persuade. Chuck Norris is not just telling us about the features and benefits of the Total Gym. He tries to persuade us to buy it. Perhaps more fundamentally, he is trying to get us to *want* to buy it. Indeed, some advertisements provide exceedingly little information about the products they aim to sell, like the Budweiser commercial we'll discuss later. In this section we consider what types of persuasion are permissible and what types are not.

3.1. The Creation of Desire

An important debate about advertising ethics began in the late 1950s. In his book *The Affluent Society*, the Canadian economist John Kenneth Galbraith argued that advertising was a pernicious force in society. Recall the story we told about the value of advertising. It begins with the idea that we want things, and then advertisers give us information that tells us how to satisfy these wants. You want a fast car, and advertisers tell us which cars are fast. You want a diamond ring, and advertisers tell us where the nicest ones can be found.

Galbraith says that this story gets things backward most of the time. Instead of giving you information that you can use to satisfy your pre-existing desires, advertisers create desires in you, which you then try to satisfy. You didn't want a fast car until advertisers told you how sexy you would feel if you owned a fast car. You didn't want to buy organic foods until advertisers told you that you would feel healthier if you ate organic goods. Galbraith called this the "dependence effect." Our desires depend on what is advertised as opposed to originating with us.

What exactly is the problem here? Galbraith says that when our wants are original to us, satisfying them has value. We are better off when these wants are satisfied. But this is not the case when the wants are created in us by advertising. Satisfying those wants is not very valuable, if it is valuable at all. It is as if I make you itchy and then scratch your itch. I have just returned you to the state you were in before. I haven't made you better off. Things may be even worse than this in some cases. Advertising may create desires in you that you can't satisfy, because you don't have the means to satisfy them. That would be like me creating an itch in you that can't be scratched.

Not all advertisements are subject to this criticism. Galbraith would probably say that advertisements for goods that satisfy basic needs like food and shelter are permissible. We have pre-existing desires for these things. But advertisements for things like fast cars and jewelry are problematic. These advertisements often create the very desires that they then try to satisfy. Galbraith thinks that, the more affluent a society is, more of its advertisements will be for things like fast cars and jewelry – things that we didn't want before we saw the advertisements for them.

Is this criticism successful? F. A. Hayek, whom we met back in Chapter 4, advanced a powerful challenge to it. Let us begin with the idea that advertising creates desires in us. This is true, Hayek said. But advertising is but one force among many that creates desires in us. Your desires are shaped by your parents, your friends, things you see on the internet, novels you read, strangers you meet on the bus, and so on. You might desire to go to college because it makes your parents proud. Or you might desire to buy a ticket to a Rihanna concert, because your friend played her music for you and you loved it. Most of our desires are produced by outside forces. Why single out advertising for special criticism? Put differently, if we think that desires produced by advertising are unimportant to satisfy because they did not originate with us, then we should also think that desires from all of these other sources – which constitute most of our desires – are also unimportant to satisfy. But this just seems absurd. Graduating from college can be one of the high points of a person's life. Attending a Rihanna concert is pretty darn fun too. It seems valuable to satisfy these desires, even though they are created in us by outside forces. If this is so, then it can be valuable to satisfy desires that are created in us by advertising. It may be true that if we had to choose, we would choose to satisfy desires for things like food and shelter instead of things like college educations and tickets to Rihanna concerts, or fast cars and diamond rings. Desires for necessities often take priority over desires for other things. But this hardly shows that satisfying desires for these other things is unimportant.

To supplement Hayek's point, we might observe that, while advertisers may create desires in us for specific products, these desires are always related to desires we already have. An advertisement creates in you a desire for a fast car.

Perhaps it does this by showing that people who drive fast cars are admired by beautiful people. You want to be admired by beautiful people. That is a desire you already have. The advertisement creates a desire in you for a fast car, but not out of "whole cloth," as it were. It leverages an existing desire of yours. The same goes for the desires advertising creates in you for diamond rings, or for things like fast food, sodas, or beer. You have certain wants, and advertising tells you how purchasing a specific product can satisfy those wants.

We might worry about desires that are created in us that we reject or repudiate. Suppose a life-long smoker is trying to quit. He really wants a cigarette, but he wishes he didn't have that want. We might say that it's not valuable to satisfy the smoker's desire for a cigarette, because he rejects that desire. It is only important to satisfy desires that people don't mind having. But there is no reason to think that the desires that are created in people by advertisements are desires they repudiate.

It might seem that Hayek's response to Galbraith so far misses the point. The point is not whether it is good to satisfy desires you have. Perhaps we should concede that it is. If you have an itch, it is good that it is scratched. The problem is that we are subjected to a constant barrage of advertising. Itches are constantly being created in us, which can only be scratched through purchasing the product advertised. We are always needing to scratch, and if we can't – say because we lack the resources to purchase the product advertised – we are left itchy. This is a bad way to live.

Galbraith may have a point here, but it is hardly decisive. As we noted, desires are being created in us all the time by all kinds of outside forces, including our friends and family. This is a necessary consequence of living together in communities. Advertising may contribute to a kind of pernicious consumerism, but since it isn't solely responsible for it, it may seem unfair to target it for special criticism.

3.2. Wrong Ways of Creating Desire?

Some have argued that the problem with advertising is not *that* it gets us to want things, but *how* it gets us to want things. Advertisers attempt not just to inform, but to persuade. Not all forms of persuasion are equally acceptable.

Consider again Chuck Norris and the Total Gym. In his infomercials, Norris points out its relevant features, demonstrates all the exercises that you can do on the system, and explains why these exercises are good for you. Norris is engaging in what is called "rational persuasion." He is articulating reasons for people to buy a Total Gym, reasons like "you can exercise all the major muscle groups in your body," "lifting weights can help you burn fat," and "it fits in a small space." The idea is that if you care about these things, then it is in your interest to buy a Total Gym.

Now consider a different type of commercial. During the 2014 Super Bowl, the brewery Anheuser-Busch ran an advertisement for its beer Budweiser called "Best Buds." On a farm, a handsome couple raises puppies for sale. One of the puppies becomes friends with a horse. They play and snuggle together. The puppy is sold to a new owner who starts to drive away. As he does, the horse breaks out of his stall and gallops after the car. Other horses on the farm follow and surround the car, which stops. In the next scene, the puppy is seen running back to the farm, escorted by the horses. As the music rises, the Budweiser logo is displayed on the screen.

Anheuser-Busch is engaging in what is called "non-rational persuasion." It is not giving us clear reasons, or reasons at all, to buy Budweiser. Instead, it is evoking powerful and positive feelings in us – friendship, family, and loyalty – and associating its product with these feelings. The suggestion is that Budweiser "goes together" with these feelings.

"Best Buds" is an example of an associative advertisement. The point of associative advertisements is not to provide facts about the product being advertised, but to associate the product with positive emotions, ideals, desires, or feelings. The idea is to persuade consumers that they can share in these emotions, ideals, etc., by purchasing the product.

It is best to think of advertisements that employ rational persuasion as on a continuum with advertisements that employ non-rational persuasion. The Total Gym advertisement and the Budweiser advertisement are extreme examples. The former is almost all rational persuasion. The latter is almost all non-rational persuasion. Most advertisements contain a mix of these techniques. They provide some information about the product while also trying to create positive associations with it, though they may contain comparatively more of the former or more of the latter. The Total Gym advertisement itself contains some elements of non-rational persuasion. The Total Gym is used in a beautiful and clean home, by attractive and fit people like Chuck Norris. This is meant to associate the Total Gym with beauty and health. The Budweiser advertisement contains some elements of rational persuasion. The logo displayed at its conclusion indicates that Budweiser is a kind of beer. You are now informed that if you want a beer, you could have a Budweiser.

Attempting to rationally persuade someone to want or to do something strikes many people as morally unproblematic. But some ethicists object to attempts to persuade someone to want or to do something non-rationally. What might be wrong with the Budweiser advertisement?

One thing that you might think is that Budweiser is lying to you, so it is running afoul of the rules against deception. In associating Budweiser with friendship, family, and loyalty, it gives the impression that drinking Budweiser will allow you to share in these experiences. This is false. Budweiser is just a beer. The mere act of drinking a Budweiser does not allow you to experience the joys of friendship, family, and loyalty. The problem with associative advertising, according to this objection, is that it often creates *false* associations in consumers' minds.

It is not clear that this objection works. Remember that, when we discussed deception, the key issue, at least according to the FTC, is whether an advertisement actually causes reasonable people to have false beliefs about a product. It is doubtful that "Best Buds" makes anyone think that the act of drinking a Budweiser, by itself, will allow them to experience the joys of friendship, family, and loyalty. So it is unlikely that this advertisement runs afoul of the rules against deception.

You might think that there is a different problem here. You might say that the problem is that, when advertisers use non-rational persuasion on us, they are trying to "go around" our faculties of rational choice. We might label this a form of manipulation.

Suppose your parents are trying to persuade you to major in accounting. To do so, they say things like "You can learn valuable skills and get a high-paying job." "Accountants are fun people and you will make a lot of new friends." "You have always loved numbers." Your parents are engaging in rational persuasion. They are presenting facts about accounting that are relevant to you given your values and aspirations. They are giving you reasons to major in accounting.

Suppose instead that, in attempting to get you to major in accounting, your parents said things like these: "See that homeless person? I heard him talking about Nietzsche" and "Do you love your mother? How about America? Then accounting is for you." They have also taken pictures of beautiful, sexually desirable, strong, and wealthy people holding accounting diplomas and pasted them all over the house. In this case, your parents are engaging in non-rational persuasion. They aren't providing you any relevant information about accounting on which to base your decision. They are just trying to create positive associations with accounting and negative associations with other majors. Moreover, the associations they are creating don't have any basis in reality.

You probably think that how your parents try to persuade you to major in accounting in the first case – where they try to persuade you rationally – is ethically superior to how they try to persuade you in the second case – where they try to persuade you non-rationally. What makes it better? The answer, you might say, lies in the fact that you are a rational agent. As a rational agent, you wish to make decisions that are supported by good reasons. You don't want to be tricked or manipulated into doing things that, upon reflection, you do not think you have most reason to do. Someone who tries to do this isn't being respectful of who you are. When your parents try to persuade you rationally to major in accounting, they are engaging directly with your rational faculties. They are providing you reasons, which you may choose to accept or not. In doing so, they are respecting your status as a rational agent. But when your parents try to persuade you non-rationally to major in accounting, they are not engaging directly with your rational faculties. They are trying to go around them, to manipulate you, by appealing to unarticulated or even subconscious desires or fears. When your parents try to persuade you non-rationally, they are not helping you to make a decision that, upon reflection, you think you have most reason to make. They are disrespecting your status as a rational agent.

You might wonder whether this is a fair characterization of what advertisers are doing when they attempt to persuade us non-rationally. You might deny that they are trying to go around or circumvent our rational faculties. They are simply suggesting an association – between Budweiser and friendship – that we may choose to accept or not. The suggested association is not slipped into your mind surreptitiously; it is made plain for all to see.

Yet it seems important to the effectiveness of these associations that they are not explicitly articulated. Imagine if there were a narrator in the Budweiser advertisement who said: "Just as this puppy formed a deep and lasting relationship with this horse, so you too can form deep and lasting relationships by drinking Budweiser. Open a can in your apartment and drink in the joys of friendship, family, and loyalty today." You would laugh. The advertisement only "works" because such things are not said. The idea is to plant them in your mind without subjecting them to your rational oversight. Things are of course much different with Chuck Norris and the Total Gym. He tries to get you to believe certain things about the Total Gym by telling or showing you exactly these things (e.g., "it fits in a small space"). Chuck Norris gives you information, which you can evaluate; Budweiser does not.

Does Budweiser actually succeed in getting you to believe that drinking Budweiser allows you to experience the joys of friendship, family, and loyalty? You might say it doesn't. Maybe Budweiser is trying to slip this association into our minds by going around our faculty of conscious choice, but it doesn't succeed. Budweiser isn't *that* clever. If this is right, then perhaps there is no problem with Budweiser's use of non-rational persuasion. It is simply a form of harmless entertainment. It is just trying to get us to remember, in an amusing way, its products.

It is hard to know how to evaluate the premise on which this objection is based. I don't think drinking Budweiser will allow me to experience the joys of friendship, family, and loyalty. If you take a moment to think about it, you would probably say that you don't either. But that's just the thing. We don't take time to think about it. We are bombarded with these types of messages and there is no time to rationally evaluate them. We are not invited to do so. It wouldn't be surprising if these messages had some effect on us. Indeed, the very fact that Budweiser and other companies use associative advertising so often suggests that they think it works. Progress on this issue must couple philosophical reflection with empirical research on the effects of advertising. If associative advertising doesn't persuade us, then there may be no problem. If it does, there may be.

4. Vulnerable Populations

We have been talking so far about advertising to people like you and me. We are rational and informed adults in (reasonably) comfortable circumstances. We are not easily deceived. We know that drinking Red Bull will not literally give us wings. We are hard to persuade. We want to experience the joys of friendship, family, and loyalty, but we know that drinking Budweiser by itself will not allow us to do so. Some people are not so fortunate. Their cognitive capacities may not be fully developed; they may lack crucial information; or they may find themselves in challenging economic circumstances. As a result, they may be harmed by products in ways that we are not. In this section we explore whether marketers have special obligations to vulnerable populations.

Infant formula is a product that parents can use to feed their children in the first months of their lives. The other option is breast milk, which most women produce naturally when their children are born. Breastfeeding is nominally "free," but it takes a lot of time and it can be inconvenient. Infants need to eat every few hours and it can be hard for women to return to work if they are nursing. So some families choose to feed their children formula. Some studies show that breast milk may be healthier for infants than formula, but formula still provides plenty of nutrition.

This brings us to the Swiss food giant Nestlé. In the 1970s, Nestlé began marketing its infant formula aggressively in the developing world. In addition to the usual assortment of advertisements in print media and door-to-door salespeople, Nestlé worked to get its products into hospitals. To entice hospitals to give their products away to new mothers, they paid for medical equipment and supplies and provided doctors funding for research and travel.

So far, so good? Not quite. There is significant poverty in the developing world, and formula is expensive. Women sometimes dilute the formula in excess of what is recommended to make it last longer. In addition, systems of sanitation and public health can be poor, so the water to which women have access may not be clean. The result is that insufficient formula is mixed with dirty water, causing infants to become sick and even die. Neither problem arises in the case of breast milk. Women produce it naturally, and what comes from the woman's body is nutritious and clean. Compounding the problem is that, once women start feeding their children formula, they stop producing breast milk. So they cannot switch to breastfeeding if they discover that they can't feed their children formula safely.

As public awareness of this problem grew in the late 1970s, some consumer groups started a boycott of Nestlé. They claimed that Nestlé was promoting a product that endangered children's health. In 1981, the World Health

Organization developed the International Code of Marketing of Breast-milk Substitutes, and in 1984 Nestlé agreed to abide by it. Among other things, the Code prohibited formula manufacturers from promoting their products as suitable for children less than 6 months of age, as equivalent or superior to breast milk, or as a replacement for breast milk. This satisfied some activists, but for others it did not go far enough. Some continue to boycott Nestlé.

Was Nestlé doing something wrong when it advertised infant formula aggressively in the developing world in the 1970s? Obviously, it is a terrible tragedy for innocent children to become sick and die. But was that Nestlé's fault? A few things can be said in its defense.

One is that not everyone in the developing world is poor or lacks access to clean water. Many people make enough money to afford adequate amounts of formula and mix it with clean water. Marketing campaigns are a "blunt instrument." Nestlé produces a single campaign designed to appeal to a large group; it can't tailor its advertisements to individual consumers. As long as many people in this group have the ability to use the formula safely, you might think, then Nestlé isn't doing anything wrong. Second, the proximate cause of children's sickness and death was not Nestlé's promoting the sale of its infant formula. It was parents using that formula incorrectly. You might say that parents are to blame, then, for their children becoming sick. If they knew that they couldn't feed them formula safely, then they should have breastfed them instead. Third, we must avoid infantilizing other people. Millions of people around the world use infant formula responsibly. Some people want Nestlé to stop advertising its infant formula in the developing world. Consider what they are saying. They are saying that some people can't be trusted even to know that it is possible to feed their children formula instead of breastfeeding them. This suggests a lack of trust in others or perhaps a disrespect for them.

These responses, however, may not take the issue of vulnerability seriously enough. Remember the main benefit of advertising. It gives people information that they can use to satisfy their wants and needs and, in doing so, carry out their plans and improve their lives. But if people are vulnerable, then they may not be able to translate information into want- and need-satisfaction in the usual way. This is the situation that many new mothers in the developing world found themselves. They wanted to know how to give their children healthy and safe food. When they acted on the information Nestlé provided, some of them gave their children food that was unhealthy and unsafe. To be clear, the formula *itself* was safe; the problem was that the women were using it incorrectly. But it was predictable that at least some women would do this, given the circumstances in which they found themselves. To sharpen the point, in the Nestlé case, it was not just that the main benefit of advertising did not materialize. It is that, for some women, advertising made things worse. It would have been better, both for these women and their children, if they had never heard about Nestlé's infant formula.

In the discussion of product liability in the previous chapter, we noted that there are two views that one could take about the sale of dangerous products. According to the contract view, manufacturers just need to disclose what the risks of a product are, and consumers should be left to make up their own minds about whether to purchase it. According to the due care view, disclosing risks is not enough; manufacturers should try to design products so that they don't pose an unreasonable risk of injury to consumers. It is possible to take similar positions about the marketing of dangerous products. If we embrace something like the contract view, we might say that Nestlé only needs to make clear in its advertisements that its formula needs to be used according to the directions and that if it isn't, serious injury or even death could result. If we embrace something closer to the due care view, we might say that Nestlé should take care to ensure that its advertisements do not cause consumers to make choices that cause harm to themselves or others. If Nestlé can't ensure this, then it should cease advertising. The same considerations of freedom and welfare that are relevant to the evaluation of the contract and due care views as applied to the sale of dangerous products are also relevant for the evaluation of these views as applied to the marketing of these products.

Whichever of these approaches we find most plausible, there is a strong case to be made that Nestlé shouldn't take the same approach to advertising its infant formula in the developing world as it does in the developed world. A simple principle of morality says that like cases should be treated alike, and different cases should be treated differently. Whatever degree of caution companies like Nestlé exercise when they advertise to non-vulnerable audiences in the developed world, they should exercise a different, higher degree of caution when they advertise to vulnerable ones in the developing world.

We have been talking about people who are vulnerable due to their economic circumstances. As noted, there are other reasons people can be vulnerable. For example, they may not be in possession of a full range of mental powers. Children are like this, and so are some adults, including some elderly people. Advertisers may need to exercise extra caution when targeting these groups. Some have argued that children should not be targets of advertising at all, since they do not typically make consumer choices. The advertising of products intended for children should be directed to the adults who make purchases for them. Another group of vulnerable people are the uninformed. The uninformed are not stupid; they just lack information that is crucial for making decisions that advance their consumer interests. Advertisers of complex financial products may need to exercise extra caution when advertising in communities with low degrees of financial literacy. Drug advertisers may need to be extra cautious when advertising to the public as opposed to medical professionals.

The reason we have focused on the vulnerable is because, compared to the non-vulnerable, the consumer choices they make can more easily lead to harm, for themselves and others. A variable we have not yet highlighted is the product being advertised. We have said that advertisers should exercise extra caution when advertising to vulnerable groups. The degree of caution they should exercise depends on what they are advertising. The Nestlé case shows that even something as innocuous as infant formula can, if used improperly, have harmful effects. But products that are intrinsically harmful, like alcohol, drugs, tobacco, guns, chemicals, and knives, must be advertised even more carefully.

This point generalizes. Just as we should want advertisers to use extra caution when advertising to vulnerable people, we should want them to use extra caution when they are advertising potentially harmful products to non-vulnerable people. It is bad to be deceived or manipulated into buying something that poses little inherent risk, like a compression brace lined with copper. At most, you wind up with a product that doesn't deliver the benefits you think it does. It is much worse to be deceived or manipulated into buying something that poses more inherent risk, like alcohol or cigarettes. Abuse or even use of these substances can result in serious harm to self and others. We may wish to restrict the advertising of such products to limit this harm.

There are of course collective action problems here. (These will be discussed in more detail in Chapters 10 and 11.) If we think that certain products should not be advertised in certain ways, or to certain individuals, we cannot rely on individual businesses to refrain from such advertising of their own accord. They will find it difficult if not impossible to do so. If one business stops advertising in the undesirable way, but their competitors do not, then it puts itself at a disadvantage. It risks losing significant revenue or even going out of business. The business will find it hard to stop advertising in this way unless it can be assured that its competitors will also stop. Traditionally, this assurance is given through law or regulation. So if we think that certain products should not be advertised in certain ways, or to certain individuals, then there need to be laws or regulations prohibiting such advertising.

5. Pricing

The part of marketing that gets the most attention in business ethics is advertising. We have seen why – advertising is an ethically fraught activity. But another activity that is traditionally understood as part of marketing has received increasing attention, namely pricing. In this section we explore ethical issues in pricing.

5.1. Is an Ethics of Pricing Possible or Desirable?

Let us begin with two background facts about prices. The first is a reminder about the role of prices in a market economy. Prices provide information about scarcity. They tell us how much people want a product, given how much of it there is. Producers, in turn, use prices to help them determine what to produce. Other things equal, they produce more of what commands high prices and less of what commands low prices. In doing so, they produce more of what people want. In this way, prices help resources to flow to their most productive uses, as determined by people's wants.

This is only true, however, if prices are set by the voluntary choices of sellers and buyers. If people want a certain item more, they will pay more for it, and over time more of it will be produced. But they can only pay more if they are permitted to pay more. If prices are set by an external authority – say the state – then prices will not convey information as accurately or at all. This is why economists typically recommend that states avoid setting prices and instead allow them to be determined by the voluntary choices of market participants. If the state sets the price of a good too high, then producers will flood into the market, and supply will exceed demand. This is a glut. If the state sets the price too low, then producers will leave the market, and demand will exceed supply. This is a shortage. When prices float free, supply and demand will align.

The second background fact is that, in the standard model of the market, all economic agents, including all firms, are "price-takers." This means that individual firms have no control over the prices that they pay for things or the prices for which they can sell things. The market rate is determined by hundreds (or thousands or millions) of buyers and sellers of that type of thing. When it buys a thing, the firm can't pay less than the market rate, because the seller can sell it to one of the countless other buyers who will pay that rate. The firm doesn't have to buy a product from a seller who is selling it above the market rate, because it can buy it from one of the countless other sellers who will sell it for the market rate. For similar reasons, when a firm goes to sell one of its products, it cannot sell it for above the market rate, and it need not sell it for below the market rate.

If we put these ideas together, we might think that an ethics of pricing is either impossible or undesirable. To talk of an ethics of pricing is to suggest that firms have some control over the prices they charge. It is to say that the market rate is one price but that firms should charge a different price, if that is what ethics requires. The second background fact tells us that firms have no control over the prices they charge. It is often said that in ethics, ought implies can. If you ought to do something, then you can do it; that is, it is possible for you to do it. This implies that if you can't do something, then you have no obligation to do it. If it is impossible for firms to change their prices (to make them more ethical), then they are not obligated to do so. On this reasoning, firms have no ethical obligations when it comes to price.

Maybe firms can't do anything about prices, it might be said, but what about states? Can't they intervene in markets to set prices? If so, then an ethics for pricing should be directed toward states, not individual firms. Here the first fact is relevant. It tells us that it is undesirable for states to try to adjust prices. It leads to problems, including gluts and shortages. Markets work more efficiently when prices float free. According to the argument so far, an ethics of pricing is impossible at the firm level and undesirable at the state level. Either way, we have no use for an ethics of pricing.

This all makes sense at the level of theory. But at the level of practice, it doesn't quite hold. The fact is, firms do have some flexibility when it comes to the prices they charge. They are able to charge more or less than the market rate. The simple explanation for this is that actual markets deviate in significant ways from perfectly competitive ones. They are rife with imbalances of power and information. In addition, in the standard model, products are assumed to be "undifferentiated," that is, all the same. But in reality products differ from producer to producer, as advertisers inform us. Because firms have some flexibility about the prices they charge, they can adjust their prices in response to ethical considerations. An ethics of pricing is therefore possible at the firm level.

What about the idea that an ethics of pricing is undesirable? On this view, prices should be determined by supply and demand, and not by anyone's – the state's or a firm's – ideas about what is right. Against this, we might observe that states *do* intervene in markets to set prices. Many states set minimum wages (a wage can be understood as a price of labor) and create price floors for agricultural products. The fact that states do these things doesn't prove that they should do them. But it is not hard to identify ethical considerations in favor of these policies. We might think that it is good for workers to earn living wages and good to secure the nation's food supply. Of course, we haven't done nearly enough to justify these policies all things considered. The point is simply that common practices give us reason to suppose that intervening in markets to set prices is not out of bounds.

We have seen at this point that an ethics of pricing is both possible at the firm level and potentially justifiable. But we need to be realistic. Firms have some ability to set prices, but their ability is not unlimited. It is constrained by market forces. Firms and states can and do set (or limit) prices, but they are reluctant to and rightly so. It follows that sellers should be largely free to price goods as they wish, with buyers being free to pay those prices, or not, as they choose. But there are some cases in which we may wish to limit this freedom. In the next two sections, we will focus on two of the most significant cases, the first involving price discrimination and the second involving price gouging.

Before moving on, let me flag another way of thinking about prices that has historically been of considerable interest. This is the idea of the "just price," which has its roots in the work of the 13th-century Catholic theologian and philosopher Thomas Aquinas. According to the standard interpretation of this idea, the price that sellers should charge for their products – the just price – is a function of how much it costs to produce them, including both the cost of the materials and the value of the producer's labor (which is in turn a function of what he needs to live decently). Insofar as Aquinas thought that the just price diverges consistently and significantly from the market price – the price that is voluntarily agreed to by buyers and sellers – most would say that his view is best forgotten. But a recent strain of scholarship argues that, for Aquinas, the just price mostly *is* the market price. In this case, there is no significant disagreement between the just price tradition and modern thinking about prices. Either way, this tradition does not merit an extensive or separate discussion.

5.2. Price Discrimination

Firms engage in price discrimination when they sell the same good to different people for different prices at the same time. When you hear "discrimination," it might call to mind invidious discrimination on the basis of protected factors like race or sex. This discrimination is universally believed to be ethically wrong, and it is almost always illegal. If firms discriminate on the basis of race or sex in their pricing – for example, if they sell the same good for a higher price to blacks than whites, or to women than men – then this would be wrong. But this is not typically what is meant by "price discrimination." Price discrimination is when firms try to sell products to consumers not on the basis of protected factors like race or sex, but on the basis of willingness to pay. The idea is to charge more to people who are willing to pay more and less to people who are willing to pay less.

If you are learning about price discrimination for the first time, you might think that it is still unfair. "You mean that firms sometimes try to charge more for products to people who want them badly?" You might think that this is a kind of exploitation. But if you take a step back, you will see that price discrimination is common, and people generally have no problem with it.

Economists typically divide price discrimination into three kinds or "degrees." Third-degree price discrimination is discrimination at the group level. This is the sort of price discrimination you see in things like senior and student discounts at movies, museums, and on public transportation. First-degree price discrimination is discrimination at the individual level. This is the sort of price discrimination that you might find in a flea market or a car dealership. Buyers and sellers haggle over the prices of products, and the final price is determined by the strength of each party's desire to transact and his or her bargaining skill. Second-degree price discrimination is an amorphous category that includes all instances of price discrimination that can't easily be categorized as first or third degree. Examples of second-degree price discrimination include things like quantity discounts and rebates. It is sometimes said that first- and third-degree price discrimination is based on who is buying, while second-degree discrimination is based on what is bought.

To observe that a pricing practice is common and accepted is not to say that it is justified. Practices can be common and yet wrong. But it's not hard to find arguments in support of price discrimination. One simple argument derives from the discussion of the market we gave in Chapter 4. There we said that if someone owns something, then they should be able to transfer it to someone else, if they receive what they regard as adequate compensation. This implies a freedom to price goods as the seller wishes, including to charge different buyers different prices. We can also defend price discrimination on consequentialist grounds. Price discrimination can increase social welfare when it enables producers to increase output. There is a mathematical proof for this, but we can understand the idea through a simple example. Drug companies routinely engage in third-degree price discrimination, selling medicines for less money in the developing world than in the developed world. They do this because people in the developing world have less money than people in the developed world. What if drug companies were forced to sell their drugs at a single price? Which price would they choose – the higher developed world price or the lower developing world price? Almost certainly, they would choose the former. If they chose the latter, they would be unable to cover their costs. In this case, people in the developing world would not have access to drugs and would be worse off.

This is not to say that all instances of price discrimination are accepted and justifiable. Online price discrimination has recently come in for criticism. In 2012, it was revealed by the *Wall Street Journal* that Staples was selling office products online to people in one zip code for higher prices than to people in another nearby zip code. Staples charged more to people who didn't live close to one of its competitors, assuming that they would be willing to pay higher prices. People were outraged. "How can they get away with that?" one customer asked angrily. Amazon was the target of a similar outcry when they were discovered to have engaged in price discrimination in their DVD sales in the early 2000s, based on people's browsing histories. Is the outrage justified?

It is not clear that it is. Staples and Amazon are just doing what flea market vendors and car salespeople do: sizing you up and trying to figure out how much you will pay. If what flea market vendors and car salespeople are doing is permissible, then perhaps what Staples and Amazon are doing is also permissible. Moreover, the arguments we gave earlier – about freedom and social welfare – apply here too. Indeed, the consequentialist case for price discrimination seems to tell more strongly in favor of the first-degree price discrimination that online retailers engage in than the third-degree price discrimination that drug companies engage in. Third-degree price discrimination increases the number of transactions that can occur. But it does so in an imprecise way, by offering different prices to different groups. The problem is that not everyone in the group is willing to pay the same amount. Personalized pricing allows for more precise discrimination. People are charged an amount that exactly equals their willingness to pay, so there is no overcharging or undercharging based on group membership. This maximizes the number of transactions that can occur.

We might still think there is something wrong with Staples's and Amazon's behavior. The problem may be one of knowledge. When we go into a flea market or a car dealership, we know what we are in for. The seller will try to sell the product to us for as much as we are willing to pay, and we will try to buy it for as little as they are willing to sell it for. When we browse around an online retailer's website, we don't know what we are (increasingly) in for. If we did, we might be able to protect ourselves, by deleting our cookies or browsing privately. It is possible that this issue will resolve itself over time, as consumers come to learn that online retailers are engaging in price discrimination. In the meantime, there is a risk that retailers are taking advantage of consumers' ignorance. That might be why some consumers indignantly wonder "how retailers can get away with that."

5.3. Price Gouging

The novel coronavirus pandemic swept the globe in early 2020. As of this writing in early 2021, it has killed more than four million people and sickened hundreds of millions more. One way the virus spreads is through touch. Infected people touch surfaces and contaminate them. Others touch these surfaces and then touch their faces, infecting themselves. One way to keep the virus from spreading, and to protect yourself from contracting it, is to keep your hands clean. Soap and water work well, but when you are on the go, hand sanitizer is valuable. As the pandemic took hold, there was a run on hand sanitizer. It became hard to find, and when you could find it, it was selling for many times its usual price.

Brothers Matt and Noah Colvin saw an opportunity. They rented a truck in their native Tennessee and drove around buying up all the hand sanitizer they could find, along with other cleaning supplies and medical equipment. Then they sold these items on Amazon for many times what they paid for them. For several weeks they raked in huge profits, until Amazon shut them down, citing Tennessee's laws against price gouging. The *New York Times* reported that, when they were shut down, the Colvins had amassed 17,700 bottles of hand sanitizer. As part of a settlement with the state, they agreed to give the bottles to a nonprofit organization to be donated to people in need.

Price gouging is typically defined as charging an unreasonably high amount for a necessary good or service in an emergency. This is exactly what the Colvins did. In most places, price gouging is illegal, and many people think it is unethical as well. (In his discussion of just prices, what Aquinas was most worried about was price gouging. He too thought that it was unethical.) But some argue that price gouging is not unethical and should not be illegal.

Critics of price gouging say that it is a kind of exploitation. As we saw in the previous chapter, to exploit someone is to take unfair advantage of them.

A bit more precisely, it is to extract an excessive benefit from them when they have no decent alternative but to accept your offer. Suppose you get bitten by a poisonous snake, but you would be cured by a vial of antidote that sells for $10. I have several vials on me and offer to sell you one for $1000. Since you don't have time to go to the store to buy one – you will die on the way – you agree.

In this case, I exploit you. I extract an excessive benefit from you – $1000 for a vial of antidote that sells for $10 – because you have no decent alternative but to accept my offer. This is the sort of thing the Colvins did. They got people to pay a lot more for hand sanitizer than it was worth, because people were desperate for it and had no good alternatives.

Defenders of price gouging may concede that it is exploitative. But they make two further observations. The first is that price gougers like the Colvins benefit the people they gouge. A 28 oz bottle of hand sanitizer might normally sell for $5. As people started buying it all up, the price rose to $20. But no one was forcing anyone to buy hand sanitizer. If people were willing to buy it – and they were – then they must have valued the hand sanitizer at least as much if not more than their $20. Perhaps price gouging is a form of exploitation, but if it is, the exploitation is mutually beneficial, good for both the exploiters and the people they exploit.

The second observation defenders of price gouging make is that permitting price gouging may be the best way of ending it. After a few months, it became possible once again to buy 28 oz bottles of hand sanitizer for $5. Why is this? Because producers saw that hand sanitizer was selling for $20 and rushed into the market to try to make a profit. Eventually enough entered the market – supply caught up with demand – and prices fell to normal levels. Remember that prices convey information about relative scarcity. When they rise, they tell producers that more of the product is wanted, and producers will respond by producing more of it. Suppose that price gouging weren't allowed. Then producers would not have rushed into the market. Supply would have eventually caught up with demand, but it would have taken a lot longer. People were able to purchase more hand sanitizer at lower prices because, early on, some people were gouged by people like the Colvins.

There are no easy solutions here. The Colvins thought that they were doing something good, for themselves and others. Perhaps they were. The state of Tennessee thought they were doing something bad. There might be truth here too. What we might really want is a way to get producers to produce more without allowing some to be exploited. We might think that this shows that markets have limits and that government intervention is sometimes needed.

6. Chapter Summary

In this chapter we considered ethical issues in marketing. We focused mainly on advertising, though we also had something to say about pricing. We began by thinking about what is good about advertising. The main benefit of advertising is that it provides consumers information they can use to satisfy their preferences, though it has other benefits as well.

We then considered some ways that advertising can go wrong. One way is through deception. Making false statements is one way advertisements can deceive, as we saw in the Beech-Nut case, but false statements are not necessarily deceptive, as the Red Bull case shows. In these cases, the key issue is whether reasonable consumers are actually misled, not whether advertisers intend to deceive them. We concluded by considering reasons why deception might be wrong.

Next, we considered advertising's persuasive function. An old criticism of advertising, made famous by Galbraith, is that it produces desires in us, as opposed to giving us information that we can use to satisfy pre-existing desires. Hayek objected to this criticism, pointing out that most desires are produced by outside forces and that anyway satisfying desires is good, however they are produced. A further issue is how advertisers attempt to persuade us. Rational persuasion is morally unproblematic, but non-rational persuasion raises some concerns. Here we considered whether associative advertisements are simply amusing attempts to get us to remember the products advertised or devious attempts to circumvent our faculties of rational choice.

Vulnerability presents special problems for advertisers. We saw this in the Nestlé infant formula case, where some women misused the product, with tragic results. We drew an analogy between marketing products to the vulnerable and manufacturing unsafe products. One approach is to disclose the risks and let consumers decide. Another is to try to prevent consumers from making unsafe choices – in this case by failing to alert them to a product, which they might use dangerously. One thing seems true. Whatever degree of caution advertisers exercise when advertising to the non-vulnerable, they should exercise extra caution when advertising to the vulnerable.

We closed with a discussion of prices, which pose interesting ethical questions not often explored in discussions of marketing ethics. We began by reminding ourselves of the function of prices in a market economy and why in general we should take a "hands-off" approach to pricing. We then considered two cases, which, according to some, call for a "hands-on" approach. We considered price discrimination, which is a common phenomenon, but which has come in for criticism when deployed by online retailers. We considered what can be said for and against it. We then considered price gouging, noting that it may be a form of exploitation, but it is one that can be mutually beneficial and has the positive effect of drawing additional producers into the market.

7. Study Questions

1. What is the main benefit of advertising? What are some of its secondary benefits?

2. Give an example of a false statement that is deceptive. Give an example of a false statement that is not deceptive. What's the difference?
3. Do you think that Copper Fit's advertising is deceptive? Explain and defend your answer.
4. What is the dependence effect, and how might it be used to criticize advertising as a practice?
5. We discussed two kinds of persuasion. Explain them with the help of examples.
6. What might someone say is wrong with the sort of non-rational persuasion one finds in Budweiser's "Best Buds" advertisement? How might Budweiser reply? Do you think there is anything wrong with this type of persuasion?
7. Why was Nestlé criticized for marketing infant formula in the developing world? What might Nestlé say in its defense? What do you think Nestlé should do?
8. Why might someone think that an ethics of pricing is either impossible or undesirable?
9. What are the standard defenses of price discrimination?
10. Do you think the Colvins did something wrong when they acquired and sold hand sanitizer during the pandemic at significantly above-market prices? Legally wrong? Morally wrong? Explain and defend your answers.

Additional Readings

Attas, D. (1999). What's wrong with 'deceptive' advertising? *Journal of Business Ethics*, *21*(1), 49–59.

Crisp, R. (1987). Persuasive advertising, autonomy, and the creation of desire. *Journal of Business Ethics*, *6*(5), 413–418.

Elegido, J. M. (2011). The ethics of price discrimination. *Business Ethics Quarterly*, *21*(4), 633–660.

Galbraith, J. K. (1958). *The affluent society*. Boston, MA: Houghton Mifflin.

Hayek, F. A. (1961). The non sequitur of the 'dependence effect'. *Southern Economic Journal*, *27*(4), 346–348.

Phillips, M. J. (1994). The inconclusive ethical case against manipulative advertising. *Business & Professional Ethics Journal*, *13*(4), 31–64.

Snyder, J. (2009). What's the matter with price gouging. *Business Ethics Quarterly*, *19*(2), 275–293.

Solomon, S. (1981, December 6). The controversy over infant formula. *New York Times Magazine*. www.nytimes.com/1981/12/06/magazine/the-controversy-over-infant-formula.html

Valentino-Devries, J., Singer-Vine, J., & Soltani, A. (2012, December 24). Websites vary prices, deals based on users' information. *The Wall Street Journal*. http://online.wsj.com/news/articles/SB10001424127887323777204578189391813881534

Zwolinski, M. (2008). The ethics of price gouging. *Business Ethics Quarterly*, *18*(3), 347–378.

7 Ethics at Work, Part I

In the previous two chapters, we examined ethical issues that attend market exchanges or business as an activity. We considered what can be sold and how it can be sold. In this and the next chapter, we consider ethical issues that attend business as a thing, that is, an entity that sells things. Our focus will be on ethical issues between employers and employees. In this chapter, we will discuss health and safety, meaningful work, control and participation, and pay. Running through our discussion is an account of working in an Amazon warehouse, with which we begin.

1. Working at Amazon

Working in an Amazon warehouse is hard, as two reporters found out recently. Adam Littler and James Bloodworth went undercover at separate Amazon facilities to see what it is like to work as a "picker." The job of a picker is to pull items off shelves in giant warehouses for packaging and transportation to customers. Littler and Bloodworth discovered that workers are on their feet for their entire shifts, which can last as long as 10 hours, and cover as many as 15 miles during them. (Yet another undercover reporter at Amazon in the U.S. said she worked a 12-hour shift and covered 20 miles.) They must move fast, because all of their movements are closely monitored through scanners they carry. When they do not move fast enough, the scanner beeps a warning. Enough of these beeps, and workers are disciplined or fired. It is difficult for workers to go to the bathroom on their shifts. Given the size of the warehouses, the bathrooms can be very far away – sometimes through a security gate – and every moment they are not "picking" is "idle time" that is counted against them. Both Littler and Bloodworth found the experience dehumanizing. They were called upon not *to think*, but merely *to do*. They received very little pay for their efforts, making at or near the minimum wage.

When approached for comment on these accounts, Amazon said that they told prospective employees about the demands of the job and had consulted with outside experts to ensure that their working conditions were not too taxing. Indeed, Amazon said that some workers valued being able to get so much

DOI: 10.4324/9781351016872-7

exercise on the job. Amazon didn't pay its workers very much, it is true, but no one has ever accused them of paying less than the legally mandated minimum wage.

Is there anything wrong with working conditions in Amazon warehouses? Of course, *you* might not want to work in an Amazon warehouse, but that doesn't mean that there is something morally problematic about this work. You might not want to be an accountant or a veterinarian, but you can still recognize that these are valuable jobs that someone might be willing to perform, especially for money. The Amazon case highlights four issues that are worth separate consideration: health and safety at work, meaningful work, control and participation, and pay. We will discuss them in order.

Before proceeding, let me mention a point that I hope is obvious. There is nothing special about Amazon. The kind of work they offer is found at many other workplaces. Amazon simply provides a useful example, given how well known it is as a business, and given how much information has been gathered about its working conditions. The lessons we will draw from our consideration of working conditions at Amazon can be applied to any other work environment.

2. Health and Safety

Pickers in Amazon warehouses are on their feet all day on hard, concrete surfaces and walk between 15 and 20 miles per day. They take only a few short breaks. It is not just the walking that is a problem. Pickers have to pull items off shelves and load them onto carts. This requires a lot of bending, squatting, leaning, and reaching. The items can be heavy, which can lead to muscle strains and tears. The journalists who worked at Amazon for a few weeks didn't suffer any long-term harm, but others who worked there longer weren't so fortunate.

Candice Dixon, 54, worked as a "stower" at an Amazon warehouse. Her job was to place items in bins, which is the step before picking. Dixon started work in April 2018. Within two months, after stowing approximately 100,000 items, she was physically unable to work. Her back was severely sprained and her spine had bulging discs. The pain from her injuries made it hard for her to do routine activities around her house, like climbing stairs or walking her dog. Back injuries can be notoriously hard to verify, but you don't have to take Dixon's word for it. As part of her workers' compensation application, her condition was verified by an Amazon-approved doctor.

Amazon is not the only place that you can find dangerous work. There were almost 3 million nonfatal workplace injuries and illnesses in private industry in the U.S. in 2018, more than 10% of which resulted in a visit to a medical facility. Work can be not just dangerous but deadly. In 2018, 5250 people died from work-related injuries in the U.S. The largest number of deaths occurred in the construction industry, but significant numbers occurred in the mining, agriculture, and transportation industries.

What steps should employers take to ensure their employees' safety? Is there any work that is too unsafe? How should we decide? In this section we explore these questions.

We might start with the idea that risk is a part of life. Pretty much anything you do imposes some risk on you. This goes not just for obviously perilous activities like rock climbing and hang gliding, but for more mundane activities like walking your dog (you might trip on crack in the pavement) and cooking dinner (you could burn yourself). Jobs too involve risk. Workers can be injured by falling debris, burned by fires, and scarred by chemicals. They may permanently damage their backs, like Candice Dixon did, lifting thousands of items into bins.

This is not to say that activities, including jobs, cannot be made less risky. The problem is that measures to make work less risky – hard hats for construction workers, ventilation systems for factory workers, extra breaks for Amazon pickers – tend to be costly. If they were free, or if they saved employers money, then employers would provide them voluntarily, since it would be in their interest to do so. Maybe employers would need to be convinced at first that a certain safety measure was cost-effective, but once they were convinced, they would be happy to provide it. It follows that if employers make work less risky, they will have less money to pay workers.

You might think that employers should just absorb the costs associated with safety measures and not reduce workers' wages, but this is not always possible. This is for the same reason that employers can't just increase their employees' wages if they want to. Markets are competitive, and there are limits to how much consumers will pay for goods. This limits how much firms can spend on their workers. So one way of understanding the question "How risky should work be?" is "What is the right mix between risk and pay (and other forms of compensation) at work?"

One answer to this question is, let market participants decide, a view we will abbreviate "LMPD." On this view, employers and employees should get together to decide what safety equipment will be installed, knowing that these costs will result in lower wages. They might decide to install better safety equipment and get lower wages, or worse safety equipment and get higher wages. Labor unions may play a role in the process, bargaining on behalf of workers with a particular employer. Alternatively, it may happen through employee choice or sorting. Different employers will offer prospective employees different mixes of risk and pay at work, and workers will sort themselves into different firms, based on their preferences for risk and pay. Risk-tolerant employees may prefer firms with riskier work and higher pay, while risk-intolerant workers may prefer firms with less-risky work and lower pay. Firms that have trouble attracting employees may need to offer less risk and more pay, or vice versa. Workers like Dixon will accept lower pay if it gets them a safer working environment.

Proponents of LMPD oppose mandatory health and safety regulations, of the sort governments routinely create and enforce, as limits on people's freedom. They say: "Let market participants – employers and employees – decide these matters for themselves." As we will see, LMPD is an approach that can be used to answer questions about various aspects of work, such as how meaningful it should be and how much privacy workers should have.

Why accept LMPD? We might see it as implied by a general presumption of liberty. According to this presumption, people should be allowed to do what they want, provided that their actions don't harm other people. One reason for this presumption appeals to personal welfare. You are the best judge of what makes you happy. No one else knows as much about your needs and wants. So you are likely to be happier if you make decisions about your life than if someone else does. Considerations of autonomy also support the presumption of liberty. People have an interest in shaping their lives according to their own plans. For a while, your parents made most of your decisions for you: what to wear, what to eat, what activities to engage in, when to go to bed, and so on. Now you make these decisions for yourself, and you probably don't want to go back to how things used to be. The LMPD extends this view to risky work. It implies that there is no limit on the degree of risk that an employer can have in their labor processes, and no limit on the degree of risk that an employee can take on. Both parties to the employment relationship can decide what is best for themselves.

While LMPD is based on an important idea – choice matters – it is implausible, in its current unqualified form. For a choice to be justified as an expression of autonomy or to increase welfare, it must be *informed*. If you don't know what you are agreeing to, it may be inconsistent with how you want to shape your life, and it may not increase your welfare. Remember that when Amazon was challenged on the working conditions in its warehouses, one of the defenses it gave was that it told workers about the risks. This recognizes the importance of information in justifying risk.

The solution to this, it would seem, is to ensure that people are informed about the risks they face at work. In fact, many scholars have argued for a "right to know" about risk, apart from its role in justifying risk. But there is debate about what it means to be informed, and whose responsibility it is to ensure that workers are informed. There may be some risks that workers themselves should know about. Perhaps any reasonable person should be able to figure out that they should handle sharp objects carefully or else they may cut themselves. But there may be other risks that only employers know about. A factory owner may know, but her workers may not, that chemicals known to cause burns are being used in the factory. The owner has a duty to disclose this danger to workers, just as Amazon disclosed the dangers of its warehouse jobs to its workers.

Just telling workers about the risks may not be enough, however. Employers may have to ensure that workers *really understand* the risks. It is possible that Dixon didn't fully appreciate the dangers of her job at Amazon until it was too late. A further question is what to do about risks that neither the employer nor the employee currently knows about, but which in principle could be known. This is probably not relevant in Dixon's case, since the risks are reasonably clear. But when people work with obscure or novel chemicals or substances, the answer is not so clear. Do employers have a responsibility to research scientific journals for information about the risks associated with these chemicals? What if there is no existing research on them? Do employers have a duty to produce new research? Who will bear the costs of producing this research?

If workers (or employers) cannot be relied upon to understand the risks they face, then the government may have to establish some minimum health and safety standards. We might see government regulation as a substitute for choices workers (and employers) would make if they did understand them.

Suppose now that everyone is fully informed about risks at work. Then should employers be free to offer work with any degree of risk, and should workers be free to accept any work, no matter how risky? You might still have doubts. In particular, you might worry about how "free" people's choices to perform risky work are. It's not like people are choosing risky work for fun, you might say, as they might choose to go rock climbing or hang gliding. They choose risky work because they *have* to, because they have no other decent option. This might have been Dixon's situation. Maybe she knew what she was getting into. Maybe she didn't want to do that kind of work, but she had to. Maybe it was the only job she could get that would pay her bills. In light of problems like this, you might think that government regulation is necessary to protect workers from very risky work.

A defender of the LMPD could hardly deny that some workers are effectively forced by a lack of options to choose very risky work. But, they say, if workers choose this, then – assuming they are informed about the dangers of the work – they do it because their other option – unemployment – is worse. So their choice of even very risky work can be autonomous, and can promote their welfare, even if it is not a choice that people would make under better circumstances. Besides, they might add, if the problem is that people are forced to choose very risky work, the solution is not to make work less risky but to make people's options better. If there were a more generous social safety net, for example, then it would be easier for people to refuse risky work.

This response is not entirely persuasive. The fact is, most societies don't have generous social safety nets – safety nets generous enough to allow people to "pay their bills" or, more generally, live decent lives without working. So we might see government regulation of health and safety in the workplace as necessary for protecting workers in the real world.

Suppose finally that workers are informed about risks at work and have decent options. Then should we trust them to decide how much risk to accept at work? Before you answer, consider that when people are left to make choices for themselves, they sometimes behave imprudently; that is, they make bad choices. For this reason, we do not allow people to drive cars without wearing a seatbelt. In some states, people are not allowed ride a motorcycle without a helmet or set off fireworks. These laws are instances of *paternalism*, that is, interferences with a person's liberty that are justified by appealing to that person's own good. We might justify health and safety regulations in the workplace in the same way. If left to their own devices, people might choose to work in conditions that are bad for them, even if they know the risks. Governmental regulation can make these choices impossible.

We have considered reasons for backing away from the "let market participants decide," or LMPD, approach to workplace health and safety. Workers may lack relevant knowledge; they may have no decent options; and they may make imprudent choices. To back away from this view is to move toward the view that there should be some governmental regulation of workplace health and safety. But this begins a new inquiry. How much regulation is needed? How do we decide?

A common answer to these questions is *cost-benefit analysis*. We add up all the costs and benefits of a proposed safety regulation. If the benefits outweigh the costs, then the regulation should be enacted. If the costs outweigh the benefits, then it should not be. In the case of safety improvements in Amazon warehouses, we might consider how much they cost Amazon to install and maintain. How much would it cost Amazon to give their employees longer breaks or to rearrange their labor processes so that their employees don't have to do as much heavy lifting? Then we might consider the benefits of these improvements for employees, including the number of injuries they prevent, such as those suffered by Dixon. Individuals engage in cost-benefit analysis on a personal level all the time. When Dixon was deciding whether to take the job at Amazon, she weighed the benefits of a steady paycheck against the costs of a risk of injury. Using cost-benefit analysis to determine whether to impose a safety regulation on a business takes this decision-making process from the individual to the social level, asking what the total costs and benefits of the regulation are for all affected parties.

You might wonder about how all the costs and benefits of a safety improvement can be estimated. Maybe it's easy to estimate the costs of hard hats for construction workers. We just look at the price of the hard hats and multiply it by the number of workers. But how do we estimate the benefits of being free of pain? Do we just look at how much the person would have paid to visit the doctor or buy pain pills? Or should we make some allowance for the fact that the person simply feels better? Things get even trickier when safety improvements save lives. Then it becomes necessary to try to estimate the benefit of additional years of human life. You might think this is impossible and conclude that cost-benefit analysis cannot be used to make decisions about safety. But this would be hasty. You make such decisions all the time in your own life. Every time you drive in a car, you risk serious injury or even death from an accident. But you judge that the benefits of getting where you want to go quickly and conveniently outweigh the costs, which is the (small) risk of injury and death. The point here is simply that cost-benefit analysis, while a valuable tool, has its limits. It gives us a framework for answering questions about safety improvements in the workplace, but difficult questions must be answered in order to fill it in.

3. Meaningful Work

Pickers work hard, but their work is not challenging. It requires little training, taking a normal person only a few minutes to master. The job is simply to do one thing: pull an item off a shelf and put it into a basket. They do this repeatedly, as fast as possible. Amazon pickers have almost no discretion. They are told exactly what to do and where to go.

By contrast, other jobs require a lot more thought, creativity, and freedom. Think of the job of a marketing executive at Amazon. They have to decide, among other things, what sort of advertising to do for Amazon and what forms that advertising should take. Should they purchase online ads? Or maybe a television spot? What sort of visuals should they use? And music? Should they hire a celebrity spokesperson or connect with influencers on social media? The possibilities are vast. Marketing executives at Amazon may be given some constraints. For example, they may be given a goal – increase brand awareness by 10% – and a budget – $1,000,000. But given this goal and budget, it is up to them to decide what to do. This is the type of work that takes significant training and experience to do well and many years to master.

The job of a picker at Amazon is what some call "meaningless work." We need to be careful here. When business ethicists talk about "meaningless work," or "meaningless jobs," they don't mean to imply that those jobs don't serve a purpose. People order all kinds of valuable stuff from Amazon, and without pickers, those things would never get from Amazon to consumers. The picker also gets something out of his job as well, minimally, a wage. A meaningless job is not a job that doesn't matter. Instead, it is a job that is monotonous and routine and requires no thought, skill, or creativity. Picking in an Amazon warehouse is a meaningless task, but so is bolting wheels onto cars, cutting grass, or sorting recycling. A person whose job consists exclusively in doing one of these tasks all day has a meaningless job.

Meaningful work is the opposite of meaningless work. Meaningful work is work that requires thought, skill, and creativity. The marketing executive at

Amazon performs meaningful work. But high-ranking executives are not the only ones who perform meaningful work. So do bankers, lawyers, teachers, electricians, plumbers, carpenters, and many others.

Before we ask whether there is anything wrong with meaningless work, it is worth asking why such jobs exist at all. The standard answer goes back to Adam Smith, whom we met back in Chapter 4. Smith is interested in the division of labor or what we might call "specialization." To explain how the division of labor comes about, Smith gives the example of pin-making. Making a pin, Smith says, requires 18 different steps. First the wire is drawn out; then it is straightened; then it is cut; and so on until the finished pin is packaged for sale. If a worker did all these steps herself, Smith says, she could make just one or two pins per day. If there were 10 workers working side by side, each doing all of the steps themselves, they would produce 10–20 pins per day. But if the 10 workers specialize in just one or two of the steps, then they would get really good at them and wouldn't waste time moving from one task to another. If workers combine their efforts, Smith says, they can produce thousands of pins per day. So Smith argues that a divided labor process is a more efficient labor process. We get a lot more production from the same number of worker hours if those workers specialize than if they do not.

But now notice that a highly divided or specialized labor process is one that features a lot of meaningless work, as we have defined it. In a specialized labor process, one worker will straighten wires for his whole shift; another will cut wires for his whole shift; and on and on. In sum, meaningless work comes from the fact that organizing labor processes into meaningless tasks makes them more efficient, and businesses have an incentive to produce goods efficiently. Initially, it may give them an edge on their competitors, but eventually, they have to do it just to keep up with them.

Having understood where meaningless work comes from, let us now consider whether there is anything wrong with it. We will consider two potential concerns.

The first concern is that workers will be forced to accept meaningless jobs. If Smith is right, the reason employers organize labor processes into meaningless segments is that it is more efficient to arrange things this way. Perhaps some firms could reorder labor processes so that, to complete their tasks, workers had to exercise some creativity and thought, but this would be less efficient. A firm that did this would be putting itself at a competitive disadvantage relative to other firms and, unless it found a way to cut costs elsewhere, would eventually go out of business.

It does seem true that some workers – especially in low-skilled occupations, such as retail and food service – have little choice but to accept one or another meaningless job. But it is obviously not the case that all jobs are meaningless. We noted that the marketing executive at Amazon performs meaningful work.

So do bankers, lawyers, teachers, electricians, plumbers, carpenters, and many others. One reason for this might be that some labor processes simply cannot be efficiently divided up into meaningless segments. Think of all of the things a plumber does when she comes into your house to fix a leaky pipe. She figures out where the leak is coming from, comes up with a plan to fix it (which itself may involve many steps), and then implements that plan. You can't efficiently assign these tasks to different people. Another, and perhaps more important, reason is that workers have some influence over how labor processes are organized. If workers do not like how firms are arranging their labor processes, they can complain, or they can leave for another job.

But what about the worry that firms *have to* arrange labor processes into meaningless segments – at least when it is possible for them to do so – just to stay competitive? In fact, as we discussed in the previous section, what firms need to do is make sure their overall labor costs do not get too high. If it costs more for the firm to arrange the labor process into meaningful segments, they can respond by lowering how much they pay workers. Some workers may prefer to perform meaningful work at a lower wage than meaningless work at a higher wage. Of course, workers may prefer to perform meaningful work at high wages, but competitive pressures may make it impossible for firms to offer this, at least to certain sorts of workers, perhaps including Amazon pickers.

So far we have been discussing meaningless work as work that workers don't really want, but which they might be forced to do because of competitive pressures or to earn enough money to pay their bills. But, according to the second concern, this doesn't take the badness of meaningless work seriously enough. According to this concern, meaningless work is not just something bad about work that workers may wish to avoid, like having to get up early in the morning, slogging through a long commute, or meeting deadlines. It is something that is deeply harmful.

In fact, Smith – who helped us to understand why labor processes tend to get divided into meaningless segments – was the first to suggest a problem with this. Smith claimed that work has *formative power*. Each person brings a certain set of inclinations and abilities to their work. In turn, Smith believes, work shapes people's inclinations and abilities. If your work calls for creativity – as the work of a marketer or a plumber does – then this will make you a more creative person outside of work. If your work calls for curiosity – as the work of a scientist or gardener does – then you will be a more curious person outside of work. But what if your work calls for you to perform a single boring task all day? Smith puts the likely outcome colorfully: "The man whose whole life is spent in performing a few simple operations . . . has no occasion to exert his understanding . . . and generally becomes as stupid and ignorant as it is possible for a human creature to become." If Smith is right, and we don't want people to become stupid and ignorant, then we should take steps to ensure that their work is meaningful.

Questions can be raised about this argument. One is whether Smith is right that meaningless work makes people stupid. This is an empirical claim that requires empirical evidence, and there is not a lot of evidence one way or the other as to whether it is true. Another question we might ask is whether it is really so bad if people's work makes them stupid or, less sensationally, dulls their cognitive capacities. Many things might dull people's cognitive capacities, including watching too much television, drinking too much alcohol, and not studying enough philosophy. Is it a problem if people do these things? Assuming that meaningless work has harmful consequences, which should be avoided, a further question is how we bring this about. Should society require private employers to redesign labor processes so that they contain only meaningful segments of work? If this costs money, for example because it makes labor processes less efficient, who should pay for this?

At this point, the debate about meaningful work begins to parallel the debate about health and safety in the workplace. If redesigning labor processes into meaningful segments costs employers money, then they will have less money for workers' wages. So the question is not simply about how meaningful work should be, but what is the right mix of meaningfulness and pay at work, and who should decide. We might, again, "let market participants decide" or LMPD. Employers can make work meaningless, and pay higher wages, or make work meaningful, and pay lower wages. Employees can sort themselves into different firms depending on their relative preferences for meaningfulness and pay. We might justify this by appealing to a presumption of liberty, according to which people should be able to do as they please, provided their actions don't harm others. But for choice to justify an outcome, it must be informed. So employees must be brought to understand the nature of the work they are doing and its likely effects on their mental health. If they cannot be, then governmental regulation of labor processes to make them meaningful may be necessary. Alternatively, or in addition, we might support such regulation on the grounds that, in a society with a weak social safety net, some workers will be forced to choose meaningless work or on the (paternalistic) grounds that workers should be prevented from making choices that are bad for themselves.

This analysis invites us to view meaningfulness, along with health and safety, as work "amenities" that employees might trade away for more money. Then the questions will be about the conditions under which the trades are made – is there sufficient information and decent alternatives? – and whether people can be trusted to make good trades for themselves. We might see other work amenities, such as parental leave, vacation time, and health services, in the same way. But there are limits to this analysis. It would be a mistake to think that workers could agree to work in *any* conditions, or be subjected to *any* treatment, in exchange for more money. Consider rules against sexual harassment. It would be wrong for employers to sexually harass their employees, even if employees agreed to be harassed. There are some things that employers just shouldn't do, even if employees might agree to them. Certain lines should not be crossed. But it is not always clear where these lines are.

4. Control and Participation

Candice Dixon performs a job that has health risks and that is meaningless. This is a bad situation for Dixon. What can be done? Here's an idea: Dixon could tell her manager to give her different work, work that is safer and more meaningful.

You might say: "That's not the way it goes. Workers don't tell managers what to do. Managers tell workers what to do. If Dixon wants to perform different work, then she has to find a different job." You would be correct, at least if you are describing the circumstances in which most workers find themselves. Most have little control over what they do. Their employers tell them what to do, and it is generally assumed that they have a right to tell them.

Why don't workers have control or at least an opportunity to participate in managerial decision-making? Should they have control or an opportunity to participate? In this section we explore these questions.

Our discussion overlaps somewhat with our previous discussion of meaningful work. Meaningful work, we said, is work that requires thought, skill, and creativity. Workers who have meaningful work – people like advertising executives, teachers, carpenters, and plumbers – have some control over their work. The plumber confronts a leak and chooses the best means to fix it. Students need to learn a new skill and the teacher chooses the best means to teach it. This is where the plumber's and the teacher's (and carpenter's and executive's) skill and creativity come in. If they didn't have some control, there would be no room for the exercise of skill and creativity.

Notice that this is "means" control. The worker (plumber, teacher, etc.) is given a task, or end, and then gets to choose the means to accomplish it. The choice of means is up to the worker. But the choice of the task is not. The worker's manager tells the worker what task to perform. So most workers lack what we might call "end" control. This shows that the discussion of control and participation is not exhausted by the discussion of meaningful work. We still want to know why workers like Candice Dixon aren't permitted to choose, or help to choose, their tasks. Put another way, what gives people like Jeff Bezos, Amazon's CEO, the right to boss around people like Candice Dixon? (Bezos stepped down as CEO of Amazon in July of 2021 and was replaced by Andy Jassy. Since Bezos was CEO when Dixon worked there, we will use Bezos in our example.)

4.1. Ownership and Control

You might say that the answer is that Amazon's owners – its shareholders – put Bezos in charge. (The idea that shareholders own the corporation might be challenged, but we'll ignore this complication for now. For a fuller discussion of the nature of corporate ownership, see Chapter 9, Section 4.3.) So Bezos, and anyone to whom he delegates authority (e.g., Dixon's manager), can issue orders to Amazon's other employees.

This answer is incomplete. Owning a piece of property doesn't give you a right to tell *other people* what to do with it. Dixon owns her shoes, but she can't direct her manager, or Bezos, to put them on and do a tap dance with them.

Nevertheless, you might say that Amazon's shareholders have a certain *power*, deriving from their property rights, which they delegate to Bezos (and which he may delegate to others), and this is all that is needed for control. If you own something, you can prevent others from using it. So Bezos can exclude others from Amazon's property, including its warehouses. In the same way, Dixon can prevent Bezos from using her shoes. So, if Dixon wants to work at an Amazon warehouse to earn a paycheck, she better do as Bezos says.

According to this argument, Bezos doesn't so much have a right to boss Dixon around as he does have the power to do so, because of his right to control who has access to Amazon property. But others think that Bezos does have a right to boss Dixon around. The source of this right, they believe, is a promise that Dixon made to Bezos (or her manager) when she agreed to work for Amazon. When you agree to work for someone, you agree – implicitly, if not explicitly – to do what they say. This is what it means to be an employee. There are of course limits to this agreement. You wouldn't be required to rob a bank if your employer asked you to. More mundanely, it might be understood that Dixon would perform tasks related to picking and wouldn't be asked to drive a forklift or file Amazon's taxes. But within broad limits, according to this argument, Dixon is obligated to do as Bezos says.

We now have a better understanding of why employers can tell employees what to do. This doesn't mean we should be satisfied with this state of affairs. We might think that it is bad for some people to be able to order others around, and we might wonder if the workplace should be arranged differently. But notice where employers' ability to tell employees what to do comes from: *property rights*. Employers like Bezos can tell employees like Dixon what to do because of who owns Amazon. So it might seem that the debate about who should exercise control in businesses is fundamentally a debate about who should own them. We might think that if we allow private individuals to own businesses, then we need to accept that those individuals will be in control. If we want to extend control to workers like Dixon, then we need to insist that businesses be publicly owned.

There is something to this argument. You will recall that we discussed the merits of the private and public ownership of the means of production – that is, businesses – in Chapter 4. Many of the arguments considered in that discussion appeal to the value of control. Ownership and control tend to go together. It would be a mistake to conclude, however, that the debate about control is *solely* a debate about ownership. This is so for two reasons.

First, public ownership doesn't guarantee worker control or at least meaningful control of an enterprise by its workers. It is possible for productive enterprises to be publicly owned and controlled by the public as a whole. Think of the United States Postal Service (USPS) or the U.K.'s National Health Service (NHS). These enterprises are publicly owned, but they aren't managed by their workers. They are managed by government agencies. To be sure, workers in the USPS and NHS can help to control those enterprises, by controlling who is in the government, but no more than any other member of the public.

Second, even if we think that it should be possible for individuals to own businesses, and that ownership implies control, it does not follow that business owners should be able to arrange their businesses however they see fit. This is a general point, one that we have relied on in our discussion throughout this chapter. If we support health and safety regulations, or interventions in labor processes to make them more meaningful, we are saying that owners' freedom to control their businesses is limited in these respects. We might say the same thing in this case. That is, we might say that business owners, despite being generally in control of their businesses, should cede some control to workers, by allowing workers to participate in the making of some decisions.

4.2. Freedom, Welfare, and Control

We now get to the crux of the matter. Why should workers have a say in managerial decision-making? Two types of reasons are generally offered.

One appeals to freedom. It is important for people to be able to shape their lives according to their own plans, in ways that reflect their preferences and values. If you don't have any control at work – if you cannot participate in decisions made at your firm – then your life will be dramatically shaped by other people's plans and their preferences and values. Assuming that the average full-time worker works 40 hours per week, 50 weeks per year, and has a 40-year career, that amounts to 80,000 hours – some of the very best hours of a person's life – under the control of someone else. Of course, you might be able to find an employer who shares your preferences and values. But you might not. Searching for a job can be difficult, expensive, and time-consuming. Some people will have little choice about where they work and who they work for. If we value freedom, the argument goes, then we must make sure that workers are able to exercise at least some control at work.

A second reason for giving workers the ability to participate in managerial decision-making appeals to workers' welfare. Decisions made by your employer can have significant effects on you. Your employer decides whether you get a raise, promoted, a bonus, relocated, or fired. For many people, these are major life events, causes of significant joy or grief, meriting congratulations or condolences. When workers lack control, their well-being is in the hands of other people. How well their life goes in crucial respects is decided by others. These decisions may benefit them, but they may not, and when they do not, they can't do much about them.

These considerations – of freedom and welfare – are found in arguments for democracy at the state level as well. When states are controlled by their citizens, citizens can shape their lives according to their preferences and values. They can vote out leaders who make their lives worse and vote in ones who make them better. They can't do these things if their leaders are not accountable to them. Interestingly, some writers make "parallel case" arguments for worker control. According to these writers, states are similar to firms. So if states should be run democratically by their citizens, then firms should be run democratically by their workers.

We have seen how considerations of freedom and welfare can be used to argue that workers should have some control at work. Freedom and welfare have also been appealed to, however, in arguments against worker control. More precisely, these values are invoked in defense of the idea that owners have a right to exclude workers from participating in firm decision-making.

Consider first freedom. One of the things you might want to do with your life is start and build a business. You might want to be the next Jeff Bezos. But this means shaping your business according to your own plans and your own preferences and values. As the business grows, you will hire employees. If you are required to allow them to participate in firm decision-making, and they decide to participate, then your ability to shape your business according to your own plans will be limited. You may no longer be able to implement your distinctive plan. You will instead implement a plan that you and your employees can agree on. Now you might be the sort of person who wants their employees to participate in firm decision-making, and you might appreciate the new plan you and your employees collectively create. But you might not. Opponents of worker control say that you should be able to pursue your own distinctive plan, if that is what you want.

Considerations of welfare can also be used to argue against worker control. The basic problem is that worker control is expensive. In the first place, it is slow. In the typical case, inviting workers into the decision-making process in a firm means getting input from a lot more people. If workers get to vote, this slows down the process even further. It's fine if a town, city, or state makes decisions slowly, some argue. But businesses need to make decisions – and more generally, act – quickly. They cannot afford a slow and cumbersome decision-making process. Worker control may also be expensive insofar as it raises the cost of capital for firms. Businesses often need infusions of cash to grow. Investors supply businesses with money at favorable rates on the assumption that the businesses will be managed in their interests. If workers have a say in the firm's decisions, then investors may worry that it will be managed in workers' interests, not theirs. They may still invest, but they may demand more favorable terms for their investment.

These considerations may make you think that worker control is impractical. But they should not. As a matter of fact, in some firms, workers *are* in control. In the U.S., firms of service professionals, such as lawyers, accountants, and consultants, are typically privately owned and managed by (a subset of) their employees. Employees are in control at some companies in the plywood and lumber industry (Columbia, Dixie), in grocery stores (Publix, Price Chopper), and at breweries (Harpoon, Left Hand). Germany has long had a system of co-determination, where by law large corporations' supervisory boards are elected by both shareholders and workers. The Mondragon Corporation in the Basque Country of Spain is one of the largest and most successful worker-managed enterprises in the world, with more than 80,000 workers and revenues in excess of $12 billion euros in 2019.

It is a matter of intense debate among social scientists why workers acquire control in some firms but not in others. We won't pursue this question here. For us, the key takeaway is that worker participation in firm decision-making is a live option. It is a choice we – as owners, workers, or citizens – could make. We should do so in full view of its advantages and disadvantages. In this section we have attempted to identify them.

5. Pay

After a 2018 raise, Amazon pickers start at $15 per hour. Workers at many other firms make a lot less. In the U.S., the federal minimum wage is $7.25 per hour, though some states and cities have higher minimum wages. The minimum wage in California and Massachusetts is $12 per hour. The cities of Seattle and New York have minimum wages of $15 per hour. At the same time, some people get paid huge sums of money. Jeff Bezos, Amazon's founder and former CEO, has a net worth in excess of $190 billion, almost all of it earned from his work at Amazon. Two of Amazon's other top executives are paid almost $20 million per year. When it comes to pay, what's fair?

5.1. Preliminaries

You might wonder whether we are asking the right question. You might think that the key issue is not how much people get paid, but how wealth is distributed in society overall. Do some people not have enough to meet their basic needs? Is there too much inequality? You might further think that the answers to these questions depend on how much *wealth* people have, and how much wealth people have is only partly a function of how much they are paid. People's wealth is also a function of how much money other people give them (e.g., as inheritances), how much they pay in taxes, and what services they receive from the government. In sum, you might think the focus on pay is too narrow.

It might be replied that changing what people are paid changes the overall distribution of wealth in society. It's still worth discussing pay, it might be said, even if our main concern is wealth.

This is true. But if it's the distribution of wealth you want to change, it is probably better to change this through the tax code than through wages. A higher tax rate can be applied to those who have too much, and a lower or even negative tax rate can be applied to those who have too little. Adjusting wealth through the tax code is a lot more precise than adjusting it through wages. Suppose we raised the minimum wage in an effort to alleviate poverty. This would benefit the working poor. But it would also benefit the dependent children of wealthy parents who have after-school jobs. We might try to address inequality through something like a maximum wage, but this wouldn't affect people who are rich because they receive large inheritances.

In addition to being more precise, it is more efficient to change wealth through the tax code than through wages. This goes back to something we considered in Chapter 4. Wages are prices, and prices send signals. More of some good is wanted relative to supply, and less of another good is wanted relative to supply. Artificially raising or lowering wages sends incorrect signals to markets, telling market participants that there is more or less demand than there really is. At the same time, as we also saw in Chapter 4, we should not let the fact that wages are prices scare us away from thinking that, in some cases, businesses or states should seek to alter them in response to ethical considerations. There are limits on what businesses and states can and should do to adjust prices – we should not distort too much the signal they provide – but some adjustment may be justifiable.

For this to be the case, a person's pay must be sometimes worth adjusting. Is it? Does pay matter? Put simply, yes. Think about your own pay. You probably think about it in normative terms – as just or unjust, fair or unfair. Maybe you think it is unfairly low. You look around and see co-workers doing less than you getting paid more. Or maybe you think your pay is unfairly high. You think you don't do enough to justify what you earn. This – the way real people think about their pay – is already some reason to think that pay matters morally. In support of this way of thinking, notice that paying a person a certain wage is a way of treating them. How people are treated is a matter of ethical significance. You can be treated justly or unjustly, fairly or unfairly. You can be treated with dignity and respect, on the one hand, or abused and exploited, on the other. Since paying people is a way of treating them, this suggests that pay is a proper subject of ethical evaluation. We have now cleared the way to fully engage the question with which we started. When it comes to pay, what's fair?

5.2. Two Views About Justice in Pay

To begin, we should recognize that agreements matter. You do not simply find yourself working for a particular employer, and an employer does not find herself employing a particular person. There has to be an agreement first. The employer agrees to hire you, and you agree to work for the employer. Part of what you will agree to is a wage.

According to one view about what makes a wage fair or just – I will use 'fairness' and 'justice' interchangeably in this discussion – is that it is agreed to. Not just any agreement counts. If you lie about your skills, or the employer lies about what the job involves, then the agreement is invalid. The same is true if you force the employer to hire you – say through threats or intimidation – or the employer forces you to work for her. But assuming there is no fraud or force, this view says, your wage is fair provided you and your employer agree to it. So, the pay of Amazon pickers, even if it is very low, is fair, assuming that Amazon and its pickers agree to this pay, and there was no fraud or force on either side. The same goes for the high pay that Amazon offers its top executives.

To justify this "agreement view" of justice in wages, we might appeal to property rights and liberty. If you own something, then you can offer it to others and demand anything you want in return. This goes both for the employer, who is offering a job, and you, who are offering your labor. The employer cannot be compelled to give away more than she wants, and you cannot be compelled to accept less than you want. If we take property rights and liberty seriously, this view says, then you should think that just wages should be understood exclusively in terms of agreements.

The agreement view has a certain intuitive appeal, but a moment's thought suggests that it is too permissive. Suppose that an employer pays a certain amount of money to a white employee and a different, smaller amount of money to a black employee. Suppose both employees accept their wage offers without fraud or force. But suppose finally that these employees do the same job equally well. The result is discrimination in compensation, which many would say is morally wrong. Implausibly, the agreement view finds nothing wrong with this result. Or suppose that a person is living in terrible poverty and cannot provide the basic necessities for herself or her children. An employer might be able to get this person to accept an extremely low wage for a difficult and dangerous job. Many would object to this result on the grounds that, in doing so, the employer is exploiting the person. But again the agreement view finds nothing wrong with this result.

We might seek to repair the agreement view by attaching more qualifications or "riders" to it. We have already said that a just wage is one that is agreed to without fraud or force. We might add discrimination and exploitation to this list and say that a just wage is one that is agreed to without fraud, force, discrimination, or exploitation.

Articulating these riders is not an easy task. Some cases of discrimination – an employer giving preference to a white applicant over a black applicant for a job for which race is irrelevant – clearly involve wrongful behavior. But are there any cases in which race is relevant? Perhaps for a job as an actor in a play or movie? What characteristics, beyond the usual ones of race, sex, national origin, and religion, should be protected?

Trying to specify what it means for an employer to exploit a worker is an even more difficult task. In general, one person P exploits another person Q when P takes unfair advantage of Q. P exploits Q when P extracts an excessive benefit from Q in a situation in which Q cannot reasonably refuse P's offer. Suppose Q is drowning, and P offers to throw him a life preserver, but only if Q agrees to become P's servant. Wanting to avoid death, Q agrees. In this case, P exploits Q.

While this is easy enough to identify as a case of exploitation, other cases are not so clear. You might think that Amazon exploits people like Candice Dixon when it pays them low wages for their work. But while Amazon might *benefit* from this arrangement (one of the conditions for exploitation), it might not benefit *excessively* (another of the conditions), if they pay those workers what they are worth. The value of the work of people like Dixon may not be very high. This does not mean that Dixon is a worthless person; it just means that what she is doing for Amazon is not particularly valuable. That is, the relationship between Amazon and its warehouse workers may not be similar enough to the relationship between P and Q to qualify as a case of exploitation.

So far we have been considering one view of justice in wages, the agreement view. According to this view, a worker's wage is just or fair if it is agreed to under the right conditions. These conditions include an absence of fraud and force, and perhaps also discrimination and exploitation. We might wish to add other riders to the list to make this view's implications conform to our intuitions about what justice in wages requires. Or we might conclude that the agreement view is fundamentally misguided. To see how, let's consider a second view of fairness in wages.

This view might be called the "desert view." (This is desert as in *deservingness*, not the hot, sandy place.) According to this view, employees should be paid the amount of money that they deserve to be paid, based on the value of their work. Instead of determining a worker's wage through bargaining, according to this view, his wage should be determined by an assessment of how much his work is worth. The first question that must be answered about this view is, what makes work valuable? We might say that it is a function of the worker's effort. A closely related suggestion is that it depends on the costs of work, that is, how much training and education it requires, or how dangerous or difficult it is. But the most common version of the desert view says that the value of a person's work is a function of the contribution that it makes to the firm.

How are we to determine the value of a person's work? One suggestion appeals to the idea of marginal product. The marginal product of labor is the contribution that the last unit of labor makes to the total product. So we might say that a worker's contribution is his marginal product, or the difference between what the firm produces with the worker and what it produces without the worker. What a worker should receive in wages, in turn, is the value of his marginal product or his marginal revenue product. If an employee's contribution is worth $60,000, then he should be paid $60,000. We might call this the "absolute" version of the desert view.

The absolute version of the desert view is hard to put into practice. Many firms are large and complicated, and employees often work together in teams. Isolating that part of a firm's product that is due to the actions of a single individual may be difficult, even impossible. In light of this, some favor a "comparative" version of the desert view. On this version, employees should be paid in proportion to their contributions, given what others contribute and are paid. If an employee contributes $60,000 and is paid $40,000, then an employee who contributes $120,000 should be paid $80,000. It is easier to say how much a person contributes compared to someone else than to say how much he contributes absolutely. When people think about the fairness of their own pay, the comparative version of the desert view is often the one they have in mind. You might think that you get paid too little. It is natural to justify this claim by pointing out that you get paid less than people in your firm whose work is equally as valuable, or is even less valuable, than yours.

We said that property rights and liberty can be appealed to in an argument for the agreement view. What about the desert view? For many of its supporters, this view seems intuitively obvious. People should get the things they deserve generally, so workers should get the wages they deserve. What people deserve, in turn, is determined by the value of what they have done.

This might seem like a rather weak argument, but intuitions about desert are powerful. To see this, reflect on the institution of punishment. Suppose that a person has committed a crime. How much punishment should she receive? It is natural to answer that she should get an amount of punishment that she deserves, as determined by the value of what she has done. If we are unsure about how much punishment the criminal deserves in an absolute sense, we might reach for comparative considerations. The armed robber should be punished more severely than the embezzler, but less severely than the murderer. Just as desert seems like the right metric to use when it comes to punishment, so desert may seem like the right metric to use when it comes to wages.

We noted that the agreement view seems overly permissive. By contrast, the contribution view may be overly restrictive. Suppose that a firm adopts a particularly "flat" or "egalitarian" compensation scheme. It pays workers at the bottom of the organizational hierarchy more than the value of their contributions and those at the top of the hierarchy less than the value of their contributions. A firm might do this because it wants to create a more cooperative work environment or because its owners are committed to egalitarian ideals. Suppose moreover that everyone in the firm accepts this arrangement. Indeed, they claim to prefer it to alternatives. We might doubt that there is anything wrong about the firm's compensation plan. We might reach the same conclusion about a firm that adopts a particularly "steep" or "inegalitarian" compensation plan, assuming that everyone agrees to it.

Which view should we choose – the (suitably qualified) agreement view or the desert view? It might be thought that we don't have to choose. It might be said that, in a competitive market, employers will have to pay workers according to their contributions. If an employer pays a worker less than she contributes, then the worker will be poached away by another firm who will make her a better offer. If an employer pays a worker more than she contributes, then the employer bears an unnecessary cost that puts him at a competitive disadvantage. Either way, market forces will pressure employers and employees to enter into agreements in which employees' pay matches their contributions. If so, then perhaps we do not have to choose between the agreement and contribution views.

There is something to this idea. Amazon would not be able to find competent people to take their most important jobs if they didn't pay them millions of dollars. At the same time, if Amazon paid its pickers millions of dollars, it could not compete with other retailers and would eventually go out of business. But businesses are not mere "wage takers," as this argument implies. They have some choice about what to pay their workers. This is a specific instance of the more general claim that firms are not "price takers," since wages are a kind of price. Firms could attempt to pay workers what they are worth, as estimated by workers' contributions. Or they could opt for a different compensation plan, perhaps one that is more or less egalitarian.

What now? We have described two views of justice in wages, considered arguments for both, but failed to decide between them. As we've learned, this is a regrettably common problem when thinking about ethical problems in business. This is not a failure, but simply a recognition that these problems are hard. In this case, however, we might also take it as reason to believe that, when it comes to pay, there is no one right view about what fairness requires. There may be compensation plans that are morally problematic, but there may not be a morally best one. Or rather, the plan that is best may differ from firm to firm, and context to context.

Let me add one more complication to the mix before moving on. Often firms need to think not only about how much pay is just or fair for their employees, but what employees' pay is likely to get them to do. Sears Automotive found this out the hard way. In the 1990s, they instituted a commission-based compensation scheme for their mechanics. People who sold more repairs got higher pay. People who sold fewer repairs, or who didn't make their targets, had their hours reduced or were assigned to different and less lucrative departments within the company. Sears got what it wanted – a booming repair business – but it was based on fraud. Sears' mechanics were selling people repairs that they didn't need, as an investigation by the state of California revealed. Lawsuits ensued, and Sears ended up paying fines in excess of $20 million for fraud and false advertising. Wells Fargo got into similar trouble in the 2010s. They paid employees on the basis of how many accounts with the bank they were able to persuade clients to open. The result was that Wells Fargo's employees opened accounts for clients that those clients never agreed to open. Investigations and lawsuits followed, and by the end of 2018 Wells Fargo had paid nearly $3 billion in fines and settlements. Thousands of workers lost their jobs. What these cases suggest is that, when it comes to pay, fairness to employees cannot be the only consideration. Firms also have to think through the probable consequences of their compensation policies.

6. Chapter Summary

In this chapter, we began our consideration of ethical issues that attend business as a thing, that is, an entity that sells things. We discussed health and safety, meaningful work, control and participation, and pay. There are many details specific to each of these issues. But they also share some common themes. One of the main themes is freedom. We might think – when it comes to health and safety, meaningful work, control and participation, and pay – that employers and employees should be able to arrange their economic lives as they see fit. Employees should be able to arrange their workplaces however they want, and employees should be free to accept whatever employment offers they receive. This is the "let market participants decide," or LMPD, approach. We might see this freedom as good in itself, because it allows people to arrange their lives according to their own choices, and good because of its effects, because individuals know best what is going to make them happy. If we believe in this freedom absolutely, we might say that we don't need to worry at all about ethical rules and legal regulations around any of these topics. Market participants can sort everything out for themselves.

But this justification works only under certain conditions. There must be adequate knowledge. People must be aware of and truly understand what they are getting themselves into. There must be decent options. People must be able to decline to take jobs that do not suit them. These conditions are not always, or even usually, met in our world. Even when they are met, we might favor the recognition of certain ethical rules and legal regulations for health and safety, meaningfulness, control and participation, and pay, on the grounds that people do not always make good choices for themselves.

One lesson to be drawn from this is that freedom is a complicated thing. Sometimes, to realize the true value of freedom, ethical rules need to be respected, and legal regulations need to be erected. Freedom without rules is self-defeating. Another lesson to be drawn is that freedom is not all that matters. Allowing employers and employees to arrange their economic lives as they see fit puts the achievement of other values – health, welfare, respect, and even life itself – at risk. These values must be weighed in the balance as we consider what ethics requires in the firm.

7. Study Questions

1. What are the conditions like for pickers in Amazon's warehouses? Identify at least one negative thing about working in an Amazon warehouse. Identify at least one positive thing.
2. One way of approaching the question of health and safety in the workplace is "let market participants decide" or LMPD. Describe this approach. Why might someone support it?
3. If we don't leave health and safety at work up to employers and employees, how might the government decide what regulations to enforce? What do you think is the best approach?
4. Our discussion of who is in control at work is connected to our previous discussion of who owns workplaces. Explain how.
5. Do you think workers should have an opportunity to participate in firm decision-making? Explain and defend your answer.
6. How is "meaningless work" usually defined? How is "meaningful work" usually defined?
7. Explain Smith's argument for the claim that the division of labor can increase productivity. What was Smith's worry about the effects of this division on workers?
8. If we are worried about the distribution of wealth in society, it may be better to make adjustments through the tax code as opposed to changing what people are paid. Why is this?
9. What is the agreement view of justice in wages? What qualifications, or "riders," do you think should be attached to this view?
10. What is the desert view of justice in wages, and why might someone support it? How do you think people's wages should be determined?

Additional Readings

Anderson, E. (2017). *Private government: How employers rule our lives (and why we don't talk about it)*. Princeton, NJ: Princeton University Press.

Arnold, S. (2012). The difference principle at work. *Journal of Political Philosophy*, *20*(1), 94–118.

Ethics Unwrapped. (n.d.). Wells Fargo fraud. McCombs School of Business, University of Texas. https://ethicsunwrapped.utexas.edu/video/wells-fargo-fraud

Evans, W. (2019, November 25). Ruthless quotas at Amazon are maiming employees. *The Atlantic*. www.theatlantic.com/technology/archive/2019/11/amazon-warehouse-reports-show-worker-injuries/602530/

Faden, R. R., & Beauchamp, T. L. (1982). The right to know in the workplace. *Canadian Journal of Philosophy*, *12*(supp. 1), 177–210.

Heath, J. (2018). On the very idea of a just wage. *Erasmus Journal for Philosophy and Economics*, *11*(2), 1–33.

Maitland, I. (1989). Rights in the workplace: A Nozickian argument. *Journal of Business Ethics*, *8*(12), 951–954.

Moriarty, J. (2005). Do CEOs get paid too much? *Business Ethics Quarterly*, *15*(2), 257–281.

Schwartz, A. (1982). Meaningful work. *Ethics*, *92*(4), 634–646.

Taddonio, P. (2020, February 14). 'You're just disposable': New accounts from former Amazon employees raise questions about working conditions. *PBS Frontline*. www.pbs.org/wgbh/frontline/article/youre-just-disposable-new-accounts-from-former-amazon-employees-raise-questions-about-working-conditions/

8 Ethics at Work, Part 2

In the previous chapter, we considered ethical issues inside the firm. Focusing on work in an Amazon warehouse, we considered health and safety, meaningful work, control and participation, and pay. In this chapter we stay inside the firm and consider additional ethical issues. First, we examine ethical issues in hiring and firing. Then we consider privacy at work. Finally, we examine whistleblowing.

These issues may not seem like they have much to do with each other. It is true that they can be treated separately. Unlike in the previous chapter, our discussion is not united by a common example. But they can also usefully be considered together. In each case we are thinking about ethical issues that have to do with *information*. With respect to hiring and firing, we consider which facts about people are relevant for making hiring and firing decisions. With respect to privacy, we ask what information employers should be permitted to know about (prospective) employees. With respect to whistleblowing, we ask whether and when employees can share information about illegal or unethical behavior that their employer is engaging in with third parties.

1. Who Is Hired? Who Can Be Fired?

Let us begin at the beginning, with hiring. We'll then consider firing.

1.1. Hiring

Suppose a firm needs to hire a worker. It has advertised the position and now has a pool of applicants. Whom should it hire? You might first think, whomever it wants. A job can be understood as an ongoing exchange of property. When you take a job at a store – for example, as a clerk at Walmart – the store agrees to exchange some of what it owns (its money) for some of what you own (your labor). Walmart is not obligated to hire anyone. So, it might be thought, if Walmart decides to hire, it can extend an offer to whomever it wants. The applicant can accept the offer, or not, as she chooses.

This is not a very plausible view. Most think that there are factors that should not be taken into account by employers when they are deciding whom to hire.

DOI: 10.4324/9781351016872-8

If the manager at the Walmart decided not to hire you simply because you are black, or a woman, or gay, then that would be wrong. To do so would be to discriminate against you, and discrimination is wrong.

There is debate about which characteristics about people should be "protected" in this way. In the law, race and sex are standardly recognized as protected characteristics, along with religion, national origin, and age. Sexual orientation is protected in some jurisdictions but not others.

There is also debate about why discrimination is wrong. Some believe it is wrong because it is demeaning. People who are discriminated against are treated as if they had lesser worth than others. Others believe it is wrong because of the harm it causes. When people are discriminated against, they lose the chance to attain scarce goods and advance themselves.

It might be said, plausibly, that discrimination is permissible in *some* cases – even on the basis of characteristics that are normally protected, such as race or sex. If a director is casting an actor to play the role of Muhammad Ali in a film, she can justifiably rule out white actors. If a swimming club is hiring an attendant to supervise the women's locker room, it can justifiably rule out men. The key question seems to be whether the characteristic in question is *job-relevant*. For most jobs, it isn't, and then discrimination based on the characteristic is wrong. But when it is job-relevant, then it is permissible.

But what does it mean for a characteristic to be job-relevant? This is trickier than it seems. Suppose a restaurant owner in the Jim Crow South needs to hire a waiter. She is not bigoted, but many of her customers are. They refuse to be served by a black waiter. Is it permissible for the owner to refuse to hire black applicants on the grounds that race is job-relevant? The black waiter cannot perform the job as well as a white waiter, because customers refuse to be served by him. Or is it impermissible for the business owner to refuse to hire black applicants on the grounds that race *should not be* job-relevant? You might say that we should answer this question by abstracting away from the environment in which the job is performed and concentrating on the functions of the job itself. When we do this, you might further say, we can see that race isn't really relevant to the job of a waiter. So, you might conclude, it would be wrong for the restaurant owner with bigoted customers to refuse to hire black waiters.

But is abstracting away from the environment always the right approach? You might have noticed that salespeople, receptionists, and other "customer-facing" employees are typically good-looking. This is not an accident. Employers treat attractiveness as a qualification for these jobs on the grounds that customers prefer interacting with attractive people. The result, of course, is that unattractive people are excluded from consideration for these jobs. You might say that this is just as unfair as excluding blacks from consideration for jobs as waiters in the Jim Crow South because customers don't want to be served by them. But perhaps we can draw a distinction between these cases. Women and minority racial groups have struggled long and hard against discrimination, and we might think that employers owe it to them – and to society as a whole – not to take their customers' bigoted preferences into account when deciding whom to hire. But the ugly and overweight are not in the same way a persecuted group. Perhaps employers should be permitted to "discriminate" against them in certain situations.

So far we have been talking about factors that employers should *not* be allowed to consider when making hiring decisions. Is that all ethics in hiring comes to – don't take into account certain factors? Some will say 'yes'. As long as you don't discriminate, you are morally in the clear. But others claim that there are certain factors that employers *should* take into account – things like education, experience, skills, and so on. The maximal version of this view is that employers have a duty to hire the most qualified applicant. So if you are the most qualified applicant for the job at Walmart, but the manager hires his daughter instead of you, then the manager has done something wrong.

Appealing to a duty to hire the best qualified applicant may ground objections to nepotism, but it may also ground objections to programs of preferential treatment. In an effort to increase diversity in its ranks, a firm might give preference to applicants from some backgrounds rather than others. The effect of such programs may be to give jobs to less-qualified over more-qualified applicants, where qualifications are measured in terms of experience, education, training, and the like.

We might wonder, however, what grounds the duty to hire the best applicant. If those who have a right to control the firm (e.g., shareholders) *want* to hire the best qualified applicants, and they direct their agents (e.g., managers) to satisfy this want, then it seems plausible that their agents have an obligation to do so. If this is what Walmart's shareholders want, then the manager does something wrong when he hires his daughter instead of you. But we might not think that the government or any other employer has this obligation independently of the will of those who have the ultimate right to determine hiring policy within an organization. So, if you are applying for a job as a clerk in a small, family-owned grocery store, and the owner hires his daughter instead of you, then perhaps there is no problem. This owner may not have a duty to hire the most qualified applicant.

1.2. Firing

Hiring is an ethically fraught process. So is firing. Ross Hopkins was a warehouse supervisor for American Eagle Distributing, a business that distributes Budweiser, Michelob, and other beers brewed by Anheuser-Busch around Colorado. One weekend evening, while he was relaxing with friends at a local bar, Hopkins was seen by a relative of the owner of American Eagle drinking a Coors, a beer brewed by the Molson Coors Brewing Company and that is distributed by different businesses. Hopkins was fired the following Monday. According to Hopkins, the reason he was given was that he was drinking the wrong brand of beer.

What should we say about American Eagle's firing of Hopkins? Laws about firing vary from state to state, but it appears that what American Eagle did was legal. (Hopkins sued for wrongful termination but eventually dropped the lawsuit.) The question was whether it was ethical. Was American Eagle's firing of Ross Hopkins ethically permissible?

There are two main approaches to the ethics of dismissal. According to the first, employers can fire employees for almost any reason. Legally, this view is known as "employment-at-will," and it is the prevailing view in most U.S. states. In its original formulation, employment-at-will, or EAW, was the view that either party could leave the employment relationship for "good reason, bad reason, or no reason at all." An employer might decide to terminate a worker's employment because the worker is incompetent, or, as in our case, because he is drinking the wrong brand of beer. According to the second main approach to the ethics of dismissal, employers must have good reason for firing employees. Legally, this view is known as "just cause," and it is the prevailing view in much of Europe and the U.S. state of Montana. Usually the only "good" reasons are those related to the employee's job performance. So an employer could fire an employee for incompetence or excessive absenteeism, but not because he drank the wrong brand of beer.

Over time, various legal exceptions to EAW have been carved out. Employers are not permitted to fire employees upon learning that they are Muslim or that they have a hidden disability. Religion and disability status are among the protected classes mentioned earlier. There are also "implied contract" and "public interest" exceptions to EAW. Employers are not permitted to fire employees if they have promised that they would not (implied contract) or if it would be seriously bad for society if they did (public interest). The public interest exception to EAW was first articulated in 1959 in the case of Peter Petermann, who was fired by his employer, the International Brotherhood of Teamsters, for refusing to lie to Congress. It is not in the public's interest for people to be coerced by their employers through a threat of firing into committing crimes.

The exceptions to EAW have brought it closer in theory and practice to just cause dismissal rules. But they are still not that close. If you embrace EAW, then you think that employers should be allowed to fire employees for any reason, with some exceptions. If you embrace just cause, then you think that employers should not be allowed to fire employees except for certain specific reasons. The set of reasons for which an employee could be justifiably fired is much larger for supporters of EAW, even with exceptions, than for supporters of just cause. Minimally, supporters of EAW and just cause would disagree about whether American Eagle was justified in firing Ross Hopkins.

We have been talking about what is legal. What does morality require? And why? Those who favor EAW often justify it by appealing to the value of freedom. To demand that employers terminate employment relationships only for certain reasons, they say, is an unwarranted limitation of employers' freedom. Defenders of just cause dismissal rules have replied that employers' exercising, or even simply having, a robust freedom to fire workers is an unwarranted diminution of workers' freedom. To be free is to be able to live your life as you choose. If your employer can deprive you of your livelihood for arbitrary reasons, like drinking the wrong beer, then you are to that extent unfree. In these circumstances, your power to shape your life as you see fit is limited.

Another important consideration is welfare. On the one hand, losing a job can be really hard for a worker. To begin with, it results in a loss of income. But it can also lead to a loss of self-esteem and disrupt social ties, since people may identify with their work and form friendships with their co-workers. Even the threat of a job loss can be a source of stress. Just cause dismissal rules offer workers some protection against this harm. On the other hand, some people believe that Europe's persistently high unemployment rate relative to the U.S. is explained by the fact that most of Europe uses just cause dismissal rules while the U.S. uses EAW. The harder it is for employers to fire employees, the more reluctant they will be to hire them in the first place. Just cause may protect workers' jobs at the cost of creating a more rigid labor market overall. Indeed, even if individual workers prefer strong job protections (and hence just cause), workers as a whole may prefer a healthier labor market (and hence EAW). Seen from this perspective, the firing of Ross Hopkins might be seen as an unfortunate event that is justified by the value of the employment system that makes this decision possible.

We have been considering the question of when an employment relationship may be terminated from the perspective of the employer. But we can also ask this question from the perspective of the employee. That is, we can ask under what conditions can an employee terminate her relationship with her employer. Can the employee quit for "good reason, bad reason, or no reason at all"? Or must she have a good reason? Not too much attention has been paid to these questions, but many of the arguments we have considered apply to them. We might say that it is important for employees' freedom to be able to quit when they want to, even if it's not for an objectively good reason. But if employees' freedom is constrained by being terminated by their employers, especially for arbitrary reasons, then employers' freedom is likewise constrained by their employees quitting, especially for arbitrary reasons. Arguments about social welfare are relevant here too. If employees believe that they will be locked into jobs unless they have good reasons to leave, then they will be less likely to take them. Here again, even if individual employers would prefer to be able to keep talented workers, employers as a whole may prefer that workers have the freedom to leave.

Why do people seem to care more about the circumstances in which it is legitimate to fire employees as opposed to the circumstances in which it is legitimate for employees to quit, that is, to "fire" their employers? The answer is that typically the employee suffers more harm when she loses a job than the employer suffers when she loses an employee. On average, it is easier for a firm to manage in the worker's absence, and find a replacement for the worker, than it is for the worker to find a new job.

We should not conclude, however, that an employee's terminating an employment relationship is always a trivial matter. Some employees may be as important to their firms as those firms are to most employees. If arguments for just cause are sound, they require at least that, when employees terminate employment relationships, they do so thoughtfully. Their pursuit of new opportunities for themselves should be tempered by a concern for the damage they do to their current employers and co-workers.

2. Privacy at Work

Once we begin talking about the ethics of hiring and firing decisions, we soon see it is necessary to talk about privacy. Hiring and firing practices can compromise our privacy. Before you are hired, employers want to know certain things about you, like your educational background, skills, and work history. They may also want details about what you might consider your "private life." The moving and storage company U-Haul would like to know if you use nicotine. If you do, you will not be hired. U-Haul instituted a "nicotine-free" hiring policy in 2019. It was not the first business to do so. Alaska Airlines instituted a similar policy in 1985, arguing that there was no time on the job for workers to take cigarette breaks. Some healthcare organizations like the Cleveland Clinic decline to hire smokers because of the negative health consequences of smoking. Firing decisions can also turn on matters that employees may think of as private affairs. The deadly "Unite the Right" rally in Charlottesville, Virginia, in 2017 was attended by significant numbers of white nationalists and neo-Nazis, some of whom chanted racist and antisemitic slogans. Afterward, there was a concerted effort on social media to identify and "out" the attendees. Many people lost their jobs.

In addition to knowing what you do outside of work, employers may wish to know what you do at work. Some are satisfied with routine evaluations, but others want much more information. We noted that the movements of pickers in Amazon warehouses are tracked closely. In addition, these workers typically must pass through metal detectors at the end of each day to ensure that they are not stealing. The package delivery company UPS has computers installed on each of its delivery trucks, recording when the driver gets into and out of the vehicle, when the seatbelt is buckled, how often the vehicle backs up, at what speed, and other movements. Close monitoring is not limited to blue-collar workers. Many employers reserve the right to monitor employees' emails and internet use. In this section we consider what information employers have a right to know about employees.

We are focusing here on (prospective) employees' privacy. What about employers' privacy? In theory we could also ask what sort of information employees have a right to know about employers. But in practice the pressing ethical issues concern employees' privacy from employers. In practice, we encounter many situations where employers want to know things about employees that some employees would prefer to keep private, not the other way around.

2.1. Why Privacy Matters

To begin, we need to think about what's at stake. That is, we need to consider what privacy is and why it is important. Privacy was originally understood in U.S. law as the right to be "left alone." Privacy in this sense has been invoked in the U.S. to challenge laws prohibiting homosexual sex and the use of contraceptives. The claim was that people should be left alone to do as they please in their own bedrooms, without state interference.

More recently, privacy has been tied to information. The issue is not what the state can tell you to do or not to do. It is what information you can keep from others. Privacy in this sense – informational privacy – can be understood in terms of *control* and *access*. Roughly, you have informational privacy with respect to a certain zone of personal information if you can determine who has access to that information. To take a simple example, you have (informational) privacy with respect to your educational or medical records insofar as you can keep me from viewing them.

Why is privacy important? A variety of reasons have been offered. Many focus on the degree of control that is central to privacy. First, privacy protects us from a variety of personal harms. It helps us to avoid people who wish to bother us or worse. A woman who is abused by a romantic partner might leave him, and privacy is then essential to her safety. Privacy protects us from more mild harms as well. You may find some facts about yourself embarrassing. These could be facts about your medical or educational history or more generally your actions and interests. Privacy enables you to avoid embarrassing disclosures. Privacy also helps us to avoid economic harms. You may have worked hard on a business idea. Privacy ensures that you and not someone else will benefit from it. More generally, privacy helps us to secure our economic resources, including by preventing fraud and identity theft.

Second, privacy is important for intimacy or closeness to another person. Our relationships with friends, children, parents, and partners are among the most important relationships in our lives. Part of what it is to be close to another person is to have that person, and not others, know certain facts about you. Your friends, not strangers, know your hopes and dreams, what you love, and what you fear. If you weren't able to control people's access to that information – if everyone could know it – then the intimacy of your relationships would be compromised.

Third and perhaps most important, privacy matters for autonomy. Privacy promotes autonomy in two ways. One has to do with action, and the other has to do with presentation. First, the autonomous person acts according to her own plans. If you cannot control who has access to information about you, you may be tempted to "edit" your plans according to society's expectations. You may be gay and wish to have sex with a person of your same gender. But if you live in a community that frowns upon gay sex, and you cannot keep your sexual activities private, you may decide it's not worth it to have sex. Autonomy is best understood in terms of self-government. But in this case your actions are being effectively governed by other people. Second, the autonomous person presents herself in public according to her own conception of who she is. You may wish to present yourself as a hard-charging corporate executive. To you this means being relentlessly focused on your job and in the little downtime you have engaging in stereotypically "corporate" past-times, like golf and tennis. But what you really enjoy is collecting cookie jars and snuggling with kittens. If you can't keep this information private, you are unable to present yourself in the world in the way that you want.

2.2. Privacy Versus Other Values: How Do We Decide?

For these reasons – and others which you may be able to think of – privacy matters. But it isn't the only thing that matters. Sometimes, privacy comes into conflict with other values. Employers might want to know whether you smoke cigarettes, because they want to promote good health among their employees or because it reduces their healthcare costs. Employers might want to track your movements to improve efficiency or monitor your email to make sure that you aren't sending pornographic or otherwise offensive materials to co-workers.

How should we decide when employees' privacy should be protected, and when employees should be able to override it in the service of other values? One approach to this question was discussed in the previous chapter. This approach is "let market participants decide" (LMPD). On this view, employers should be free to afford employees whatever level of privacy they want, and employees should be free to work under those conditions, or not, as they choose. U-Haul is free to decide to hire only nonsmokers. This will make no difference to nonsmokers, but it does affect smokers. If you smoke, and you want to work at U-Haul, you will have to make a choice between the two. According to LMPD, UPS is free to track the movements of its delivery trucks. If a person doesn't want to be tracked so closely at work, then they will choose not to work at UPS.

The LMPD approach treats privacy as a value that individuals can trade off for other things. U-Haul doesn't allow you to smoke, and this will be a cost for some people, but if they are willing to quit to work for U-Haul, this is evidence that U-Haul makes it worth it to them to quit. Perhaps U-Haul is able to share some of its savings from its lower healthcare costs with employees. This seems to be what UPS has done. They monitor their drivers extremely closely, and while some find this intrusive – like "big brother," one said – UPS has been able to achieve huge gains in efficiency, some of which have been shared with employees. According to their union, UPS drivers make about twice today what they made in the 1990s. We might think that the LMPD approach is best because it allows employers and employees to determine the mix of privacy and other benefits they prefer most.

As in the case of other aspects of work to which we applied the LMPD approach, including safety and meaning, for this approach to workplace privacy to be at all plausible, employees must know what they are getting into, that is, what level of privacy they will enjoy at work. So an employer would not be justified in spying on employees, or attempting to discover private information about them without their consent. They would need to be forthright about how they intended to use the information that they collected. Beyond truthfully disclosing what level of privacy employees will enjoy at work, however, employers have no other privacy-related obligations to employees, according to the LMPD. The level of privacy is a matter to be negotiated by employers and employees.

We noted in the previous chapter some limitations of the LMPD approach. It seems most attractive when a person is comfortable financially and is deciding which of multiple jobs to take. They might decide to take a job for more money and less privacy, or less money and more privacy. But things don't always or even usually work this way. A person might just have one job offer, or one job offer that allows them to pay their bills, and they feel forced to take it, even if it involves what they regard as serious infringements of their privacy. We might support restrictions – enforced by the government – on what information employers can collect, and how they can collect it, to prevent people from having to agree to such infringements. We might also support such restrictions because, left to their own devices, people sometimes make imprudent choices. A person might agree to share information with an employer, not fully understanding how it might be used against her.

In fact, few believe that employers should be able to ask for *whatever* information they want from employees. In the U.S., your employer is not allowed to ask for genetic information about you, such as whether certain diseases run in your family. They are not allowed to ask if you are disabled or how severe your disability is. In some states, employers are not allowed to ask how much money you made at your previous jobs. Some states also have "off-duty" conduct laws, which prevent employers from asking questions about things that people do outside of work. In fact, U-Haul was only able to implement its nicotine-free policy in 21 states. The other 29 have laws that prohibit such policies.

It is not hard to see why governments have instituted these laws. Privacy matters to people. They want to be able to keep information out of the hands of their employers, often in an effort to continue living their lives the way they want. It is true, as the LMPD assumes, that some people might be willing to share this information in order to get a job or get a better job. But some governments have decided that you shouldn't have to do this. Insofar as we are sympathetic to these regulations, we are recognizing the limits of the LMPD approach to workplace privacy.

Some might object at this point that an employer's simply asking questions cannot be understood as an infringement on privacy. The employee can always refuse to answer, thereby blocking access to the information. This is true, but acknowledging an employee's right to refuse to answer questions is obviously not tantamount to protecting her privacy. If an employer is able to impose a cost on an employee for declining to answer questions – by denying her a job or firing her – then the employee will feel pressured to answer. Her privacy is in jeopardy. This is why those who seek to protect employee privacy seek to prevent employers from asking certain questions, not simply letting employees know that they can refuse to answer them while suffering the consequences.

Asking questions is the most common way that employers acquire information about employees. But it is not the only way. As seen, employers may wish to track or search employees, and these practices raise additional concerns. For the defender of the LMPD approach to privacy, this matter too will be settled by agreement between market participants. Employers must simply announce what types of methods they will use to collect information about employees, and employees can choose to work for the employers understanding that they will be subjected to those methods, or they can choose to work elsewhere. But, just as we might seek to protect what information employers can collect about employees, we might also seek to protect how they can collect it. Certain ways of coming to know things about a person are degrading and even humiliating. We might think, for example, that it is permissible for Amazon to send its warehouse workers through metal detectors to prevent theft, but we might object if it decided to strip-search them. When jobs are scarce, employers might be able to get employees to agree to these sorts of humiliating intrusions, but this would not eliminate their wrongness. They seem incompatible with respect for employees.

Suppose we want to protect certain kinds of information, as some governments have chosen to do. How do we decide what information should be protected, and what information is fair game for employers to collect? In the next section we consider this question.

2.3. Job Relevance as a Criterion

Whether employers should be permitted to keep certain information private, or not, is traditionally thought to depend on whether that information is job-relevant. If you are applying for a job as an accountant, your employer is permitted to ask you whether you have a degree in accounting and whether you have ever worked as an accountant before. But she is not permitted to ask you whether you have a family history of breast cancer or whether you use a wheelchair. The former – educational credentials and work experience – is relevant to the job for which you are applying. The latter – family history of disease and wheelchair use – is irrelevant.

Earlier we noted that job-relevance is the criterion often used to determine whether hiring decisions are discriminatory. Employers are permitted to make decisions on the basis of factors that are relevant to the performance of the job, and factors like race and sex typically aren't. It is no surprise, then, that job-relevance should also be the criterion for determining what information employers can request from employees. If it is permissible for employers to make decisions based on certain facts, then it seems permissible for them to learn those facts.

The criterion of job-relevance is an appealing one. Privacy is important to us. We want to be able to limit who has access to personal information about us. At the same time, employers need to be able to find out certain information about us. They need to be able to ask us specific questions – like what training and experience we have – and make our getting a job contingent on our answering truthfully. Otherwise they could not run their businesses effectively.

But the criterion of job-relevance does not end the discussion, as we saw in our discussion of hiring. "Job-relevance" is a vague term, and there is disagreement about what it means in certain cases. Consider U-Haul's policy of not hiring nicotine users. Is nicotine use – by smoking cigarettes – job-relevant? To answer this question, we have to think about the kinds of jobs people perform at U-Haul. U-Haul employs accountants, mechanics, IT professionals, sales associates, and call center operators, among others. If you think about what these people do, it seems clear that nicotine use by itself doesn't interfere with the performance of any of these jobs. Of course, if an employee were taking unauthorized breaks to smoke cigarettes because he is addicted to them, then that would be a problem. But the problem would be with taking unauthorized breaks, not with nicotine use. If we think of things this way, then it seems that U-Haul is infringing on employees' privacy, by asking for information that isn't job-relevant.

By way of explanation of its nicotine-free hiring policy, U-Haul says that nicotine use, especially smoking, is dangerous, and they want their workforce to be healthy. Does this make nicotine use job-relevant information? Probably not. By this logic, a company could make *any* trait job-relevant just by saying that they want their employees to have this trait.

But suppose – and this may be the real reason for U-Haul's new hiring policy – that they want to know whether prospective employees use nicotine because they want to lower their healthcare costs. Smokers are more expensive to provide health insurance for than nonsmokers. U-Haul operates in a competitive industry, and they have to cut costs where they can. Then is information about nicotine use job-relevant? You might say 'yes'. Nicotine use is relevant to how costly a person is to employ, and how costly a person is to employ is job-relevant information.

Note that if we accept this reasoning, all kinds of information about an employee become job-relevant. An employee with a family history of disease, or who has children or is thinking about having children, or who has a hidden disability, may all in various ways be more costly to employ than employees who do not meet these criteria.

We might try to answer this question by thinking even more carefully about what it means for a certain piece of information to be job-relevant. We might inquire about the nature of jobs, what it means to perform them, and what it means for an action or trait to be relevant to the performance of a job. If we define job-relevance narrowly, we might conclude that employers can ask prospective employees very few questions. If we define it broadly, we might grant employers permission to ask a wider range of questions. But it is unclear that "job-relevance" is a sufficiently robust concept to support this sort of analysis. We might instead appeal to other values. That is, we might say that job-relevance isn't the only thing we should be thinking about when we consider what information employers can request from employees. Job-relevance may act as a kind of filter so that, if a question isn't job-relevant, it can't be asked. But even if a question is job-relevant, we might decline to give employers permission to ask the question to protect other social values. We might think that people should be free to engage in legal off-duty activities (like smoking or attending political rallies) or to have children without limiting their employment prospects. The same goes, we might say, for people with hidden disabilities or genetic predispositions to diseases. Protecting this freedom may come at a cost to employers, but this is a price that we may decide that employers should bear. This is not just a question for employers and employees. It's about how we want to live as a society.

3. Whistleblowing

In the late 1980s, Jeffrey Wigand, a PhD in biochemistry, was hired as Vice-President for Research and Development at the tobacco company Brown & Williamson (B&W). (Brown & Williamson no longer exists. In 2004, it merged with R. J. Reynolds to form a new company, Reynolds American, which was later purchased by British American Tobacco, the largest tobacco company in the world.) Wigand's research for the company led him to become concerned about some of the ingredients that it was adding to its cigarettes, especially ammonia and coumarin. B&W added ammonia to increase potency and coumarin for flavor. Wigand said that ammonia made cigarettes more addictive, and that coumarin was a carcinogen. He argued that B&W should take these ingredients out of its cigarettes to make them safer. The CEO disagreed, and their disagreements eventually led to Wigand's firing in 1993. As part of his severance agreement, Wigand signed a nondisclosure agreement with B&W. He agreed not to discuss what he knew about B&W's cigarettes with anyone.

As Wigand tells it, his conscience eventually got the better of him, and he decided to share what he knew with Mike Wallace, a reporter at *60 Minutes*, in 1996. One thing Wigand shared was that cigarettes were addictive and that tobacco companies knew this. This might not seem newsworthy now, but in the mid-1990s, tobacco companies were still denying that cigarettes were addictive. Wigand went on to say that cigarettes were dangerous, and tobacco companies knew this too and that B&W was making its cigarettes even more dangerous by adding ammonia and coumarin. Needless to say, all of this went against the nondisclosure agreement that Wigand signed when he left B&W.

Wigand is a whistleblower. He "blew the whistle" on what was going on in B&W and in the tobacco industry more generally. There are many definitions of 'whistleblowing' in existence and each is slightly different. But most would agree that a whistleblower is typically (1) an employee or other insider with access to nonpublic information about an organization, (2) who reports information about activity in that organization that he perceives to be unethical or illegal, (3) outside of the normal reporting channels within that organization, and (4) in particular, to a person or entity that he perceives to have the power to do something to stop the activity. Jeffrey Wigand is thought to have engaged in whistleblowing when he gave an interview to *60 Minutes* about the ingredients in B&W's cigarettes. As a former high-ranking executive at B&W, Wigand (1) had access to nonpublic information about the ingredients, especially ammonia and coumarin, in its cigarettes. He further (2) thought that these ingredients were unusually dangerous. Wigand (3) reported this information to *60 Minutes*, because (4) he thought the public attention would cause B&W to stop.

In our discussion we will focus on Wigand's whistleblowing on B&W. But there are many other examples we might have focused on, such as Roger Boisjoly at Morton Thiokol, Sherron Watkins at Enron, Cynthia Cooper at Worldcom, Edward Snowden at the National Security Agency, and Tyler Shultz at Theranos.

There are two questions traditionally asked about whistleblowing. The first is, when is whistleblowing permitted? The second is, when is it required? Framing the issue this way supposes, however, that whistleblowing needs a justification – that when it happens, some reason for it must be provided, or else it was unjustified, that is, neither permitted nor required. The explanation typically given for this is that whistleblowing is an act of disloyalty, and people (like Wigand) have reasons to be loyal. This is meant to establish a presumption against whistleblowing. In the following section we examine the nature and value of loyalty and consider what it means for people like Wigand.

3.1. Why Not Blow the Whistle? The Question of Loyalty

Loyalty is complex. To begin to understand it, we might reflect on the types of things that people are loyal to. They are loyal to siblings, parents, children, friends, religions, states, countries, towns, sports teams, political parties, brands, and more. Now think about your relationships with one of these. What does it mean to be loyal to them?

To be loyal to a person or group is, in the first place, to have some sort of positive feeling about that person or group. Perhaps you are loyal to your friends. One thing that means is that you feel positively about them. You like them. But loyalty is not just a feeling. It is also a disposition or an inclination to act in certain ways on certain occasions. Your loyalty to your friends means that you will sometimes help them out when they need it. You will give them a ride to the airport or let them cry on your shoulder when they are sad. Note that these actions are costly for you. Giving a ride to your friend costs you time and gas money. Letting a friend cry on your shoulder also takes time and is emotionally draining. But being loyal requires the bearing of costs. A loyal fan will cheer for her team even when there is no hope of winning, and she is guaranteed to feel the sting of loss.

That's what loyalty is. Now why should anyone be loyal? One reason that some people give is that being loyal can be good for you. Your relationships with others make your life go well, and maintaining these relationships requires loyalty. If you got rid of your friends and found new ones every time they needed your help, you wouldn't have meaningful friendships. Second, loyalty may be beneficial not just personally but socially. This social value of loyalty is especially clear when the object of our loyalty is a group like a family, religion, or country. These groups provide significant benefits to society, but they will not hold together over time unless their members make sacrifices for them. A third common reason given for loyalty is gratitude. Those to whom you owe loyalty are often those who have provided you benefits first. These may be your parents, siblings, friends, religions, countries, and other persons and groups. Loyalty – feeling positively about and being disposed to benefit – may be simply what you owe them for what they have done for you.

Note that these reasons for loyalty are contingent on certain facts. The first depends on the object of your loyalty being loyal to you in return. Meaningful relationships are not one-sided. The second depends on whether the group in question provides value to society. Some groups, like families and charitable societies, do, but others, like the Nazi party and the KKK, do not. The third depends on the other party's providing benefits to you. If loyalty is based on the provision of benefits, then it is misplaced when the object of loyalty does not or cannot reciprocate.

Now consider the Wigand case. Whistleblowing is typically understood as an act of disloyalty. What a company like B&W wants is for its employees like Wigand to keep quiet about the things it is doing. B&W assumed, correctly, that if the public found out, they would be upset, and the company would have to change the way it did things. This would be embarrassing and costly. So the loyal employee, it might be said, would help the company by keeping quiet, even at the cost of living with a guilty conscience. A whistleblower like Wigand is disloyal.

But why should Wigand be loyal to B&W? Following our earlier discussion, we might think that Wigand should be loyal in order to enjoy a more meaningful relationship with B&W, or to allow B&W to continue to provide significant benefits to society, or because Wigand owes loyalty to B&W after everything it has done for him.

At the same time, also following this discussion, we have seen that the reasons in favor of loyalty depend on certain facts, and these facts do not obtain in every relationship that a person has. Consider Wigand's relationship with B&W. First, there is the question of whether B&W is an organization that is capable of loyalty to employees like Wigand. Some have argued that businesses, and especially publicly traded corporations like B&W, cannot afford to be loyal. If it is in their financial interest to cut ties with an employee, or even many employees, they will. If B&W is not or cannot be loyal to Wigand, then he cannot develop a meaningful relationship with it. Second, there is the question of whether B&W provides significant benefits to society. Loyalty is admirable among the Red Cross's employees and donors, because of the good this organization does, but condemnable in the members of the Nazi party, because of the destruction this organization wreaked on the world. These of course are extreme cases. Where do tobacco companies fall on the spectrum? On the one hand, they manufacture a product that some consumers genuinely want, and they provide employment and income for thousands. On the other hand, their products cause health problems and shorten people's lives. Reasonable people will disagree about whether tobacco companies benefit society overall. Third, there is the question of the benefits that B&W provides to Wigand. Does Wigand owe B&W loyalty, in the form of silence, because it gave him an important job and a high salary? Some will say 'yes'. B&W did something good for Wigand, and now he should return the favor. But others will say 'no'. Wigand has already "returned the favor" by working diligently for B&W for years; he owes them nothing more.

We have been assuming thus far that loyalty requires Wigand to keep quiet about what he knows about B&W's cigarettes. If you are loyal to someone, you have a reason to promote their interests, even at some cost to yourself. B&W

certainly wanted Wigand to keep quiet about the ingredients in its cigarettes, but was that really in B&W's interests? You might say 'no'. Maybe Wigand was doing B&W a favor by telling what he knew about B&W's cigarettes. In the short term, this would be embarrassing and costly to B&W, but looking back, the embarrassment and cost were inevitable. Eventually people were going to realize that cigarettes were addictive and harmful and that tobacco executives had known this all along. Might as well just get it over with. Or we might say that it is never in a person's or a company's interests to mislead and harm people, even if this is what they say they want. So Wigand did a favor to B&W by stopping them from misleading and harming people.

We have considered at this point the nature and value of loyalty and the reasons Wigand might have to be loyal, and in particular, not to disclose what he knew about B&W's cigarettes to the media. Our discussion has taken several twists and turns, but if we had to sum it up, we might say that Wigand *might* have loyalty-based reasons not to disclose what he knew. I say "might" because, as we have seen, the reasons people normally have for being loyal may not apply, and loyalty may not require nondisclosure, in Wigand's case. However this matter is resolved, we must remember that Wigand had an additional reason not to disclose what he knew. He signed a contract stating that he wouldn't disclose. So we might say that, either because of loyalty or because of a promise, Wigand had a good reason not to blow the whistle on B&W. This does not, however, settle the question of what Wigand should do. No one thinks whistleblowing is never justified, either in the sense of being permitted or required. Put another way, everyone agrees that in some cases the presumption against whistleblowing can be overturned. Next we consider what can be said in favor of blowing the whistle.

3.2. Reasons in Favor of Whistleblowing

The most common justification of blowing the whistle appeals to the harm that employees can prevent by doing so. You should be loyal to your friend, but if your friend says that he is going to set his neighbor's car on fire, you should tell someone. You should blow the whistle on your friend. The harm you can prevent makes it (at least) permissible for you to do so.

Wigand knew that cigarettes were addictive and that B&W was adding chemicals to its cigarettes to make them more addictive and more harmful. If people smoked B&W's cigarettes, they were putting themselves at risk for a variety of heart, lung, and circulatory diseases, ones that could take years off of their lives. Wigand helped to prevent this harm by alerting people to the nature and effects of B&W's cigarettes. We can expect that fewer people will smoke B&W's cigarettes because of the dangers they pose to their health.

The point is not simply to help people avoid diseases and live longer. If that were our only goal, we would have to outlaw cigarettes entirely, along with other drugs like alcohol and marijuana, fatty foods like pepperoni and salami, and dangerous activities like mountain climbing and hang gliding. The point is to help people live what they regard as good lives, given their goals and preferences. To do this we need to factor in the risks associated with our activities. Our lives go worse – we are in a sense harmed – when we are given incorrect information about these risks. Wigand helped to remedy this problem by blowing the whistle on B&W.

Some scholars object that the focus on harm is too narrow. What justifies blowing the whistle, they say, is not that the conduct is harmful, but that it is wrongful. Wrongful conduct is often harmful. Consider murder, torture, assault, and robbery. These are wrongful actions that cause harm to identifiable victims. But we might think that some actions are wrongful but not harmful. Insider trading – when a corporate insider engages in a securities transaction on the basis of nonmaterial, nonpublic information – is generally considered to be wrongful, but scholars disagree about whether it is harmful. The parties directly involved in the transaction benefit, and it is not clear whether anyone else is harmed. The National Security Agency's (NSA) formerly secret surveillance program may not have been harmful, at least not in the way that murder and robbery are. But it was illegal, and we might think that this fact alone justifies Snowden's blowing the whistle on the NSA. If we claim that employees are justified in blowing the whistle only when they prevent harm, this would imply that they are not justified in blowing the whistle on insider trading schemes or government surveillance programs, insofar as these activities are not harmful. We avoid this counterintuitive result by shifting the focus from harm to wrong and claiming that whistleblowing is justified when it helps to bring an end to wrongful conduct.

The harm- and wrongdoing-based justifications of whistleblowing make the justification of whistleblowing depend in part on how likely it is that the whistleblower will succeed. If the whistleblower has little or no chance of preventing the harm (or wrongdoing) by disclosing what he knows to a third party, then he may not be justified in blowing the whistle. The alleged benefits of whistleblowing do not materialize.

Why wouldn't whistleblowing succeed? It isn't a matter of a whistleblower being unable to share what he knows. The plethora of social media outlets makes this easier than ever. The problem is that the whistleblower may not be believed. Businesses engaged in wrongdoing have powerful incentives to get the public to discount what the whistleblower is saying.

The Wigand case is illustrative. B&W hired a law firm to prepare a massive file detailing Wigand's alleged personal and professional transgressions. It then marketed the dossier to media outlets in an effort to get them to run negative stories about Wigand. This didn't work in the end. Wigand was believed, and tobacco companies were forced to admit their products were addictive and remove coumarin from them. Wigand helped to bring these outcomes about, but he wasn't solely responsible for them. Wigand had the good fortune to be interviewed by Mike Wallace of *60 Minutes*, one of the most trusted news reporters in the U.S., on one of the most trusted news programs in the U.S. As Wigand was speaking out, lawsuits filed by dozens of state attorneys general were winding their way through the courts. Wigand's disclosure by itself would probably have done little to change the way tobacco companies operate, especially given B&W's enormous efforts to discredit him.

While Wigand's whistleblowing did seem to have the intended effect, many whistleblowers will not be effective. On the harm- and wrongdoing-based justifications of whistleblowing, it seems that these whistleblowers will not be justified in blowing the whistle. They don't produce the effects that could justify their behavior. This might seem like an odd result. It implies that the more effective a business is in undermining the truth of what the employee says, the less reason the employee has to blow the whistle. The business is rewarded for bad behavior.

A different way of justifying whistleblowing may avoid this odd result. This justification appeals to complicity. The point is not so much to prevent something bad – harmful or wrongful – from happening, but to make sure that you don't contribute to its happening. Wigand seems to have interpreted his own whistleblowing in this way. He said that, after he disclosed what he knew about B&W's cigarettes, he felt "clean." Wigand seemed to think that he was, through his silence, complicit in B&W's "dirty deeds." When he disclosed what he knew, he removed himself from the chain of events that began inside B&W and ended in harm and wrongdoing to consumers.

"Clean" and "dirty" are metaphors. We might understand what is really going on here in terms of integrity. "Integrity" is a vague term that is sometimes used to mean "truthfulness" or "committed to ethics." But we can understand integrity a bit more precisely in terms of "wholeness" and, in particular, in terms of a union between a person's values and her actions. If you have integrity, your actions are consistent with your values. If you care about the environment, you do not roll coal in your truck. If you care about animal welfare, you do not kick your dog. You are not a hypocrite. You can understand Wigand as saying that his integrity was compromised when he didn't speak out about the dangers of B&W's cigarettes. He cares about people's health, but he wasn't doing anything to protect it, even though he could.

The complicity-based justifications of whistleblowing do not depend on the probable success of whistleblowing, as the harm- and wrongdoing-based accounts do. This means that complicity-based accounts have the potential to justify more instances of whistleblowing than harm- and wrongdoing-based accounts. As seen, it can be difficult for individuals, even if they have good evidence, to stop a company from doing something bad (harmful or wrongful). But it is easy for someone to notify a third party that their firm is doing something bad.

Complicity-based accounts face their own problems. First, complicity-based justifications of whistleblowing, even if they increase the probability that any given act of whistleblowing is justified, decrease the number of disclosures that count as acts of whistleblowing. This is because they limit the number of people who qualify as whistleblowers. In fact, on complicity-based accounts, Wigand is almost certainly not a whistleblower. At the time he disclosed what he knew about B&W to the media, he was no longer an employee at B&W. There may be disagreement about who precisely within a large organization is responsible for the organization's bad behavior, but it is extremely unlikely that a person who is not an employee of the organization is responsible. This strikes many people as a counterintuitive consequence of complicity-based accounts. Whistleblowers are traditionally "insiders," like Wigand, but need not be directly involved in the bad behavior.

Second, and more importantly, it is not at all clear how whistleblowing eliminates complicitly. Suppose you work for a company that is illegally dumping toxic waste into a river. Your job is to help load the waste onto the trucks that drive to the river at night. You tell this information to a journalist, who writes a story about it. But you keep loading the waste onto the trucks. It seems that you are still involved – still complicit – in the company's bad behavior. Disclosing it doesn't help you to avoid complicity. If you want to avoid complicity in the company's bad behavior, minimally, you need to ask to perform a different job in the company, one that is unrelated to the dumping. Perhaps you need to quit the company entirely. Now it might be said at this point that blowing the whistle on your company might remove your complicity in the company's bad behavior if it causes the bad behavior to stop. Then there will be no more bad behavior for you to be complicit in. But this reduces the complicity-based justification of whistleblowing to the harm- and wrongdoing-based justifications.

3.3. Do I Have to?

Let us suppose now that an employee has good reasons to blow the whistle. They have really good evidence that their company is doing something wrong, and really good reason to believe that their evidence will be believed, and will cause the company to stop their wrongdoing. We might be confident at this point that blowing the whistle is justified in the sense of being permissible. What about justified in the sense of being required?

Consider again your friend who is planning to set his neighbor's car on fire. Surely it is permissible for you to blow the whistle, say by calling the police. Your friend is planning to do something seriously wrong, which will inflict significant harm on his neighbor.

But you might think that this – a permission – doesn't go far enough. Shouldn't we go further? Isn't it ethically *required* for you to blow the whistle?

The short answer is, not necessarily. It depends on whether blowing the whistle would be effective and how personally costly it is for you to blow the whistle. Suppose that no one would believe you if you blew the whistle. Your friend is an upstanding member of the community, and a great supporter of the police, and they wouldn't even take your call. Or suppose that if you did, your friend would set *your* car on fire. Then we might say that, while you are permitted to blow the whistle on your friend, and it would be a good thing if you did, you are not required to blow the whistle. Philosophers call this a "supererogatory" act, one that goes beyond the call of duty. In general, you are not required to put yourself at a great risk of harm by doing something that isn't likely to have good effects.

This is a made-up example. Does it have any relevance for the real world of whistleblowing? Regrettably, yes. We considered the issue of effectiveness in the previous section and won't retrace our steps. Suffice it to say that if blowing the whistle on a company won't do any good, because you won't be believed, then the case for blowing the whistle is weakened. Here we will focus on the costs of blowing the whistle. These costs can be considerable, as the Wigand case again illustrates.

Humans are a tribal species. If you betray the tribe, it may seek revenge. In an interview with the *New York Times*, one of Wigand's associates recounted an incident at a bar. As Wigand was chatting with some friends, a stranger approached them and started screaming at Wigand: "How does it feel not to be making big money anymore? Look at your cheap shoes!" The stranger "pointed to a tobacco company logo on his shirt and pulled a wad of bills from his pocket, thrusting it under Mr. Wigand's nose. Big tobacco money! Remember what this looks like?" This was not even close to the worst that Wigand suffered. He had already lost his job at B&W. Blowing the whistle meant he could never work in the tobacco industry again. Who would hire a traitor? Instead he worked as a high school science teacher for $30,000 per year, 1/10th of his previous income. The strain caused his marriage to fall apart. He received death threats. At 56, Wigand had to rebuild his life.

Other whistleblowers suffered similar fates. Edward Snowden, the NSA whistleblower, sought asylum in Russia from U.S. authorities. Roger Boisjoly was hounded out of Morton Thiokol by his colleagues. Sherron Watkins, a whistleblower at Enron, never worked in corporate America again. Tyler Shultz was only 24 years old when he blew the whistle on Theranos. His parents spent hundreds of thousands of dollars defending him from lawsuits filed by Theranos's powerful and well-connected lawyers. Other whistleblowers have suffered less drastic consequences, but that is probably only because the stakes were lower. When a person blows the whistle on his or her employer, many employees are negatively affected. They may take out their anger on those in their company who are responsible for the wrongdoing, but history shows that they also take it out on those who report the wrongdoing.

The lesson of this section is that whistleblowing can be personally costly, and while it is permissible and even admirable for individuals to bear these costs, it is not obligatory for them to do so, if the costs are too high. In these circumstances, whistleblowing is supererogatory. At the same time, we need to be careful not to let potential whistleblowers off the hook too easily. Ethics makes demands on us, and sometimes these demands are hard to meet. You might prefer to leave your dog's poop in the public park, but you should clean it up. You might prefer to speed away after backing into another person's car in the parking lot, but you should leave a note. If a business is doing something wrong, and you stand a good chance of putting a stop to it by disclosing information about the wrongdoing to the public – that is, blowing the whistle – you have good reason to do so. It might be personally costly for you to blow the whistle – you might wish someone else would blow it, or you might wish that you never learned about the wrongdoing in the first place – but that is just your tough luck. The personal costs you might bear for blowing the whistle are simply one of the many considerations you must take into account in deciding what to do. Doing the right thing can be hard sometimes.

4. Chapter Summary

In this chapter we continued our discussion of ethical issues at work. We considered ethical issues in hiring and firing, privacy, and whistleblowing. These issues can be considered separately, and for the most part that's how we approached them, drawing on unique examples and different arguments. But they share a common theme, which is information.

In the case of hiring, we asked what factors should be taken into account when it comes to making hiring decisions. Almost everyone agrees that employers should not discriminate against employees, though there is disagreement about why discrimination is wrong and what counts as discrimination. A further question is whether employers should go beyond nondiscrimination and hire the best candidate. In the case of firing, we considered what factors should be taken into account when deciding whether to fire someone. Here again the fundamental question is how much freedom employers should have. Some think they should be able to fire an employee for (almost) any reason, while others think they should be able to fire an employee for just a handful of reasons. There are costs and benefits to each approach.

Privacy was our next topic. This makes sense, because hiring and firing practices can compromise our privacy. We considered what privacy is, why it is valuable, and how we should go about deciding what information employers should be able to request from employees. We considered a version of the "let market participants decide" (LMPD) view from the previous chapter but also highlighted reasons for thinking that it doesn't give us exactly the right answers. Indeed, we saw that some states have enacted regulations, which take decisions about what information employers can request out of the hands of market participants. According to these regulations, employers can only ask for information about employees that is job-relevant. We noted that while this provides a good starting point for discussion, there is disagreement about what makes information job-relevant, so more work is left to be done.

We concluded the chapter with a discussion of whistleblowing. Here the question is whether employees should be allowed to share information about illegal or unethical activity in which their employers are engaged with third parties, in an effort to stop that activity. For many, the default position is that employees should not share such information, because they should remain loyal to their firms. So we began with a discussion of the nature and value of loyalty. But many also believe that it is sometimes appropriate to move away from this default position if there are good enough reasons to do so. We then considered reasons for employees to disclose what they know. According to various accounts, employees are justified in blowing the whistle when they can prevent harm or wrongdoing or avoid complicity in harm or wrongdoing. But the costs of blowing the whistle can be high, so even when employees have good reasons to do so, they may not be required to do so. Ethics sometimes requires personal sacrifice, but there are limits.

5. Study Questions

1. Some people argue that "job-relevance" is a key factor in determining whether an employer can consider a certain trait in a hiring decision. Explain why. Is it always clear whether a trait is job-relevant?
2. What is the difference between employment at will and just cause dismissal rules? Which approach do you think is better?
3. Was it permissible for Ross Hopkins to be fired for drinking the wrong brand of beer? Legally permissible? Morally permissible?
4. Identify at least two reasons why privacy is valuable.
5. How would an adherent of the "let market participants decide" (LMPD) approach decide what information an employer can know about an employee, and how she can know it?
6. Some people argue that "job-relevance" is a key factor in determining what information an employer can request from an employee. Explain why. Is it always clear whether a piece of information is job-relevant?
7. In your view, is U-Haul's nicotine-free policy acceptable? Or should they get rid of it?
8. There is a presumption that insiders shouldn't blow the whistle – that they should remain loyal to their firms. What reasons can be given for being loyal?
9. Common justifications for overriding this presumption – for blowing the whistle – appeal to the prevention of harm or wrongdoing. Explain these justifications.
10. Do you think Jeffrey Wigand was justified in blowing the whistle on B&W? Was his blowing the whistle ethically permissible? Was it ethically required?

Additional Readings

Brenkert, G. G. (2010). Whistle-blowing, moral integrity, and organizational ethics. In G. G. Brenkert & T. L. Beauchamp (Eds.), *Oxford handbook of business ethics* (pp. 563–601). New York: Oxford University Press.

DeGeorge, R. (2010). Whistle-blowing. In his *Business ethics* (7th ed., pp. 298–318). New York: Pearson.

Desjardins, J., & Duska, R. (1987). Drug testing in employment. *Business & Professional Ethics Journal*, *6*(3), 3–21.

Hellman, D. (2008). *When is discrimination wrong?* Cambridge, MA: Harvard University Press.

Kleinig, J. (2017). Loyalty. In E. N. Zalta (Ed.), *The Stanford encyclopedia of philosophy*. https://plato.stanford.edu/entries/loyalty/

Lyman, R. (1999, October 15). A tobacco whistle-blower's life is transformed. *New York Times*. www.nytimes.com/1999/10/15/us/a-tobacco-whistle-blower-s-life-is-transformed.html

McCall, J. J., & Werhane, P. H. (2010). Employment at will and employee rights. In G. G. Brenkert & T. L. Beauchamp (Eds.), *The Oxford handbook of business ethics* (pp. 602–627). New York: Oxford University Press.

McCarthy, K. (2020, January 2). U-Haul announces nicotine-free hiring policy in 21 states. *ABC News*. https://abcnews.go.com/US/haul-announces-nicotine-free-hiring-policy-21-states/story?id=68030799

Mulligan, T. (2018). On the distribution of jobs. In his *Justice and the meritocratic state*. New York: Routledge.

Tavani, H. T. (2007). Philosophical theories of privacy: Implications for an adequate online privacy policy. *Metaphilosophy*, *38*(1), 1–22.

9 Corporate Social Responsibility

Some people who pick up a book on business ethics will think: "Oh, this is a book about whether corporations have an obligation to give money to charity." When people talk about business ethics, this is often the issue they are talking about.

By now you will have realized that business ethics includes a lot more than this. It includes the study of the limits of markets, the ethics of advertising, employee rights and duties, and much more. But whether firms have obligations to society – obligations that might be discharged through charitable giving – is an important topic in business ethics and the topic to which we now turn.

1. Understanding the Issue

One simple way of asking the question that we will be concerned with in this chapter is, what are businesses' duties to society? A slightly more complicated refinement is, do businesses have a duty to benefit society, even at a cost to themselves?

To be clear, businesses *already* benefit society in the course of their normal operations. They make goods and services that people want; they provide jobs to people who need them; they pay taxes to support governmental programs. The question is whether they have a duty to provide benefits to society beyond what they provide in their normal operations.

Here is another way to understand the problem. Businesses make money. Once they have done whatever they need to do to satisfy their legal obligations – pay wages and taxes, install pollution control systems, etc. – what should they do with it? Are they *ethically* free to spend all of the money on themselves – say by generating higher profits and giving shareholders larger dividends? Or do they have a duty to spend the money on other groups, say by cutting pollution below the legally required limit or by donating a playground to a local community? Of course, it may be the case that cutting pollution below the legally required limit or donating a playground to a local community generates higher profits and larger dividends for shareholders. People may want to purchase goods from businesses that benefit the community in these ways. Then there is little question about what

DOI: 10.4324/9781351016872-9

should be done. Our question is whether businesses have moral duties to benefit others even if their doing so does not yield benefits for themselves.

In fact, this is not a question unique to businesses. It is one that we all face in our lives. You probably have some money in your pocket right now. You have to use some of this money to pay your bills – your rent, car payment, tuition, taxes, and so on. What about the rest? You could spend it on yourself, perhaps by going to the movies. But you could also use this money to benefit other people. You could give it to a friend to pay for a dental procedure or you could donate it to an organization like Oxfam to help people living in poverty in developing countries. Now the question you have to ask yourself is, do you have a *duty* to help needy people, or are you permitted to spend all of your money on yourself?

We have described the problem at hand as one about businesses' duties to benefit others, even at a cost to themselves. I think that this is the simplest and most helpful terminology available. But scholars sometimes ask these questions in different terms. They ask whether businesses should engage in *philanthropy* or acts of *corporate social responsibility*. They attempt to assess the *social performance* of businesses. They ask questions like these: should businesses be *good corporate citizens*? Should they operate in a *sustainable* way? Should they measure their performance not in terms of a single bottom line (viz., financial performance), but in terms of a *triple bottom line* (viz., financial, environmental, and social performance)? New labels seem to be created continually. As long as you can keep them all straight, there is no problem with this. Indeed, it can be helpful to think about problems using different concepts or terms. Despite the different labels, however, the fundamental issue seems to be the same. The question is whether corporations have a duty to benefit society, beyond what they are required to do by law, and even at a cost to themselves.

The most commonly employed terminology to talk about the moral duties of businesses to society is the language of *corporate social responsibility* or CSR. This is not ideal terminology. A corporation is a specific legal form that a business can take. Other business forms are partnerships, cooperatives, and sole proprietorships. So when people talk about corporate social responsibility you might think they are talking about the duties of corporations only. But 'corporate' in the phrase 'corporate social responsibility' usually refers to all business forms. Despite its drawbacks, we will use the language of corporate social responsibility, or CSR, in this chapter. But we should not lose sight of the essence of the issue, which is about the duties of businesses to groups other than themselves.

In this chapter we will focus on a case where a company has to make a decision about whether to benefit a group of people by developing a medicine for them. We might call this a social benefit. But we might just as easily have focused on a case whether a company has to make a decision about whether to benefit the environment in some way. You may have noticed that there is no separate chapter on environmental issues in this book. That is because these issues lend themselves to the same kind of analysis as social issues. In each case, the question is the extent to which corporations need to go beyond what the law requires to provide a benefit. The considerations in play are the same whether we are dealing with a social or an environmental benefit.

2. The Kind of Corporate Responsibility We Are Interested In

Before considering the example that will inform our discussion in this chapter, first we need to discuss the issue of responsibility. We are talking about corporate responsibility or the duties of businesses. You might wonder whether businesses are the kinds of things that can be responsible.

We need to be careful. There is a debate in business ethics that is carried on under the label of "corporate moral responsibility." This is a debate about whether corporations, or businesses more generally, are the kinds of things that can be morally responsible for their actions. To be morally responsible is to be an appropriate target of praise or blame, respectively, for actions that are (very roughly) good and bad. Typical human adults are morally responsible for their actions. If I step on your foot and cause you pain, you will blame me for what I did. But if a very small child steps on your foot and causes you pain, you will not – or at least should not – blame him for what he did. The same is true if a branch falls out of a tree and lands on your foot, causing you pain. The small child is not a morally responsible agent, and the tree is not an agent at all. Blame is inappropriate in these cases. The question of corporate moral responsibility is the question of whether businesses are more like typical human adults or more like small children or trees. There is intense philosophical debate about what makes typical human adults capable of moral agency, so there is intense debate about whether corporations can be morally responsible.

Our question in this chapter is not the question of whether corporations can be responsible in this sense. We are interested in the question of whether corporations have responsibilities – duties or obligations – to promote social ends. This question is different from the question of whether corporations are morally responsible for what they do.

Yet it might seem that these questions are connected. If corporations aren't the kinds of things that can be morally responsible, then why suppose that they are the kinds of things that can have duties or obligations at all? Very small children and trees aren't morally responsible for what they do, and neither do they have duties or obligations to do things. If this is right, then it might seem that the question of what responsibilities (obligations, duties) corporations have turns on the question of whether they can be morally responsible in the first place.

This is a complicated issue, and we can't pursue it in detail here. But we have reason to think that these issues are separable. First, most scholars think that the kind of agency needed to have a duty is different than the kind of agency needed to be an appropriate target of praise and blame. So businesses can have duties even if they can't be blamed for failing to discharge them. This might surprise you, but perhaps it shouldn't upon reflection. There may be a point in time at which children are old enough to have duties but not old enough to be blamed for neglecting them.

Second, and more importantly, the debate about what responsibilities – in the sense of obligations or duties – corporations have may actually be a debate about what to do with the resources corporations have. The question is whether these resources should all be directed toward increasing firm profitability and shareholder wealth or whether some of them should be directed toward promoting other social values. A separate question is *who* should be doing the directing. That might be corporations themselves, as distinct entities, or the individuals who are their managers. If we understand the issue this way, the debate about the robustness of corporate agency – whether they are appropriate targets of praise and blame, whether they have duties, or whether they aren't agents at all – is an entirely separate debate and one that has little practical significance. The key issue is what is to be done with corporate wealth. Having identified and addressed this potential confusion, we can now set it aside.

3. Merck and River Blindness

In the 1970s, scientists at the pharmaceutical company Merck were testing soil samples in search of new compounds that might prove medically useful. They discovered that one sample – taken from a plot of land near a golf course in Japan – had anti-parasitic qualities, which means that it kills parasites such as worms and mites in living organisms. Merck's scientists realized that this compound could be turned into a very lucrative drug. Millions of animals each year get infected by parasites. Many become very sick and die. The animals at risk include people's pets, but more importantly, the billions of animals the world consumes as food every year. Farmers and ranchers would pay a lot of money for a drug that would keep their animals safe from parasites. Through extensive research and testing, Merck was able to isolate the compound and develop it into a drug, which they called ivermectin. This drug was an enormous commercial success for Merck.

As Merck's scientists were developing the drug, an intriguing possibility emerged. Ivermectin was safe and effective against parasites in animals. Could a version of it be created to fight parasites in humans? The disease *onchocerciasis*, also known as river blindness, was an especially promising target. This disease begins with a bite from a black fly, which transmits worm larvae onto a person's skin. The larvae enter the body and begin multiplying rapidly. As the worms spread throughout the body, they cause intense itching and other painful skin conditions. Eventually, they enter the eyes, causing extensive scarring, which results in blindness. At the time of the development of ivermectin, river blindness affected millions of people.

While the science of a drug to treat river blindness was promising, the economics were not. It would cost hundreds of millions of dollars to develop the drug, and the people who needed it lived in some of the poorest countries in the world, mostly in sub-Saharan Africa. Merck could try to seek funding from a government agency or a nonprofit organization to support its work, and if the drug were successful, it might get some good publicity. But drug companies make most of their money from drug sales, and Merck couldn't make money on this drug.

This is in contrast to the version of ivermectin for animals. While parasites affect pets and livestock in poor countries, they also affect them in wealthy countries, and people in wealthy countries were ready to pay a lot of money to protect their animals.

Creating a drug to treat river blindness would be an instance of corporate social responsibility, as we have defined it. Merck would be providing a benefit to society, but at a cost to itself. So Merck had to make a choice. Should they develop thc drug or not?

One of the main ways this question is approached is by thinking about the purpose of the firm, that is, what goals the firm should be managed so as to achieve. The thought is that if we know what corporations should be doing in general, we will be able to tell what they should be doing in the particular case of corporate social responsibility. Now we will consider the two most important views about corporate purpose. The first is that of Milton Friedman, the 20th-century American economist, who says that firms should be managed so as to maximize shareholder wealth. The second is that of R. Edward Freeman, an American business ethicist who is currently active, who says that firms should be managed so as to balance the interests of all stakeholders.

A word about scope. This chapter is a little different than most of the other chapters in this book. Most chapters give an overview of debates to which many scholars have made contributions. This chapter offers a close examination of the views of two writers. But you will find that Friedman and Freeman loom large in business ethics, so it is worth considering their views in detail.

4. Milton Friedman and Shareholder Theory

We met Friedman back in Chapter 4, when we discussed the merits of the private ownership of productive property. Friedman also had influential views about the purpose of the firm, and in particular, whether firms should be socially responsible.

4.1. Friedman's Arguments for Shareholder Theory

The classic source for Friedman's views on the purpose of businesses and CSR is his 1970 *New York Times Magazine* article "The Social Responsibility of Business Is to Increase Its Profits." Friedman advances two arguments against CSR in that article. We can call the first the "ownership argument" and the second the "tax argument."

According to the ownership argument against CSR, corporate executives are employees in the business, which is owned by shareholders. To use language that is popular in some academic fields, shareholders are *principals* and executives are their *agents*. The idea is this. Shareholders own the business, but they do not run it themselves. Rather, they hire people to run it for them. These people are the corporate executives. But the owners of the business do not let executives run the firm however they (i.e., the executives) wish. Rather, they demand that executives manage the business so as to maximize their (i.e., shareholders') wealth. Executives agree to this when they accept employment at the business. When, instead of doing things that maximize wealth for shareholders – for example, funding a new advertising campaign designed to increase sales – managers do things that are socially responsible but reduce wealth for shareholders – for example, funding an afterschool program for at-risk youth – executives do something that they have no right to do. Indeed, they do something that is inconsistent with the agreement that they made with shareholders.

There is something to be said for this argument. Suppose you hire me to buy you groceries from the store. You give me $100 and a list of things to buy. I go to the store and get what's on your list, and it costs $80. Then I return to you with your groceries and $15 in change. I explain that your groceries cost $80, but on my way out of the store I gave $5 to a homeless person. You might not be pleased with this outcome. You might demand an additional $5 from me. Maybe you would fire me on the spot. Friedman thinks that corporate executives are in this position with respect to the owners of the business when they engage in acts of corporate social responsibility. Executives were hired, Friedman says, to make money for shareholders, not to provide benefits to other people.

The other main argument that Friedman gives against CSR is the tax argument. Friedman says that, when executives engage in CSR, they are effectively imposing taxes. CSR is going to cost the corporation money. Perhaps this money will come out of workers' paychecks – then it is a tax on workers. Perhaps it will come out of shareholders' dividends – then it is a tax on shareholders. Or perhaps it will be paid for through higher prices for consumers – then it is a tax on consumers.

Friedman says that these taxes are wrong for two reasons. One has to do with a moral principle. Taxing people to provide governmental services, Friedman says, is the job of the public as a whole, not a handful of corporate executives. You might think of this moral principle as a principle of democracy. The people as a whole should decide how the state should be run, including what services should be publicly provided. When these decisions are made by corporate executives under the banner of CSR, this democratic principle is subverted. The other reason the taxes associated with CSR are wrong, Friedman says, has to do with the expertise of corporate executives. Executives are skilled in making decisions that are good for their businesses, not in making decisions that promote the public welfare. If you task the CEO of Coca-Cola with increasing sales of Powerade, he can probably do this. If you task him with reducing poverty, he probably can't. Or at least he will be a lot less effective at reducing poverty than genuine experts in this field, such as development economists.

Some people, once they hear Friedman describe the costs associated with CSR as "taxes," will immediately leap to the conclusion that CSR is wrong. For some people, "tax" has a negative valence. Taxes are bad, and imposing new taxes in the form of CSR must be wrong. I suspect Friedman uses the "taxation" rhetoric to appeal to people like this. But in this case Friedman's rhetoric inflames more than it illuminates. First, almost everyone thinks *some* taxes – to fund national defense forces or the construction of sewers – are justified. Describing a certain cost as a "tax" does not tell us whether it is justified. Second, firms impose "taxes" – or less sensationally, *costs* – on all kinds of people all the time. A corporation might decide to cut workers' wages in an economic downturn. Or it might decide to raise prices because they want to increase their profits. It would be absurd to say that these actions are wrong because they impose "taxes" on people.

Does this mean Friedman's tax argument should be rejected? No. In fact, Friedman's "tax argument" doesn't actually depend on thinking of the costs of CSR as taxes. Remember again *why* Friedman thinks CSR "taxes" – let's call them costs from now on – are wrong. They are wrong because they subvert a principle of democracy. Society as a whole, not a handful of corporate executives, should decide what benefits will be publicly provided. They are also wrong because they are likely to be wasted. Corporate executives are experts in business, not social responsibility. These reasons are no less compelling if we describe CSR activities as costs than if we describe them as taxes. Put another way, you can object to CSR because it is anti-democratic, and because it is going to lead to waste, and your objections do not have to mention taxes at all.

The ownership argument and the tax argument are very different. The ownership argument appeals to the idea that corporations are owned, and executives accept employment on the condition that they will do what the owners want. The tax argument appeals to the ideal of democracy and the value of expertise. But they have the same conclusion. Executives should not engage in CSR. Instead, they should focus exclusively on maximizing shareholder wealth.

Friedman did not give his theory a name, but it will be convenient to give it one here. Following what is now common practice, let us call it "shareholder theory." This label is appropriate because Friedman thinks that shareholders' interests should get priority in corporate decision-making. When executives engage in socially responsible actions, they attempt to benefit parties other than shareholders, even if this costs shareholders money. So Friedman is opposed to CSR.

What would a shareholder theorist like Friedman say about the Merck case? He would probably say that Merck should not develop a drug to treat river blindness. Merck's executives should be maximizing profits, and a drug that costs a lot of money to make, but that generates little or no revenue, is likely to reduce profits. Of course, in business, as in life, you can never be completely sure how your decisions are going to turn out. Maybe through a strange twist of fate a decision that looks very likely to cost you money (e.g., leaving your wallet full of cash on the subway) will actually make you money (e.g., a stranger returns it to you with even more cash stuffed into it). But you have to play the percentages. The odds that a product that costs you a lot of money to make, and which you can only sell at a steep loss, will in the end make you money are very low. So a shareholder theorist would recommend that Merck not develop a drug to treat river blindness.

4.2. Understanding Friedman's Theory Better

In this section I want to clarify a few elements of Friedman's view. This will help to address common criticisms that result from misunderstandings of it.

The first thing to note is that, while Friedman thinks that corporate managers should try to maximize shareholder wealth and not pursue social objectives, he does not think that managers should take *any* action that they think will maximize shareholder wealth. Indeed, Friedman says that managers should try to maximize shareholder wealth within the bounds of "law and ethical custom." It is illegal to burn down your competitor's factory or steal their intellectual property. So managers should not do these things, even if doing them would increase shareholder wealth. Friedman's reference to "ethical custom" is more mysterious. But the idea seems to be that there are things that we all think are wrong but which are not illegal. It is not illegal to call an employee "stupid" for making a mistake, but this seems unethical. Friedman is saying that managers should not do these sorts of things either, even if doing them would increase shareholder wealth. The point is, for Friedman, there are legal and ethical constraints on managers' behavior. But, within these constraints, they should be trying to maximize shareholder wealth, not advance social objectives.

The second thing to note about Friedman's view is that it applies to business forms that feature a separation of ownership and control. The corporation is the most familiar example of such a business. In a corporation, the people in control of the business on a day-to-day basis are the managers, but they don't own the corporation. The shareholders do. (Or at least most people think – more on this later.) Friedman is saying that the controllers should be doing what the owners want, and what the owners want is to maximize profits. But suppose the people who own the business are not separate from the people who control the business. In a sole proprietorship – for example, a small local coffee shop or gas station – the owner of the business exercises control over it. In this case, Friedman says, it is perfectly fine for the manager not to maximize her wealth and instead to pursue social objectives. She is not going against the owners' wishes when she does this. She is the owner.

The third thing to note about Friedman's view is its scope. It applies to managers *in their role as managers*. He is not saying that socially responsible behaviors such as fighting poverty and eliminating inequality are wrong and people should never engage in them. Friedman is not advocating a kind of universal selfishness. He is saying that if you are a corporate manager, then *your job* consists of managing the business in a way that maximizes shareholder wealth. But you are perfectly free to use your salary to pursue social objectives. You could give it to organizations dedicated to fighting poverty, inequality, or environmental degradation. What Friedman thinks is wrong is the manager's taking *some of the corporation's money* and using it, against shareholders' will, to engage in socially responsible behavior.

We have said that, when it comes to how managers should manage businesses, Friedman is "for shareholders, and against CSR." But what about when being for CSR is good for shareholders? This brings us to a fourth thing to note about Friedman's view. Friedman knows that, in some cases, doing something good for the public could be good for shareholders, in the sense of making shareholders wealthier. A business might donate playground equipment to a local school. It might then highlight its actions in a public relations campaign. This may lead to goodwill in the community, which may lead to increased sales, which may lead finally to increased shareholder wealth. In fact, Friedman thinks that a lot of social responsibility by businesses is just a thinly veiled strategy to increase shareholder wealth. He wishes that consumers wouldn't look to businesses to address social problems like run-down parks, underfunded schools, or global poverty. That should not be their job. But if consumers are looking to businesses to address social problems, and are willing to reward businesses for addressing them, then Friedman reluctantly agrees that businesses should do so.

4.3. Criticisms of Friedman's Arguments

In the previous section, we refined our understanding of Friedman's view. In this section we return to his arguments for the view and critically evaluate them.

Remember that Friedman's argument begins with the claim that shareholders own the corporation. Because shareholders own the corporation, they get to hire the people to run it, and the people they hire agree to run it in the way that shareholders want, which is to make as much money as possible. Some legal scholars have argued that shareholders do not, in fact, own the corporation. To make sense of this claim, we have to say a bit more about what ownership is.

To own something is to have a bundle of rights with respect to that thing. Think about the things you own – your shoes, your computer, your books. You can use them, sell them, rent them out, destroy them, or just keep them around. The shareholders of a corporation don't have any of these rights with respect to the corporation. I own a few shares of Walmart stock, as it happens. I cannot use one of Walmart's delivery trucks – say, to help me move. I cannot rent a Walmart store out for a party. I cannot go into a Walmart store and throw away a bunch of merchandise. (You might say that the problem is that I don't have the permission of all of the other owners of Walmart's stock. But in fact I could not do any of these things even if I did.) My ownership of a few shares of Walmart stock gives me some rights with respect to Walmart. I can vote to elect its board of directors. If the board decides to issue a dividend, then I will receive some of that money. But that's about it. This is a much different, and much more limited, set of powers than the powers I have with respect to my shoes, computer, and books. Considerations like these make some legal scholars think that shareholders don't *really* own corporations. At best, shareholders have a few of the powers normally associated with ownership.

You might have two questions about this argument. First, you might wonder: "Well, shareholders own something. So if it's not the business, then what do they own?" The answer that is often given is, "Shares of stock, which is a type of financial instrument." Second, you might wonder: "If shareholders don't own the business, then who does own it?" The answer often given is, "No one." This might seem strange. How can a business be unowned? Doesn't someone have to own it? The answer is no. Consider the state in which you live. People own things in this state; people work for this state to produce things; people control the state by exercising power in political offices; the state can enter into agreements with other states. But no one owns the state in which you live. There is nothing strange about this at all. In fact, it would be strange if someone did own the state.

Friedman's argument begins with the idea that shareholders own the corporation, and they get to decide who runs it and for what purpose. So it might seem that Friedman's argument collapses if shareholders do not in fact own the corporation. In a sense this is right. But there is another argument in the neighborhood of Friedman's argument that does not depend on shareholders owning the corporation and which reaches the same conclusion.

We begin again with the idea of shareholder ownership. But instead of saying that shareholders own *the firm*, we can instead say that shareholders own *capital*. That is, they own the money that can be transformed into buildings, machines, computers, and so on. For capital to be productive, labor is required.

There must be someone there to manage the buildings, run the machines, and type on the computers. Owners of capital do not supply this labor themselves. Rather, they hire other people to supply it. They do so, according to this new argument, on the condition that these people labor in such a way that shareholders' wealth is maximized. This argument gives us the conclusion that managers should try to maximize shareholder wealth because of a promise that managers made to providers of capital, but without relying on the claim that shareholders own the firm.

You might wonder how it could be known that shareholders hired workers, not the other way around. People claim to be able to see who was hired, and who did the hiring, based on who is ultimately in charge in corporations. In typical corporations – ones you are probably most familiar with, like Wells Fargo and Coca-Cola – these are the shareholders. Of course in these corporations there are many individuals who exercise control. At Coca-Cola, a shift supervisor might exercise control over workers on a bottling line. At Wells Fargo, a director of research might exercise control over a group of analysts. But these exercisers of control are subject to the control of a more senior person. A plant manager at Coca-Cola might exercise control over a group of shift supervisors; a vice-president at Wells Fargo might exercise control of a group of research directors – and so on up the organizational hierarchy. Eventually we reach the chief executive officer or CEO. But the CEO himself or herself is controlled by the corporation's board of directors. That is, the board hires and fires the CEO. Who controls the board? The answer is, shareholders. That's where the line of control stops. There is no one who controls the shareholders. You don't find the workers at the top of the line of control in a typical corporation. If you did, then it would be correct to say that, in that corporation, labor hires capital.

This is a better argument. The claim that shareholders own the firm is dubious, and even if it turns out to be true, it is better for an argument not to rely on dubious claims. But that does not mean that this argument cannot be challenged. It relies on many of the same claims as Friedman's original argument, including the claim that managers agreed to maximize shareholder wealth and that shareholders asked them to maximize their wealth. Both of these claims can be questioned.

Consider the claim that managers accept employment on the condition that they attempt to maximize shareholder wealth. Many people have wondered how plausible this is. Think about the jobs you have held. Did your employer make you promise to try to maximize shareholder wealth, or owner wealth more generally, when you accepted employment? Probably not. Maybe you are thinking that, even if your employer did not make you explicitly promise to maximize shareholder wealth, when you accepted employment, you made an implicit promise to do so. There was a shared understanding between you and your employer that this was the ultimate goal of your employment. This is a trickier matter, but in general we need to be careful about assuming that there is an agreement to do something where no one has explicitly agreed to do anything. The political philosopher Robert Nozick, whose theory of justice we discussed in Chapter 4, once said about implicit (or tacit) consent that it "isn't worth the paper it is not written on." Nozick's point is that implicit agreement is not real agreement.

So far we have been assuming that shareholders want managers to maximize shareholder wealth (and get managers to promise to do so). Scholars have also objected to this claim. I own shares of stock, and you might also. What do you and I want the corporations in which we are stockholders to do? Do we really want them to maximize our wealth? Or do we want them to pursue social objectives as well? I do not recall being asked, and I bet you weren't either. The question of how shareholders want firms to be managed is an open one. It might vary from firm to firm and from time to time. Some shareholders may want firms to be managed so as to maximize their wealth, but others may want firms to pursue other objectives. To be clear, I am not now arguing that shareholders actually do want firms to pursue objectives other than maximizing shareholder wealth. I am simply pointing out that the opposite claim – that shareholders want firms to maximize their wealth – is in need of justification.

5. R. Edward Freeman and Stakeholder Theory

We have considered one major view about the purpose of corporations. Now we will consider the second. This is stakeholder theory, and its main proponent is R. Edward Freeman.

5.1. Freeman, Stakeholders, and CSR

Freeman devised stakeholder theory as an alternative to shareholder theory. Shareholder theory tells managers to maximize shareholder wealth. On this theory, shareholders' interests always get priority. Stakeholder theory, by contrast, tells managers to balance the interests of all stakeholders. Instead of always giving shareholders' interests priority, managers should sometimes give priority to the interests of other groups.

Freeman gives two definitions of "stakeholder." On the narrow definition, a stakeholder is anyone who is essential to the survival and success of the corporation. Freeman says that this group includes employees, suppliers, consumers, the local community, and shareholders. Without employees, the business could not exist. There would be no one to work to create the business's products and services. Without suppliers, the business wouldn't have any raw materials for the employees to work with. Similar stories could be told about the other narrow stakeholders. On the wide definition, a stakeholder is anyone who can affect the corporation or who can be affected by the corporation. This includes all of the stakeholders on the narrow definition, but many other people as well. Businesses can affect and be affected by (in addition to all of the narrow stakeholders) governments, the media, and competitor firms. Indeed, for very large businesses like Walmart, Amazon, and Alphabet Inc. (the parent company of Google), pretty much anyone in the world could be affected by them or could affect them, at least in some small way. When stakeholder theorists claim that managers should balance the interest of all stakeholders, they usually have the narrow group in mind.

If managers should balance the interests of all stakeholders, what does this mean for CSR? In fact, Freeman does not have much use for the concept of CSR. He thinks that if the manager is balancing the interests of all stakeholders, then she is doing the right thing, and she doesn't need to worry about CSR. In balancing all stakeholders' interests, she will be taking into account the interests of community members, among others. This does not mean that firms managed according to stakeholder principles will never do things that qualify as acts of CSR. Quite the opposite. Freeman would likely support a manager's diverting some of the firm's revenues to social causes, instead of giving them all to shareholders in the form of increased profits, on the grounds that doing so helps to balance the interests of all stakeholders. To do this sort of thing is to engage in an act of CSR.

What would a stakeholder theorist like Freeman say about the Merck case? For reasons that will become apparent shortly, it is not clear exactly what he would say. (A preview: it is not obvious what "balancing" stakeholders' interests requires.) But stakeholder theorists will certainly be more sympathetic to the claim that Merck should develop a drug to treat river blindness than shareholder theorists. Developing the drug would probably reduce shareholders' profits. But since stakeholder theorists do not think that managers should always prioritize the interests of shareholders, this is not a conclusive reason on their view not to develop the drug. Stakeholder theorists will consider other stakeholders' interests too, and there is reason to think that other stakeholders will be benefitted by this decision. In developing a drug to treat river blindness, Merck would do a lot of good for one of the communities in which it operates; it would provide continued employment for a group of employees; and it would do additional business with its suppliers of lab equipment and materials. These benefits may be enough to counterbalance the costs to shareholders and justify a decision to develop the drug.

5.2. Arguments for Stakeholder Theory

When Freeman first presented stakeholder theory, he argued that there was a certain descriptive truth to it. In the early to mid-20th century, managers had a relatively free hand to promote shareholders' interests. That is, managers were not much constrained by laws and regulations that required them to pay attention to the interests of other stakeholders. But new laws and regulations changed this. In the U.S., the Clean Air Act (1970) and Clear Water Act (1972) required managers to take into account the interests of the members of the communities in which they operate, specifically, their interest in a clean environment. Court decisions like *Greenman v. Yuba Power Products Inc.*, discussed in Chapter 5, assigned strict liability to corporations for harm that their products cause, requiring managers to think carefully about consumers' interests. The Occupational Safety and Health Act (1970) required employers to provide a working environment free of known hazards to their employees, which means that managers must take into account their employees' interests. Similar laws and regulations can be found in many countries. In sum, Freeman believes, managers have to pay attention to all stakeholders' interests, because this is (now) what the law requires.

Freeman is certainly right that firms and their managers increasingly operate in a world in which they must be responsive to the interests of multiple stakeholders. But this is not really an argument for stakeholder theory. Shareholder theorists like Friedman think that managers should obey all laws and regulations too. The difference between shareholder theory and stakeholder theory is not whether managers should obey laws, including laws that require them to take into account stakeholders' interests. The difference is what managers should do once they have obeyed these laws. Shareholder theorists think that managers should maximize shareholder wealth. Stakeholder theorists think they should balance all stakeholders' interests. An argument for stakeholder theory is an argument that managers should try to balance all stakeholders' interests, even after they have obeyed all of the relevant laws. Freeman has offered three such arguments, which we will consider now.

One argument appeals to a philosophical device we encountered in Chapter 4. This is the veil of ignorance, which Rawls uses to select his principles of justice. The idea is that we imagine that we don't know certain facts about ourselves, such as our social status, our wealth, what makes us happy, and so on. In ignorance of these facts – "behind the veil" – we select principles to govern the distribution of advantages in society. Those are the principles of justice, Rawls says. Freeman argues that if we use this device in the context of the corporation, we will think that stakeholder theory is correct. Imagine, he says, that you don't know which *stakeholder* you are. You don't know whether you are a shareholder, a supplier, an employee, a community member, or a consumer. Now choose a set of principles that you would like to govern the distribution of advantages in the firm. What principles will you choose? Freeman says that you won't choose the principles that comprise shareholder theory, because this directs managers to always prioritize shareholders' interests, and you might not turn out to be a shareholder, once the veil is lifted. It would make more sense for you to choose stakeholder theory, because this theory directs managers to take your interests into account, by balancing them, no matter what stakeholder you turn out to be.

Another argument that Freeman gives for stakeholder theory appeals to rights. Shareholders invest their money in the corporation and receive in exchange the right to elect the corporation's board of directors and the right to the firm's residual earnings. But there are limits to these rights. Just because a shareholder can exercise a certain sort of control over the corporation, doesn't mean that she can use it to do whatever she wants. Other stakeholders have rights too. Employees have a right to be paid wages; the community has a right that corporations obey local laws and regulations; suppliers have a right that the corporation pays its bills in a timely fashion. The danger of shareholder theory, Freeman says, is that it risks overinflating the value of shareholders' rights and directing managers' attention away from the legitimate rights of other stakeholders. Stakeholder theory is a superior theory, he thinks, because it directs managers to pay explicit attention to the rights of all stakeholders.

A third argument appeals to consequences. Most businesses are complicated entities and need the cooperation of many parties. They need labor from employees, parts from suppliers, infrastructure from the local community, and so on. Suppose that a manager decides that she will put the interests of shareholders above the interests of every other stakeholder in the firm. This doesn't mean that she will violate her commitments to other stakeholders (e.g., fail to pay her employees or suppliers), but whenever there are resources left over, they will go into shareholders' pockets. What, Freeman asks, would it be like to be a stakeholder in this firm? You would probably feel quite marginalized. You wouldn't go the extra mile to help the firm out if it ever got into trouble. If you were a worker, you wouldn't work nights or weekends on a big project. If you were a supplier, you wouldn't tolerate late payments. Indeed, you might look to do business with someone else. This would be bad for the firm. The business world is competitive. To be successful, a firm needs the help of many stakeholders. But in a firm managed according to shareholder principles, they will not be inclined to help. For this reason, Freeman thinks, stakeholder management is likely to have better consequences for the firm than shareholder management. A firm will perform better – and in fact be more profitable – if managers seek to balance all stakeholders' interests than if they try to maximize shareholders' profits.

5.3. Criticisms of Stakeholder Theory

Like shareholder theory, stakeholder theory has been the target of considerable criticism. One set of criticisms has focused on the formulation of the theory. Another set has focused on the arguments for the theory. We'll take these sets of criticisms in order.

5.3.1. What Does the Theory Actually Say?

Stakeholder theory tells managers to balance the interests of all stakeholders. Some critics have wondered what this really means. It is not clear who the stakeholders are or what it means to balance their interests.

Consider first the issue of who the stakeholders are. Freeman distinguishes stakeholders in the narrow sense – those who are vital to the survival and success of the firm – from stakeholders in the wide sense – anyone who can affect or be affected by the firm. As we said, stakeholders in the narrow sense include employees, shareholders, suppliers, customers, and the local community, and stakeholders in the wide sense includes all of these groups plus many others, including the government, the media, and competitor firms. We might wonder about the significance of this distinction. Freeman says that managers should balance the interests of all stakeholders, and he typically means stakeholders in the narrow sense. But does this mean that managers should ignore the interests of "secondary" stakeholders, that is, groups who are stakeholders in the wide but not narrow sense? This seems arbitrary. What would be the reason for taking into consideration some stakeholders' interests but not others? On the other hand, it seems a bit odd to take into consideration the interests of some groups who are stakeholders in the wide sense, such as competitor firms. Should managers really take into consideration – in the sense of try to promote – their competitors' interests?

The larger point is this. Stakeholder theory tells managers to balance the interests of some group of people. It makes a great deal of difference who is in this group and who is out of it. If you are in the group, then your interests will be promoted by the manager. If you are not, then they won't be. But stakeholder theory does not provide an adequate account of who is in the group and who is out of it. While we are told who the key groups are, we are not told why these groups are key.

Now consider balance. What does it mean to balance the interests of all stakeholders? Since stakeholder theory was offered as an alternative to shareholder theory, we know at least that it means that managers should not always give priority to shareholders' interests. What else does it mean?

The concept of balance has *some* content. It is common to talk of ecosystems being in or out of balance. It might be in balance if there are appropriate numbers of predators and prey. It might be out of balance if there are too many predators and not enough prey. Sometimes people talk about finding a work-life balance. Typically, this is said by people who are working too much and want to find more time to engage in leisure activities. Similarly, when stakeholder theorists direct managers to balance the interests of all stakeholders, they are saying that managers should not give too much weight to the interests of one group of stakeholders and too little weight to the interests of other groups.

Still, the concept of balance has its limits. Suppose I want to achieve a work-life balance, and I am trying to decide whether to take a day off to hang out with friends. If I never took a day off, that would probably be inconsistent with achieving a work-life balance. I would be working too much. At the same time, if I took multiple days off per week, then that would probably also be inconsistent with having a work-life balance. I would be working too little.

That information is helpful, but not *that* helpful. It doesn't tell me whether to take a particular day off. The same goes for stakeholder theory. The requirement to balance all stakeholders' interests tells us not to always give priority to the interests of one group of stakeholders. But the idea of balance does not tell us how much attention these interests should receive relative to other interests. Put another way, we are told not to give the interests of any one group of stakeholders too much weight, but we are not told what "too much" means.

We might see these two issues as deep problems with stakeholder theory, that is, as reasons to reject it. Or we might see them as gaps in the theory that require filling in. Either way, they require attention. Until they are addressed, stakeholder theory cannot be said to provide managers specific direction about what to do.

5.3.2. What Reason Do We Have to Accept the Theory?

Suppose the questions about what stakeholder theory says are resolved. A further question is why we should accept it. That is, why should managers seek to balance the interests of all stakeholders? Questions can be raised about each of the arguments for stakeholder theory we considered.

Consider the argument from the veil of ignorance. The main problem here is that Freeman has not provided an argument for why it is proper to use this device in the context of corporate governance. Rawls, whose device it is, does not think that the veil of ignorance should be used to make every distributive decision. He limits it to the choice of principles of justice for society as a whole, on the grounds that the knowledge that individuals lack behind the veil – knowledge about talents and social status – is irrelevant to the determination of how society's resources should be justly distributed. But there are many decision-making contexts in which information about who we are seems relevant to justice. Imagine that you go out to dinner with friends. You go to settle the bill, and someone proposes that you decide how much each pays behind a veil of ignorance, where you don't know what each person ordered. This seems like an odd suggestion. It seems better – more just – for people to pay for what they ordered. Or suppose that a firm has a great year and is trying to decide how to distribute bonuses. It might make this decision behind a veil of ignorance and blind itself to knowledge about what each employee has contributed. But it seems better for it to decide in light of this information. The same goes, we might think, for dividing corporate revenues among stakeholders. Freeman suggests that principles for just distribution in corporations should be determined behind a veil of ignorance, where you don't know which stakeholder you are. But information about who you are and what you have done is often relevant to determining what you should get. It seems relevant in the corporate context too. If this is right, then it doesn't make sense to choose a theory of corporate resource distribution behind a veil of ignorance.

Consider next the argument from property rights. The main problem with this argument is that it isn't really an argument for the core element of stakeholder theory, which is that managers should balance all stakeholders' interests. The argument from property rights notes that shareholders' rights are limited, and other stakeholders have rights too. This is correct. But shareholder theorists agree. The core debate between shareholder and stakeholder theorists is not about whether people's *rights* should be respected; the debate is about whose *interests* should be promoted. Shareholder theorists say "shareholders only," while stakeholder theorists say "all stakeholders."

What about Freeman's point that if managers are directed to prioritize shareholders' interests, they will forget about stakeholders' rights? It is hard to know what to make of this claim. We don't normally forget about other people's rights when we are promoting a certain party's interests. I prioritize the interests of my children over other people's children, but I think I still do a good job of respecting other people's rights. Perhaps I would do an even better job if I stopped always prioritizing my children's interests over other children's. Maybe I should do more for other people's children at the expense of my own. In the end, this is an empirical claim in need of empirical verification. That is, we would need to gather a lot of data about how having certain priorities affects respect for rights.

Consider finally the argument from consequences. Freeman believes that firms that are managed according to stakeholder principles will perform better than firms that are managed according to shareholder principles. That is, managers will achieve better results, even for shareholders, if they seek to balance the interests of all stakeholders than if they try to maximize profits for shareholders. It is hard to know what to say about this argument as well. On the one hand, it seems plausible to think that if a manager ignores one of the firm's key stakeholder groups – for example, its employees or its customers – then that firm may suffer. Stakeholders will be disinclined to "go the extra mile" at the moment the firm most needs their help. On the other hand, some scholars have argued that assigning managers multiple objectives leads to worse organizational performance because it gives managers more discretion – discretion which they may use to benefit themselves at the expense of the firm. The key issue is oversight. It is easier to tell when a manager is failing to maximize profits for shareholders than when she is failing to balance all stakeholders' interests. If it is hard to tell when a manager is doing her job, then she may be able to get away with self-serving behavior.

Notice something else about this argument. If it is true, then it turns out that shareholder theorists should embrace stakeholder theory as a business strategy. Shareholder theorists think that the goal of management should be shareholder wealth maximization. What the argument from consequences says is that balancing all stakeholders' interests is a means to this end. So if the argument from consequences is correct, then there is no debate between shareholder and stakeholder theorists. Balancing all stakeholders' interests leads to the maximization of shareholder wealth. Is this argument correct? We don't really know. And no amount of armchair speculation or philosophical reflection will answer this question. This is another empirical claim in need of empirical verification.

5.3.3. A Different Way of Thinking About Stakeholder Theory

Stakeholder theory has been subjected to criticisms related to its content and justification. Critics have wondered who the stakeholders are and what it means to balance their interests. They have questioned why all stakeholders' interests should be balanced.

It is sometimes said, in reply to these criticisms, that stakeholder theory is being misconstrued. Its purpose is not to offer determinate advice to managers, but simply to get them to think about corporate management in a different way. Every firm is embedded in a complex web of relationships – with shareholders, employees, suppliers, communities, consumers, and others – and no firm will be successful if it fails to attend to these relationships. This means that managers must give stakeholders' interests due consideration. If a group of stakeholders comes to believe that a manager is merely *using* them to promote someone else's interests (e.g., shareholders'), then they will not have a positive relationship with the firm, and the firm will not succeed. On this view, stakeholder is best understood as a "mindset," that is, a useful way of looking at the firm.

This conception of stakeholder theory avoids the problem of what it means to balance the interests of a certain group of stakeholders by removing the concept of balance from its formulation. But this comes at a cost. It makes it even less clear what stakeholder theory's content is. It reduces it to something like the claim: "Pay enough attention to all the firm's stakeholders," without attempting to say how much attention is "enough." And it combines this claim with an empirical claim about what paying enough attention to the firm's stakeholders will do, namely, lead to firm success. Again, while intuitively plausible, this is an empirical claim that requires empirical verification. But without a definition of "enough," it is hard to know how to even begin to evaluate it.

6. CSR, the Shareholder/Stakeholder Debate, and Beneficence

You might think that the issue of whether firms should act in socially responsible ways depends on the outcome of the debate between shareholder theorists like Friedman and stakeholder theorists like Freeman. You might think: "If Friedman is right, then firms should do everything they can to maximize shareholder wealth, within the law. There is no room for socially responsible acts, understood as acts intended to benefit other stakeholders at shareholders' expense." You might also think: "If Freeman is right, then socially responsible acts are sometimes required, because shareholders' interests shouldn't always get priority. Sometimes firms should benefit other stakeholders, even if this costs shareholders money." According to this view, the debate about CSR boils down to who is right, shareholder theorists or stakeholder theorists.

It is correct to think that stakeholder theory leaves more room for acts of social responsibility than shareholder theory. But this is not the whole story. In fact, the debate about whether firms should engage in socially responsible acts is in an important way independent of the debate between shareholder and stakeholder theorists.

To see this, consider an example due to the contemporary philosopher Peter Singer. Imagine you are walking across your college campus early in the morning, going to meet a friend for coffee. You are passing by the college's ornamental fountain, and you see a small child drowning in it. You could easily rescue the child – while the water is deep enough for the child to drown, it only comes up to your knees – but it would come at a cost to you. You would be late for your friend, and you would get your clothes wet. You are the only one around, however, and it seems like only a matter of moments before the child goes under the water. Should you rescue him?

The answer to this question is clear. Yes! Imagine that you didn't, and someone – maybe his parents – asked why. Would they be satisfied with your saying that you didn't want to be late for your friend and get your clothes wet? I doubt it. No one would be. Rescuing the child is clearly the right thing to do. Failing to rescue him is very wrong.

The lesson of this story is that people have a duty of beneficence. That is, they should sometimes help other people out, even at a cost to themselves. It is normally permissible for people to do what's best for themselves, but they are required in certain circumstances to benefit others. Rescuing a drowning child from an ornamental fountain is one of these circumstances. The duty of beneficence can be understood as a moral constraint on people's behavior. Whatever a person is trying to do, there are constraints on how he can behave. One of the constraints is beneficence.

This lesson applies to the business context as well. Consider the Merck case with which we began. Millions of people were suffering and dying from a terrible disease. Merck had the ability to help them, and it was arguably the only firm that could help. To be sure, developing the drug would cost Merck, but it could do so much good for so many others. So it might be said that Merck had an obligation to develop the drug. It might further be said that Merck had this obligation whether its goal was to maximize shareholder wealth or balance all stakeholders' interests. The duty of beneficence functions as a constraint on Merck's pursuit of its ends, whatever those ends might be. In the circumstances in which Merck found itself, it might be said, the duty of beneficence requires developing the drug.

Now you might object that the Merck case and the case of the drowning child are different in morally relevant respects. You might say that the cost that Merck would have to pay for developing the drug (hundreds of millions of dollars in research funding) was much higher than the cost that you would have to pay for rescuing the child (being late for a friend and getting your clothes wet). You might also say that, in the case of the drowning child, you have an obligation to help because you are the only person who can help. No one else can get there in time. But, you might go on, Merck wasn't the only organization that could have helped people with river blindness. Once Merck discovered the promising chemical compound, a nonprofit group or government might have stepped in and shouldered the costs of developing it into a safe and effective medicine for the disease. So, you might insist, it is unfair to blame Merck if they don't rescue those suffering from river blindness.

But notice what we are doing here. Developing a beneficial drug that people will be too poor to afford to purchase is clearly an act of social responsibility. It is an act that Merck considered taking in order to provide a benefit to society, but that would not benefit its own shareholders. What we are doing here is debating whether Merck should perform an act of social responsibility. We are doing this without appealing to either shareholder theory or stakeholder theory. We are instead appealing to the existence and scope of the duty of beneficence.

I will not try to bring this debate to a conclusion. This is a difficult issue, and we don't have the space to explore all of the complications. My point here is simply that we can think about what ethics requires businesses to do without thinking about what goals they should ultimately be managed to achieve. Less depends on the debate between shareholder theorists and stakeholder theorists than is sometimes thought.

You might be wondering what, in the end, Merck decided to do. Merck decided to develop the drug. It takes many years to develop a safe and effective drug to treat a medical condition in humans, but by the mid-1980s Merck had succeeded in doing so. Since there was no plausible path to making money on the drug, Merck decided to donate it, "as much as needed for as long as needed." As of 2019, and in concert with several nonprofit groups, Merck had given away 2.7 billion treatments for river blindness, and the disease has been eliminated in several countries, including Ecuador, Colombia, and Guatemala. As you consider whether Merck made the right choice, you might reflect on the value of what Merck did, what it cost them, and what rights and duties were at issue.

7. Relying on Corporations

One question is what we should think of a specific business trying to solve a specific social problem – like Merck and river blindness. Another question is what we should think of CSR as a general practice. There are lots of problems in the world and lots of ways corporations could help. Should we rely on corporations to solve social problems?

Friedman identified several problems with CSR. It takes away money from the corporation that should be used to increase shareholder wealth; it wrongfully intrudes into the public sphere; it gives managers a task that they have no expertise in. We are raising another problem with CSR, now understood as a practice. The worry is that society puts itself in danger if, as a rule, it "outsources" the solving of social problems to corporations.

Suppose there is another disease like river blindness that afflicts people, but that businesses find unprofitable to solve. Suppose in our society, corporations usually solve social problems, but this one is going unsolved. What are we, the members of society, to do? We could ask a corporation to solve the problem. Perhaps we let Merck off the hook because of its work on river blindness, so we ask another drug company, like AstraZeneca or Pfizer. They refuse. What now?

The problem is that we can't compel any corporation to take action to solve the problem, because we do not control it. The ultimate decision-makers in the corporation are the members of the board, and they are appointed by shareholders, not the public. We can speak to the corporation, but we have no right even that they listen to us.

Things would be different if the government were in charge of solving social problems. We do control the government. Perhaps we cannot tell it what to do directly, but we control who serves in it. If we want a certain problem addressed, we can elect people who promise to address that problem and un-elect them the next time around if they don't. Some people are cynical about politicians. They wonder whether their president, senator, or congressperson is really listening to them. They may have a point. But people in these roles have thousands if not millions of constituents. They do not have time for every single one of them. Moreover, many social problems are solved not at national but at state and local levels. People in these roles have more time for each constituent. In any event, the question we are asking is who is more likely to act when the public calls for a social problem to be addressed, a corporation or a government. It seems clear that the government is. For this reason, social problems are more likely to be solved by our government than by a corporation.

You might say that this doesn't mean that we shouldn't outsource social problems to corporations. All it means is that, when we come across a social problem that corporations won't solve, we should solve it ourselves, through our government. But if we have become accustomed to having corporations solve our problems, then own our ability to do so may have deteriorated. Suppose you hire someone to mow your lawn. They do it for years. Now they stop, and you can't get anyone else to do it. But your lawn needs mowing. You must do something. But you don't have a mower, you don't know where to find one, and even if you did, you wouldn't know how to operate it. If we outsource our social problems to corporations, we may find ourselves in a similar position one day. If we don't practice solving social problems ourselves, we may be unable to solve them when we need to.

8. Chapter Summary

In this chapter we have discussed corporate social responsibility and corporate purpose. Through their usual operations, businesses provide benefits to society. But businesses are sometimes able to do more. Merck had a chance to do more in the 1970s by developing a drug to treat river blindness, and they took it. This decision cost Merck a lot of money. It probably would have been better for shareholders if Merck put this money into a drug to cure cancer, heart disease, or even baldness. The question we have asked in this chapter is whether Merck did the right thing in developing the drug to treat river blindness. We defined this as the issue of corporate social responsibility – whether businesses have a duty to benefit society, beyond their legal obligations, even at a cost to themselves.

The standard way of answering this question is by thinking about corporate purpose. What ends should businesses be trying to promote? One answer, given by Friedman, is that businesses should be run in the interests of their owners, which in the case of corporations (according to Friedman) are the shareholders. Shareholders want to maximize their profits, so this is what managers should be trying to do. Another answer, given by Freeman, is that businesses should be run in the interests of all of their stakeholders. Managers should balance the interests of shareholders, employees, suppliers, community members, and consumers. If shareholders' interests should be prioritized, then Merck probably made the wrong choice when it decided to develop the drug. If all stakeholders' interests should be balanced, then it is possible that Merck made the right choice.

Thinking about corporate purpose isn't the only possible way of thinking about whether firms like Merck should engage in acts of corporate social responsibility. We can also approach this problem by thinking about beneficence. You have a duty to help those in need – like the drowning child – no matter what your goals are, and even if fulfilling this duty imposes some costs on you. Similarly, it might be said, whatever a firm's goals are, it has a duty of beneficence, and this requires it to be socially responsible, even if fulfilling this duty impedes the achievement of its goals. We concluded by reflecting on CSR as a practice. Even if we think that it can be justified in some cases, we might worry about relying on corporations too heavily to solve social problems.

9. Study Questions

1. What is corporate social responsibility or CSR?
2. What is Friedman's ownership argument against CSR? What is his tax argument against CSR?

3. Many legal scholars think that shareholders don't really own corporations. Does this undermine Friedman's ownership argument? Why or why not?
4. If stakeholder theory is true, then what goal should managers of corporations be trying to achieve?
5. Some people think that the concept of "balance" is vague. Why is this a problem for stakeholder theory?
6. One argument that Freeman gives for stakeholder theory appeals to the veil of ignorance, an idea from John Rawls's political philosophy. Explain this argument. Do you think it succeeds?
7. What is one reason for thinking that stakeholder management will lead to superior corporate performance? What is one reason for thinking that it will not?
8. The debate about CSR doesn't have to be seen as a debate between shareholder and stakeholder theorists. It can also be seen as a debate about the nature and scope of the duty of beneficence. Explain how.
9. What might Friedman say about the Merck case? What might Freeman say? What do you think Merck should have done?
10. Do you think it's a good idea for businesses to make a habit of solving social problems? Explain and defend your answer.

Additional Readings

Business Roundtable. (2019, August 19). Business Roundtable redefines the purpose of a corporate to promote 'an economy that serves all Americans'. www.businessroundtable.org/business-roundtable-redefines-the-purpose-of-a-corporation-to-promote-an-economy-that-serves-all-americans

Freeman, R. E., & Reed, D. L. (1983). Stockholders and stakeholders: A new perspective on corporate governance. *California Management Review*, *25*(3), 88–106.

Friedman, M. (1970, September 13). The social responsibility of business is to increase its profits. *New York Times Magazine*, 32–33, 122–124.

Friedman, M., Mackey, J., & Rodgers, T. J. (2005, October). Rethinking the social responsibility of business. *Reason*. https://reason.com/2005/10/01/rethinking-the-social-responsi-2/

Hansmann, H., & Kraakman, R. (2001). The end of history for corporate law. *Georgetown Law Journal*, *89*(2), 439–468.

Merck. (2019, December 1). Over 30 years: The Mectizan donation program. www.merck.com/stories/mectizan/

Orts, E. W., & Strudler, A. (2009). Putting a stake in stakeholder theory. *Journal of Business Ethics*, *88*(4), 605–615.

Phillips, R., Freeman, R. E., & Wicks, A. C. (2003). What stakeholder theory is not. *Business Ethics Quarterly*, *13*(4), 479–502.

Singer, P. (1972). Famine, affluence, and morality. *Philosophy & Public Affairs*, *1*(3), 229–243.

Stout, L. A. (2002). Bad and not-so-bad arguments for shareholder primacy. *Southern California Law Review*, *75*(5), 1189–1210.

10 Business and Politics

Businesses engage in political activity. They support candidates for public office, lobby government officials, and take public stands on controversial issues. Should they? This is the question we will explore in this chapter. We begin by identifying some of the ways that businesses engage in political activity. Then we will see what can be said for and against this engagement. We conclude the chapter by considering a kind of political activity in which businesses are not themselves political actors but instead are targets of political activity. This is ethical consumerism.

1. Varieties of Corporate Political Activity

Let us begin by identifying some of the ways that businesses engage in political activity. As we move through the list, you might begin to doubt that the activities identified are properly described as "political." We'll address this issue briefly at the end.

1. *Money*. One thing that businesses do is support candidates for political office. In the U.S., businesses can't give money to candidates directly, but they can give to political action committees (PACs), and PACs can support candidates for office. It is also possible for businesses to give money to political parties, which can mobilize voters on behalf of candidates. In 2010, the U.S. Supreme Court decision *Citizens United v. Federal Election Commission* gave businesses the right to spend unlimited sums of money in support of political causes. Common vehicles for these expenditures are independent expenditure-only political action committees, known as "super-PACs." In 2018, the Las Vegas Sands Casino gave \$28 million to super-PACs in support of conservative causes, while Paloma Partners, an investment firm, gave \$23 million to liberal super-PACs.
2. *Speech*. In U.S. law, money is treated as speech. Giving money to PACs and political parties, and spending it on political advertisements, is protected by the legal right to freedom of speech. But there are ways that businesses engage in political activity through speech understood in the usual sense.

DOI: 10.4324/9781351016872-10

First, they lobby government officials. To lobby someone is to attempt to convince them, through speech, to do something. In the U.S., businesses spent approximately $3 billion lobbying the federal government in 2018. Large firms – especially those who do a lot of business with the government, like healthcare providers and defense contractors – employ dozens of full-time lobbyists. A second speech-related political activity businesses engage in is taking stands on controversial political issues. For example, the Corn Refiners Association (CFA) runs ads seeking to allay consumers' fears about the health risks of high fructose corn syrup. Following the mass protests and social unrest caused by the killings of George Floyd, Breonna Taylor, Ahmaud Arbery, and other black people in 2020, many companies released statements supporting Black Lives Matter.

3. *Exercising property rights*. Another way that businesses exert political power is through exercising their property rights. They can communicate information about what they will do with their property if certain laws are passed, or certain candidates are elected to public office. In 2010, the Indiana legislature passed the Religious Freedom Restoration Act, a law ostensibly designed to protect religious freedom. But there was a worry that some businesses would use this freedom to discriminate against LGBT people on religious grounds. In response, large companies like Salesforce and Angie's List cancelled plans to expand in the state and threatened to leave it altogether. Indiana responded by passing an amendment to the Act explicitly protecting LGBT people from discrimination.
4. *Self-regulation*. Businesses engage in self-regulation, sometimes individually but more often in groups. For a firm to self-regulate is for it to agree to abide by a certain set of rules – rules that are not promulgated by the state or other governing authority but by a private actor or set of private actors. A notable example is the Forest Stewardship Council (FSC). The FSC is an organization whose goal is to ensure that the world's forests are used responsibly. Its members include businesses, nongovernmental organizations, research institutes, and trade unions. To obtain FSC certification for products sourced from forests, including timber but also many kinds of paper products and packaging, a business must agree to follow certain rules, and not just the rules and regulations of the country they are operating in. They must respect indigenous people's rights to use forest lands and reduce the environmental impact of logging, among other things. Additional examples of self-regulation include the Roundtable on Sustainable Palm Oil (RSPO), the Extractive Industries Transparency Initiative (EITI), and the United Nations Global Compact (UNGC).
5. *Promoting the public welfare*. A final way that businesses engage in political activity is by promoting the public welfare. Of course, most businesses promote the public welfare simply by making things that people want to

> buy. But businesses can promote the public welfare directly through their charitable activities. In Chapter 9, we considered Merck's development and distribution of Mectizan, the drug for river blindness. You can understand this as a contribution to public health. Through its KidSmart Early Learning Program, IBM introduces young children in underserved communities to basic concepts in science and math. This can be understood as a contribution to public education. Walmart contributed to disaster relief when it mobilized its employees and leveraged its vast supply chain to assist victims of Hurricane Katrina in 2005.

All of these kinds of activity have been classified by scholars as "political activity." As we went along, however, you might have been less and less convinced that the activities in question are properly described as "political."

The first two – (1) giving money to political candidates and (2) speaking out in favor of controversial issues – strike most people as obviously political. When firms engage in (1) or (2), they are inserting themselves directly into the formal political process.

(3) Exercising property rights strikes some people as less obviously political. You might say that when businesses threaten to take action in response to a political decision, like the passage of a new law, they are doing things with their own property, and these actions primarily concern the business. But decisions like these have a political source – the passage of a law – and a political end – a change in the law. Indeed, they may have a greater political impact than giving money to a candidate for public office or speaking out in favor of a controversial issue.

The final activities – (4) engaging in self-regulation and (5) contributing to the public welfare – may seem even less like political activities. When companies self-regulate, they are just deciding on their own how they will behave. What is political about that? It's just, you might say, a private economic actor making a choice for itself. And why is it political when a corporation does something good for the public, like addressing pressing problems of public health or education? Isn't this just some helpful philanthropy?

These are good questions. Against them, however, it is worth observing, first, that (4) and (5) are things states normally do. States are the ones who make the rules that businesses follow, not businesses themselves. States are the ones who play a leading role in the provision of public health, education, and disaster relief. When businesses take on these roles, they are doing things states normally do, and for this reason their activities may be classified as political. We might also reflect, second, on what it means for an activity to be "political." You might think of politics as the process of deciding how to set up and run a society or other group. When businesses make rules for commerce and provide public goods to the masses, they are making decisions about how society is run. By this definition, businesses engage in political activity when they do this. You might also remember from Chapter 9 that one of Milton Friedman's objections to activities like (5) was that they were political expenditures that didn't result from democratic political processes.

You may still be skeptical, and your skepticism would be reasonable. These questions may not admit of definitive answers. 'Political' is a vague term, and there is disagreement about what it means. In the end, it does not matter too much whether every activity in our list, or only some of them, is properly described as political. The important question is whether businesses should engage in these activities. That is the question we will address.

Before moving on, a brief terminological note is in order. Political activity by businesses of the sort we have been talking about is typically referred to as "corporate political activity" or CPA. We will follow that practice. Strictly speaking, a corporation is an organization with a certain sort of legal structure. In doing so, we are not implying that we are interested in political activity by organizations with this legal structure. 'Corporate' in "corporate political activity" just means 'business'. When we speak of corporate political activity, or CPA, we mean political activity by businesses. This is the same allowance we made when speaking of "corporate social responsibility" in Chapter 9.

2. Corporate Political Activity That Makes the World a Better Place?

You might think that one reason to allow corporations to engage in political activity is that sometimes, when they do so, they make the world a better place.

In 2013, the Rana Plaza building in Bangladesh collapsed, killing more than 1100 workers and injuring hundreds more. (We will have more to say about this case in the next chapter.) In response, businesses came together to create guidelines for worker safety in Bangladesh. European companies created the Accord on Fire and Building Safety in Bangladesh, and North American companies created the Alliance for Bangladesh Worker Safety. The Alliance and Accord set standards that all companies in the garment industry in Bangladesh must adhere to if they want to supply goods to Western multinationals. They are examples of (4), self-regulation by businesses. The Alliance and Accord made things better in the garment industry in Bangladesh. To be sure, some Bangladeshi companies chafe under their restrictions. But the regulations seem to be doing what they were meant to do, which is to prevent another tragedy of the sort we saw at Rana Plaza.

We noted also that (5) providing for the public welfare can also be understood as a political activity. When Merck makes and distributes ivermectin for free to treat river blindness, it is improving public health. When IBM makes learning opportunities in science and technology available through its KidSmart program, it is contributing to public education.

We might even think that businesses do good when they engage in political activity by (1) contributing money to political campaigns, (2) lobbying politicians and regulators, and (3) exercising their property rights. Some political outcomes, you might say, are good, and when businesses help to bring them about, they are doing something good.

This argument has significant limitations. The main one is that there is disagreement about what is good. This might be obscured when we talk about political activity like (4) and (5). That there is disagreement about the good becomes clear, however, when we consider political activities like (1), (2), and (3). There are few candidates, laws, and regulations that everyone agrees on.

There is another, more general, issue here. When we understand instances of CPA as making the world a better place, we are understanding them as instances of corporate social responsibility, or CSR. Indeed, many scholars believe that these categories overlap. Some acts count as both CPA and CSR. This means that these acts of CPA can be evaluated as acts of CSR. So what we said for and against CSR in Chapter 9 can be said about these acts of CPA. We might defend these acts as necessary for balancing all stakeholders' interests or as required by the duty of beneficence. Alternatively, we might see them as misuses of the firm's money, which should be spent instead on increasing shareholders' wealth or as ill-conceived efforts to promote social ends by people who lack the relevant expertise. My point is not that we should approve or disapprove of these acts of CPA. It is simply that what we say about them will, in part, mirror what we said about CSR previously. Since we have already considered that debate, let us move on to consider distinctive reasons for and against CPA.

3. Corporate Political Activity and Private Interests: Against and For

The previous section was about businesses promoting the public good through political activity. You might have been thinking: "Ha! When businesses engage in political activity, they are promoting their own good, not society's." This claim might feature in simple arguments both for and against CPA. Let's begin with the simple argument against.

3.1. CPA and Private Interests: Against

Consider Jaguar Land Rover North America. They told the state of New Jersey that they were considering moving across the Hudson River to an office park in New York because their taxes were too high. This is type (3) political activity. New Jersey responded by offering them millions in tax breaks. Donald Trump ran for President of the U.S. in 2016 in part on a "get tough on China" platform. U.S. steel producers contributed to his campaign. This is type (1) political activity. When Trump was elected, he raised import taxes on steel from foreign countries, including China. This helped U.S. steel producers compete more effectively against their Chinese rivals.

Some critics say that political activity by businesses of these forms is "rent-seeking" behavior. "Rent," in this sense, is a term from economic theory. It is a sum of money in excess of the amount required to bring a factor of production to market. If I would work for my employer for $8 per hour, but she pays me $10 per hour, then I earn a rent of $2 per hour. Intuitively, the idea of a rent is "money for nothing." You would produce the same value for less money.

So the problem with political activity, according to this objection, is that it yields benefits for the business "for nothing." Businesses are able to get something from society without providing any additional benefit to it. Jaguar Land Rover North America provides benefits to the state of New Jersey by employing workers and paying taxes. Its political activity allowed it to pay less in taxes – that's the benefit to the company – without doing more in any other respect for the state. Chinese steel used to be less expensive than U.S. steel. After the Trump administration imposed tariffs on foreign steel, the price of Chinese steel increased. The U.S. steel industry received a benefit – they were able to sell more steel – but without providing an additional benefit to society. In fact, the benefit the U.S. steel industry received from the government came at the expense of others in the U.S., including appliance and car manufacturers, who now had to pay more for the steel they used in their factories.

It is not clear that this objection succeeds. One problem is that one person's private rent-seeking is another person's public benefit. While some claim that companies like Jaguar Land Rover North America are seeking rents when they ask for special tax breaks, others will claim that they are just trying to survive in a competitive market, and the state needs a healthy private sector to provide jobs. The U.S. steel industry recognizes that it is trying to protect itself from competition by foreign firms, and in the process, making U.S. customers pay more for steel. But they say that their foreign competitors receive unfair subsidies from their governments, and anyway, it's in the U.S.'s interests to have a thriving steel industry. In a time of war, we cannot depend on other countries for steel to make our weapons. In sum, the same policies that some decry as "rent-seeking" others say are necessary for promoting the public good. Of course, to say that a political activity by a corporation promotes the public welfare is not necessarily to say that it is justified. The point here is simply that activities that may be classified as rent-seeking may also be classified in other, more positive ways.

There is a deeper problem with the rent-seeking objection. Suppose that, when they engage in political activity, businesses are merely rent-seeking. So what? It is not clear that there is anything wrong with trying to get what you want, even at someone else's expense, when it comes to politics. It seems permissible for you to threaten to leave your town or state unless your taxes are lowered (not that it would do much good!), or to donate to a candidate for political office who shares your values, or to campaign for a subsidy for an industry in which you are employed. You might think that there is something wrong when *businesses* do these things – we'll consider some arguments for this conclusion in Section 6. Even if there is something wrong with this, however, it doesn't seem that what makes it wrong is that it is an instance of pursuing one's own interests in politics.

3.2. CPA and Private Interests: For

In the previous section we considered the suggestion that corporate political activity is wrong because when corporations engage in political activity, they are just trying to promote their own private interests. It might next be suggested that this fact actually provides a good reason for corporations to engage in political activity.

The U.S. steel industry helped itself out a lot when it successfully lobbied the Trump administration to impose tariffs on steel from China and other foreign producers. By making the competition's steel more expensive, U.S. companies were able to sell more of their own steel. Jaguar Land Rover North America was able to win millions in tax breaks from the state of New Jersey by threatening to move its operations to New York. U.S. corn processors like Archer Daniels Midland receive millions of dollars in subsidies, which they protect through aggressive lobbying and public relations efforts. These examples can be multiplied. They all show that engaging in political activity can make businesses a lot of money.

Is this a good argument for allowing corporations to engage in political activity – because it can make them richer and more successful? In a word: no. Just because something is in your interest, does not make it permissible for you to do. Suppose you are backing out of a parking spot and you hit a car behind you, breaking one of its headlights. Assuming no one saw you, it might be in your interest to speed away. But that doesn't make it right for you to speed away. The right thing to do is to leave a note with your contact information, admitting to what you did.

You might think that the fact that political activity can sometimes be in a firm's interest generates a permission for the firm to engage in that activity, because of the firm's other obligations. The obligation in question, it might be said, is the obligation to maximize profits for shareholders or perhaps simply to maintain the firm's prosperity. But an argument we made in our discussion of corporate social responsibility previously shows that this reasoning is incorrect. An obligation not to lose money, or to maintain prosperity, does not provide a blanket permission to do whatever it takes not to lose money or maintain prosperity. You still need to observe your moral obligations. You would not be permitted to burn down your competitor's factory, even if that would help you make money.

We have now considered some simple, but flawed, arguments for and against CPA. Now we turn to better reasons for and against political activity by businesses. We begin with an argument in defense of CPA, which appeals to freedom of expression.

4. Freedom of Expression

Here is something you might say in defense of CPA. Why *shouldn't* corporations be permitted to engage in political activity? In asking this question, you may be suggesting that the default position is that businesses should be permitted to engage in political activity, unless good reasons can be given for thinking they can't.

We might find some evidence for believing that this is the correct default position by thinking about who is permitted to engage in political activity in general. Consider yourself for a moment. Perhaps you engage in political activity. You may give money to political candidates or take public positions on controversial topics. You may exercise a modicum of political power through the exercise of your property rights and provide for the public welfare in your own small way. Is it permissible for you to do these things? Surely the answer is yes. We might understand these activities as protected by your freedom of expression, which is a foundational right in a democratic political system.

In fact, we might say that not only do you have a right to engage in political activity in these ways, it is a good thing when you exercise this right. People disagree about politics and, more generally, about how to live. J. S. Mill, whom we met back in Chapter 3, argued that the best way to make progress in this area is to hear a multitude of ideas and arguments. If we never hear opposing views, then we have no chance to correct beliefs of ours that are false. Even if we hold the correct belief, if it is never challenged, it will be held merely as a "dead dogma, not a living truth." When you engage in political activity, you add to public debate and help society to make progress.

So you – an individual – can engage in political activity. What about you together with others a group? You might wish to engage in political activity as part of a group because you think you can make a bigger difference if you coordinate your activity with like-minded others. In a society of any significant size, it can be hard for individuals to get their voices heard. It seems clear that it is permissible for groups to engage in political activity too. Consider nongovernmental organizations like the National Rifle Association (NRA), whose goal is to protect the right to own guns; the Sierra Club, whose goal is to protect natural and wild spaces; and the National Right to Life Committee (NRLC), whose goal is to end abortion. People will disagree about whether the goals these groups pursue are worth pursuing, but there is little doubt that they should be permitted to pursue them, and more specifically, that they are legitimate participants in the political arena. We can see their activity as justified in the same way that the political activity of individuals is justified, through the right to free expression and the value of that expression. Groups like the NRA, the Sierra Club, and the NRLC are simply tools that individuals use in order to express themselves more forcefully.

You can see where this is going. If groups like the NRA and the Sierra Club can engage in political activity, why not groups like Jaguar Land Rover North America and Archer Daniels Midland, that is, why not businesses? We understood the value of political activity by nongovernmental organizations, like the value of political activity by individuals, in terms of the right to and value of political expression. These groups are exercising a right that is fundamental in a democratic society and provide a benefit when they do so, insofar as they add new information and arguments to public debate. So, it might be said, do businesses when they engage in political activity.

In fact, you might think that businesses are especially important participants in the political arena. When politicians make laws, they need to do so with as much knowledge as possible about their impact. Businesses are a valuable source of this information. For example, we might as a society want to increase employment by creating job training programs. If so, we will need to hear from employers to know which skills are in short supply. Or we might want to reduce the rate of serious accidents in the construction industry. We need to hear from contractors to figure out how people get hurt and what we can do to make construction sites safer. Employers are not the only or necessarily the most objective sources of information. They may try to shade the truth in their favor. So policy-makers will want to consult other experts too, such as management consultants and university professors. But policy-makers would be foolish not to call on businesses to share what they know.

We have now presented a case for thinking that corporations should be permitted to engage in political activity. We think it is permissible for individuals like you and me, and groups like the NRA and the Sierra Club, to engage in political activity. They have a right to do so, and it is good, on the whole, when they exercise this right. It follows, it might be said, that businesses should also be able to engage in political activity. In the next two sections, we will consider arguments against this case.

5. Corporate Political Activity and Democracy: Power and Equality

The objections we will consider are variants of a single basic concern. That concern is that corporate political activity is a threat to democracy. The first variant focuses on power; the second focuses on representation.

Some corporations are large and powerful. If they want something done, they have ways to try to make it happen. As noted, when large corporations like Salesforce became convinced that Indiana's Religious Freedom Restoration Act (RFRA) would permit discrimination against LGBT people, they threatened to leave the state. The Indiana legislature responded by passing an amendment to the Act explicitly protecting LGBT people from discrimination.

It is quite possible that the point of the original Act was to allow discrimination against LGBT people on religious grounds. Some of the original supporters of the Act said that the amendment effectively undermined it. This goes to show the power of corporations. When they threatened the state with financial consequences, the state passed a law that the corporations wanted.

If you or I lived in Indiana, and we threatened to leave when the legislature passed the RFRA, the Indiana legislature would probably not have cared. This is a problem, it might be thought, because equality is central to democracy. The equality that is central to democracy is familiarly expressed in the principle of "one person one vote." But it shows up in other parts of the political process as well, like the right of all people to stand for political office, to join political groups, to express their political opinions, and to make their voices heard. When powerful players exert disproportionate influence in the democratic process, an inequality is created. This is what is problematic about CPA, it might be said. Businesses can exercise disproportionate power in the political process and undermine the ideal of equality at the heart of democracy.

This argument needs to be qualified, and some of its limitations need to be recognized. First, not all corporations are large and powerful. If a very small business declared that it might leave Indiana in response to the passage of the RFRA, this might be given the same attention as if you or I had made this threat, namely, very little. Second, some governments are larger than others. Suppose that the U.S. federal government passes a law similar to Indiana's RFRA. If Salesforce threatens to leave the U.S. (e.g., for Canada), the U.S. federal government might not pay much attention. Salesforce is a large business, but it is not that large. So the objection from democracy to corporate political activity, as articulated so far, doesn't apply to all corporations and all of their political activities but only some corporations in only some contexts. But that doesn't mean that the objection has little force. It may still be a potent objection in the contexts in which it does apply.

The problem, of course, is not just that some businesses have a lot of power. It is what they can do with this power. They can extract benefits from the state that others cannot. Jaguar Land Rover North America pays a lower rate of tax in New Jersey than Middletown Sprinkler Company, a small family-owned irrigation business. Why is this? The answer is that Jaguar Land Rover North America is powerful, and Middletown Sprinkler Company is not. The production of corn and sugar is heavily subsidized in the U.S., while the production of grapes and apples is not. Why is this? There are many possible reasons, but one of them is surely that corn and sugar growers are more organized and powerful than growers of grapes and apples. Disproportionate political power raises the specter of corruption. Those with more power are able to bend government officials to their will, while those with less power simply have to take what they get. Put another way, instead of being treated in an even-handed way by the state, the more powerful receive better treatment than the less powerful.

It might be claimed that this argument proves too much. Some businesses exercise disproportionate power in the political process. But that is true, it might be said, of some individuals and groups. It is true of the groups mentioned earlier, like the Sierra Club and the NRA. It is also true of wealthy individuals like Sheldon Adelson and Tom Steyer, two major donors to conservative (Adelson) and liberal (Steyer) causes. Because of their money, and the access and influence it buys them, these groups and individuals exercise far more political power than you or I. So if we object to political activity by businesses on the grounds that it undermines the ideal equality at the heart of democracy, we should object to political activity by groups like the NRA and individuals like Tom Steyer.

We might at this point run the argument the other way. That is, we might say that we *shouldn't* object to political activity by groups like the NRA and individuals like Tom Steyer. There is nothing wrong with what they do. It follows that there is nothing wrong with political activity by businesses, even large and powerful ones. So whatever the ideal of equality central to democracy requires, we might say, it doesn't require individuals like Tom Steyer, groups like the NRA, or businesses like Jaguar Land Rover North America to abstain from political activity.

Alternatively, we might hold the line. We might say that it is in fact wrong for certain individuals and groups, including businesses, to exercise so much power in the political process. The U.S. and other nations have laws that are designed to limit the influence of money – from all sources, not just businesses – in the political process. There are limitations on how much individuals and groups can give to candidates for political office, among other political causes. We might say that these limitations make sense and wish for even more severe limitations.

We need to be consistent in our thinking. If we are worried about disproportionate power, we should be just as worried about businesses as we are about other powerful political actors, like wealthy individuals and well-organized groups. If we are not worried about political activity by these actors, then perhaps we should not be so worried about political activity by businesses. We have identified what the stakes are in this debate but have not said where the balance of reasons lies. This matter calls for further reflection.

6. Corporate Political Activity and Democracy: Representation

In the previous section, we considered an objection to political activity by businesses that applies to other powerful actors. But some think that there is a problem with political activity by businesses specifically – a reason that businesses should stay out of politics that does not apply to individuals like Tom Steyer and groups like the NRA. The problem is one of representation.

Suppose we all belong to the university Scrabble club. If the club is democratic, then all of us – all members – should have a say in how the club is run, and our say must be equal in some sense. We should all be able to support candidates for club president and offer opinions about what the club should do, for example, what type of Scrabble boards and tiles to purchase, what dictionary to use, when to play, and so on. If our Scrabble club is very large – and why wouldn't it be? – individuals may band together into groups to get their voices heard. Suppose there is the "morning Scrabble group," or MSG, which tries to get the club to schedule its tournaments in the morning, and the "afternoon Scrabble group," or ASG, which tries to get the club to schedule its tournaments in the afternoon. The MSG and ASG support candidates for club office who are sympathetic to their positions and promote those positions in public debate.

Is it permissible for groups like the MSG and ASG to participate in political activity in the Scrabble club? It seems like the answer should be 'yes'. These groups are just collections of individual members of the club who come together based on their support for a particular view. The MSG and ASG represent their members' views in the political arena. We have agreed that it is permissible for individual members of the Scrabble club to engage in political activity. It likewise seems permissible for the MSG and ASG to do so, on behalf of those they represent.

Now suppose the Scrabble club is so large that small businesses have been set up inside of it to sell goods to members – things like boards, tiles, dictionaries, and alarm clocks. One of these businesses is "Clocks Etc," or CE, and they specialize in alarm clocks. If groups like the MSG and ASG should be able to participate in political activity within the club, should groups like CE be able to do so as well? CE might wish to lobby the club's leadership to schedule the tournaments early in the morning, thinking that this would boost the sale of alarm clocks. You might say 'yes'. If the MSG can advocate on behalf of its members for early start times, then CE should also be able to advocate on behalf of its members for early start times. The individual members of the Scrabble club, we agree, are permitted to engage in political activity. They should be able to do so, it might be said, through any groups to which they belong, whether these are advocacy groups like the MSG or businesses like the CE.

This line of argument has been challenged. Some argue that there is a crucial difference between groups like the MSG and businesses like CE. The difference is their representativeness. MSG is the collection of club members who have come together based on their preference for playing Scrabble in the morning. The whole point of the group is to raise awareness of and secure acceptance for this point of view in the club. So individuals join or leave the group based on their commitment to this view. Thus, when the MSG advocates early morning Scrabble tournaments, it can plausibly be said to be representing its members' views. This is not the case with CE. The point of CE is to make and sell alarm clocks, not to advocate a particular point of view. The members – owners and operators – of CE do not come together based on shared preferences, but for economic reasons. Very roughly, they come together to make money. Thus, when the CE advocates early morning Scrabble tournaments, they may not be representing the views of their members. Indeed, it is possible that most of CE's owners and operators prefer to play Scrabble in the afternoon. In this case, if CE were to advocate early morning Scrabble tournaments, it would give the wrong impression about its members' preferences.

The implications that our extended analogy has for the real world should already be clear. But let us make them explicit. In a society that is democratically run, individuals like you and me, and Sheldon Adelson and Tom Steyer, are legitimate participants in the political arena. A democratic society is one that is run by its members, and we are all members. Groups like the NRA and the Sierra Club are also legitimate participants in the political arena. This is because they represent, or speak on behalf of, individuals. But businesses like Archer Daniels Midland and Jaguar Land Rover North are not legitimate participants in the political arena, according to this line of reasoning, because they are not representative organizations. They exist to sell things and make money, not to promote a particular point of view.

You might object: if you work for a certain firm, and a certain political outcome is in your firm's economic interests, then isn't that outcome in your economic interests as well? So when the firm advocates that outcome, isn't it speaking on your behalf? Not necessarily. People are complicated, and the outcome that benefits their employer, or even themselves, financially is not necessarily going to be the outcome that they think is best, all things considered. It might be to the advantage of Raytheon Technologies if the U.S. goes to war with Iran. If it does, the U.S. is likely to buy more weapons from Raytheon Technologies, and this will be good for the bottom line. But that hardly means that all of the employees of Raytheon Technologies think it would be good for the U.S. to go to war with Iran (or anyone else). Besides this, the political causes that a firm supports will not necessarily be connected with its economic self-interest. We noted that, in 2018, the Las Vegas Sands Casino gave $28 million to super-PACs in support of conservative causes, while Paloma Partners, an investment firm, gave $23 million to liberal causes. This has more to do with the politics of the people who control these organizations than any economic benefits that the firms would get from certain political results.

Next you might object that certain firms have deliberately cultivated political identities, and workers and investors embrace those identities when they associate with them. The fast-food restaurant Chick-fil-A has a religious and socially conservative identity. Its corporate purpose is "to glorify God by being a faithful steward of all that is entrusted to us and to have a positive influence on all who come into contact with Chick-fil-A." Until recently, it gave money to political groups that opposed same-sex marriage. You might say that, in supporting these groups, Chick-fil-A was speaking on behalf of its members, including its owners and employees. The ice cream maker Ben & Jerry's has a progressive identity. Among the issues it cares about, and takes action on, are racial justice, democracy, and GMO labeling. When Ben & Jerry's supports liberal causes, you might think that they too are speaking on behalf of their members. But there is reason for skepticism about these conclusions. In any large business, not every member will accept the business's purpose or values, and not everyone who accepts them will understand them in the same way. Many Christians see no problem with same-sex marriage, and people disagree about what actions promote social justice. So even Chick-fil-A and Ben & Jerry's are imperfect speakers on behalf of their members. And these businesses are atypical. Most businesses have no explicit political or social identity and have no claim to speak on behalf of their members at all.

As a final objection, what about the idea, mentioned earlier, that businesses have specialized knowledge, which is valuable in the political process? If we tell businesses to stay out of politics, because they aren't representative organizations, or because they are too powerful, then we risk closing off a valuable source of information for policy-makers and making society worse off.

In theory, there is a simple solution to this problem. Allow businesses to be involved in the political process, but tell them simply to provide information without promoting a particular point of view. This solution will be difficult to implement in practice, however. If a business is welcomed into the political process, it may try to highlight information that advances its own interests and downplay information that doesn't. This is not because businesses are especially bad actors in the political sphere. It is simply because they are made up of human beings with ordinary human inclinations.

7. Ethical Consumerism

So far in this chapter we have been considering political activity by businesses, identifying and examining reasons for and against allowing businesses to engage in politics. But there is another way that businesses can be involved in politics. They can be the target of political activity by consumers. Consumers can choose to buy, or choose not to buy, goods from firms based on political considerations.

We mentioned Chick-fil-A's religious and socially conservative identity. This identity derives from the commitments of its founder, S. Truett Cathy. In a radio interview in 2012, Dan Cathy, son of S. Truett and current CEO of Chick-fil-A, said that the company was "very much supportive of the family – the biblical definition of the family unit." He went on: "I think we are inviting God's judgment on our nation when we shake our fist at him and say, 'We know better than you as to what constitutes a marriage'." These statements, combined with Chick-fil-A's previous donations to religious groups, especially ones that opposed same-sex marriage, ignited a firestorm. LGBT rights groups and their allies organized a boycott of Chick-fil-A. They encouraged local governments not to grant licenses to new Chick-fil-A restaurants. Students at some universities led efforts to keep the restaurant chain off of their campuses. In response to these protests, other groups organized counter-protests. Mike Huckabee, former Governor of Arkansas, declared August 1, 2012, "Chick-fil-A Appreciation Day," encouraging his followers on social media to eat at Chick-fil-A in support of its values.

Consumers normally decide which goods to buy on the basis of factors like quality and price. When they make consumer choices on the basis of moral or political considerations, as some did in the case of Chick-fil-A, this is known as "ethical consumerism." In this section, we consider what can be said for and against ethical consumerism. Some of the arguments we will consider will be familiar from our critical examination of CPA.

Before beginning, let me address a possible terminological confusion. We have been talking about corporate *political* activity. Now we are talking about *ethical* consumerism. Aren't politics and ethics different? Well, yes. But ethical consumerism has a lot in common with corporate political activity. When people make consumer choices for ethical reasons, they are trying to bring about an outcome that can reasonably be described as political. They are trying to change the way businesses operate in society. One way to do this is to change economic laws and regulations. Another way is to apply economic pressure to businesses. The latter is what ethical consumers do. In the case of Chick-fil-A, they are trying to prohibit corporate donations to political groups opposed to same-sex marriage. Consumers who boycotted Nike in the 1990s were trying to get Nike to change its labor standards for foreign suppliers. Ethical consumerism can be understood as political activity of type (3), that is, an attempt to influence political outcomes through the exercise of property rights.

7.1. A Permission to Ethically Consume?

The first thing you might say is: "Is there really a problem here?" You might be thinking people should be able to buy what they want, for whatever reason they want. We might recognize that some goods – goods like kidneys and drop-side cribs – should not be for sale. But if something is legitimately for sale, you might think, then people should be able to buy it, and it doesn't matter why they buy it. If people want to make consumer choices based on ethical considerations, then they are permitted to do so.

We can support this conclusion by thinking back to the justification of the market in Chapter 4. "The market" is just another way of referring to voluntary exchanges of property. One reason to allow people to engage in these exchanges derives from the concept of a property right. What it means to own a thing is to have a bundle of rights with respect to that thing. That includes, you might say, exchanging that thing for some other thing for ethical reasons. Another reason to allow people to engage in exchanges of property has to do with freedom. It is good if people are able to live their lives as they please, again within limits. We don't think that people should be permitted to do anything they want, like assault or defraud others. But we might say that people should be allowed to make consumer choices in accord with their ethical beliefs. Indeed, we might think that this is an especially important form of freedom.

This last claim can be sharpened by reflecting on what we might say about a person who didn't consume ethically, at least sometimes. Consider Fred, who is in a loving and fulfilling same-sex marriage. Fred also eats regularly at Chick-fil-A. Chick-fil-A is (or at least was, until recently) contributing to organizations that oppose same-sex marriage and who think that Fred's relationship is sinful. We might say that Fred is complicit in the production of outcomes that are, by his lights, bad. When he purchases food at Chick-fil-A, he gives them some of his money, some of which goes to organizations that are working to undermine the legitimacy of his marriage. We might also say that Fred lacks integrity. We encountered this concept in Chapter 8 in our discussion of whistleblowing. There we said that while "integrity" is sometimes used loosely to mean "committed to truth or ethics," it is more precisely defined in terms of "wholeness." If a person has integrity, his actions are aligned with his values. Fred's aren't. His actions promote an outcome that is inconsistent with his professed values. Fred can avoid complicity in what he regards as bad outcomes, and preserve his integrity, only by consuming ethically, which means stopping eating at Chick-fil-A. For this reason, we might recognize the permission to consume ethically as an especially important kind of permission.

Remember that, in addition to the rights- and freedom-based justifications of markets, there is also a welfare-based justification. Societies that allocate productive resources mostly by markets tend to have a higher standard of living than societies that allocate productive resources mostly by planning. One of the reasons has to do with incentives. If you can satisfy people's needs and wants better than others – say by making better products or lowering their cost, or both – you can make a lot of money. Another reason has to do with information. When the prices of goods are set by the forces of supply and demand – that is, through people's voluntary exchanges – this directs resources to their most valuable uses, as determined by people's wants.

Now consider what happens to this justification when people start making consumer choices based on ethical considerations. Instead of having an incentive to produce higher quality, lower-price goods, businesses have an incentive to adopt certain ethical values. Productive resources will be directed to their most productive uses, not simply as measured by what people want, but as measured by what they want *and* what they think is ethically right. You might think this is fine. People are still getting what they want; it's just that what they want is informed by a combination of their ethical and non-ethical preferences. What will be produced in this market is not the tastiest chicken sandwich, but the tastiest chicken sandwich that morality allows. We might worry, however, that this kind of market comes up short. It makes us less well off, in a certain respect, than we could have been.

Even if the welfare-based justification of ethical consumerism fails – and it may not – there is still the rights- and freedom-based justifications. The freedom-based justification is especially important, given its connection to personal integrity. If we say that in general people should be allowed to exchange their property for other people's property, within broad limits, then it seems that we should say that people should be allowed to exchange their property for other people's property *for ethical reasons*, within the same limits. So far, ethical consumerism seems permissible.

7.2. A Positive Reason to Ethically Consume?

You might think that we can go beyond simply a permission to consume ethically. Ethical consumerism is a way to bring pressure on businesses to change their behavior. If a business is doing something wrong, and people stop making purchases from it in response, then the business may stop. Similarly, a business may start doing the right thing if it believes that it will cause consumers to buy its products. In this way, ethical consumerism can make the world a better place. You might say that this gives people a positive reason to consume ethically, not just a permission to do so.

In the following discussion we will focus on "negative" ethical consumerism, or choosing not to spend money at a business for ethical reasons. There is of course "positive" ethical consumerism, which is choosing to spend money at a business for ethical reasons. These are two sides of the same coin. Money spent at one business is money not spent at another business. We focus on negative ethical consumerism for the sake of simplicity only.

In response to the claim that ethical consumerism can make the world a better place, two things can be said. First, boycotts and other consumer actions against businesses don't often work. The reason is that these are collective action problems. In a collective action problem, the interests of a group do not align with the interests of each of its members. For a boycott to work, everyone or almost everyone has to participate. But if everyone is participating, then it won't matter if you don't. You can "defect" and make a purchase from the target of the boycott. Now suppose that no one or almost no one is participating in the boycott. Then it won't make a difference if you don't participate. So whatever everyone else is doing, it is in your interest to defect. This logic is available not just to you but to every consumer. So it is in the interest of every individual consumer to defect, whatever anyone else is doing. But since the group is just the collection of its members, the boycott is likely to fail. (After Dan Cathy's controversial 2012 interview, Chick-fil-A did stop contributing to organizations that opposed same-sex marriage. But it is unclear that the boycott forced them to do so, since the boycott may not have cost them any money, as a result of the counter-boycott.)

Second, and more importantly, for any policy or action that some people think is bad, others will think it is good. The Chick-fil-A case provides a prime example. Many people think same-sex marriage should be permissible and that there is nothing wrong with same-sex relationships. But other people think same-sex marriage should not be permissible and that there is something wrong with same-sex relationships. Some people thought the labor standards Nike asked its foreign suppliers to adhere to in the 1990s were deficient. Others thought they were acceptable. These examples can be multiplied. The point is this. To say that people have a reason to engage in ethical consumerism because they can bring about good outcomes is to assume that these outcomes really are good. But in a pluralistic society, people will disagree about what outcomes are good. This is not to say that there is no reason to bring about good outcomes. It is only to say that, for any given instance of ethical consumerism, we cannot say to everyone's satisfaction that it brings about a good outcome.

7.3. Concerns About Ethical Consumerism

We have considered the case for thinking that ethical consumerism is permissible, and that there may be reasons to consume ethically, at least on some occasions. Now let's consider what can be said against it. Several worries come to mind.

The first derives from our description of ethical consumerism. We said that it is a form of political activity. Instead of trying to change how businesses operate in society through the political process, consumers use economic pressure to achieve this result. You might find this objectionable in itself. Political outcomes, you might say, should be achieved through the formal political process, which is designed to get input from many different voices. This might not be a problem if consumers could not exercise much power. But they can. So you might further object to certain instances of ethical consumerism as exercises of disproportionate political power. To be sure, compared to a business, any single consumer typically isn't very powerful. But when consumers unite – and thanks to social media, they can unite quickly in large numbers – they can exercise enormous power. Over 600,000 people RSVP-ed 'yes' to Governor Huckabee's counter-boycott of Chick-fil-A. Even if only a fraction of these people showed up, this represents a significant boost to Chick-fil-A's daily sales.

A second and related concern about ethical consumerism is that it can be a form of mob justice. We have been understanding ethical consumerism as an attempt to change the way businesses operate in society. But it is also plausible to understand it as an attempt by some consumers to *punish* businesses for engaging in behavior that they think is wrong. LGBT activists and their allies meant to punish Chick-fil-A for its CEO's statements about same-sex marriage and its history of contributions to groups hostile to LGBT rights. The punishment they meant to inflict was financial. They wanted to prevent Chick-fil-A from opening new stores and otherwise reduce its revenues.

Punishment is serious. It should not be imposed without sufficient justification. When it is imposed, the punishment should fit the crime. Perhaps the punishment that LGBT activists inflicted fit Chick-fil-A's crime. Perhaps it didn't. Perhaps Chick-fil-A committed no crime. The mob can't be relied upon to make these judgments accurately. It acts from a sense of moral outrage. Mob justice is therefore imperfect. In the actual criminal justice system, people who are outraged by certain events don't get to decide who should suffer for them and how much they should suffer. That job is given to professionals within the system, neutral parties who have received extensive training and are bound by clear rules. They are more likely to bring about just results than a mob.

This brings us to a third concern about ethical consumerism: it can harm innocent parties. (This same concern arises for divestment movements, considered in the next chapter.) LGBT activists meant to impose harm on Chick-fil-A because of the statements of its CEO and its donations to groups hostile to LGBT rights. Just one person is responsible for the statements, and at most a handful of people are responsible for the donations. But the harm was imposed on the company as a whole. If the company is forced to close stores as a result of the boycott, the CEO and other executives may suffer some small penalty. Their pay may go down slightly. The people who will suffer the most are the minimum or near-minimum wage workers who lose their jobs. Even if they share the views of Chick-fil-A's CEO and other executives, they aren't responsible for the actions that are said to merit the boycott.

A fourth and final problem with ethical consumerism is a social one. Imagine if you tried to be a thoroughgoing ethical consumer, and made all of your consumer decisions based on ethical considerations. If you are a liberal, you might make all of your purchases from liberal-leaning firms, that is, firms with mostly liberal executives or who make business decisions that promote liberal values. If you are a conservative, you might make all of your purchases from conservative-leaning firms, that is, firms with mostly conservative executives or who make decisions that promote conservative values. Would that help to make your society better or worse?

You might say: it makes my society better, because it makes it more likely that a certain set of values – my values – will be the dominant ones. It is true that ethical consumers can change society by using economic pressure to change the way that businesses operate in it. If you have enough economic resources on your side, your values may indeed come to dominate.

But there is reason to think that a thoroughgoing ethical consumerism of the sort we have just described could make society worse. The 18th-century French writer Voltaire said, on a visit to England:

> Take a view of the Royal Exchange in London, a place more venerable than many courts of justice, where the representatives of all nations meet for the benefit of mankind. There the Jew, the Mahometan and the Christian transact together as though they all professed the same religion, and give the name of infidel to none but bankrupts.

Voltaire was observing that business brings different kinds of people together. In doing so, they learn how to live harmoniously with each other, despite their differences. This is a good thing, since there really is no other choice. It is unlikely that you will find a society where everyone shares all of your beliefs. The worry about ethical consumerism is that it allows or even encourages people to segregate themselves according to their differences. Instead of pushing out in shared spaces, doing business with conservatives and liberals, ethical consumers retreat into their separate spheres, doing business only with people who share their values. Business can help us get along with each other; ethical consumerism might do the opposite.

8. Chapter Summary

In this chapter we considered business and political activity. Most of our attention was focused on political activity *by* businesses. This is known as corporate political activity or CPA. We noted that it comes in various forms. Businesses (1) support candidates for public office, (2) take public positions on controversial issues, (3) exercise their property rights to influence political outcomes, (4) engage in self-regulation, alone and together with others, and (5) provide public goods.

We then considered some simple arguments for and against allowing businesses to engage in political activity that appeal to what businesses aim to do. According to one, when businesses engage in political activity, they sometimes make the world a better place. This argument has a limited scope, however, since there is disagreement about what makes the world better. It is perhaps more common to claim that, when they engage in political activity, businesses aim to promote their private interests. Some criticize this behavior as "rent-seeking," but it is not clear that it is wrong for a group, including a business, to promote its interests in the political sphere.

A better argument for CPA appeals to free expression. In a democratic society, its members should have an equal say in deciding how it is set up and run. This is guaranteed in part by the right to free expression, the exercise of which is also valuable. When people add their voices to public debate, they introduce new information that can help governments to make wise choices. In a society of any size, individuals naturally band together into groups to make their voices heard. If groups like the NRA and the Sierra Club are legitimate participants in the political sphere, some claim, then so are businesses like Archer Daniels Midland and Jaguar Land Rover North America.

Reflecting on democratic ideals leads some to conclude that it is permissible for businesses to engage in political activity. But it leads others to conclude that it is impermissible. One worry is about equality. Due to their size and wealth, some businesses can exercise disproportionate power in the political process. So their political activity presents a challenge to the ideal of equality at the heart of democracy. This worry applies not just to businesses, but to wealthy individuals and groups. Some believe, however, that there is a special problem with businesses being involved in politics. The problem is that they are not representative organizations in the way that groups like the NRA and the Sierra Club are. When businesses speak or otherwise participate in the political arena, they may not be speaking on behalf of their members.

We concluded the chapter by discussing another kind of political activity – political activity whose target is businesses. This is known as ethical consumerism. Ethical consumers make consumer choices for ethical reasons and, in doing so, aim to change the way that businesses operate in society. You might say that consumers have a right to consume ethically, because it is their money, and if they want to buy goods for ethical reasons, they have a right to do so. But we identified some concerns about the practice of consuming ethically. It can be a source of unaccountable, disproportionate political power. It can be a kind of mob justice. Ethical consumers can end up punishing the "innocent" along with the "guilty." Finally, ethical consumerism threatens to weaken or eliminate the power that business has to bring together people with different views. In certain circumstances, we may be permitted or even required to consume ethically, but careful reflection is required.

9. Study Questions

1. This chapter identified five kinds of corporate political activity. Which ones do you think are the most common? Which cause you the most concern?
2. You might say that businesses should be permitted to engage in political activity because when they do, they can help make the world a better place. What might someone say in response to you?
3. What does it mean to say that, in the political arena, businesses are "rent-seekers"? Are they? If so, is this a problem?

4. Freedom of expression is thought to be a right as a well as a value in a democratic society. What does this mean?
5. Some businesses are powerful. How might this fact be used to argue that political activity by these businesses is wrong?
6. In what way is a business such as Jaguar Land Rover North America unlike a group such as the Sierra Club?
7. Do you think Jaguar Land Rover North America did something wrong when they told the state of New Jersey that they would be moving to New York unless they received tax incentives? Or is this behavior permissible?
8. What is ethical consumerism?
9. Why might consuming ethically be a matter of personal integrity for some people?
10. Do you think the boycott of Chik-fil-A was justified? Explain and defend your answer. Are there any other businesses that you think deserve to be boycotted? Are there any that you think deserve to be supported?

Additional Readings

Boatright, J. R. (2009). Rent seeking in a market with morality: Solving a puzzle about corporate social responsibility. *Journal of Business Ethics*, *88*(4), 541–552.

Christiano, T. (2010). The uneasy relationship between democracy and capital. *Social Philosophy and Policy*, *27*(1), 195–217.

Hussain, W. (2012). Is ethical consumerism an impermissible form of vigilantism? *Philosophy and Public Affairs*, *40*(2), 111–143.

Hussain, W., & Moriarty, J. (2018). Accountable to whom? Rethinking the role of corporations in political CSR. *Journal of Business Ethics*, *149*(3), 519–534.

Ostas, D. T. (2007). The law and ethics of K Street: Lobbying, the First Amendment, and the duty to create just laws. *Business Ethics Quarterly*, 33–63.

Schwartz, D. T. (2017). *Consuming choices* (2nd ed.). Lanham, MD: Rowman & Littlefield.

Sepinwall, A. J. (2012). Citizens United and the ineluctable question of corporate citizenship. *Connecticut Law Review*, *44*(3), 575–615.

Severson, K. (2012). Chick-fil-A thrust back into spotlight on gay rights. *New York Times*. www.nytimes.com/2012/07/26/us/gay-rights-uproar-over-chick-fil-a-widens.html

Stark, A. (2010). Business in politics: Lobbying and corporate campaign contributions. In G. G. Brenkert & T. L. Beauchamp (Eds.), *The Oxford handbook of business ethics* (pp. 501–534). New York: Oxford University Press.

Swiatek, J. (2015, April 2). Salesforce packed a punch in galvanizing RFRA opposition. *IndyStar*. www.indystar.com/story/money/2015/04/02/salesforce-packed-punch-galvanizing-rfra-opposition/70842680/

11 Business Ethics Across Borders

In this chapter we consider ethical issues that arise when business is done across borders. Some of the issues that we will consider are peculiar to international business ethics. Others are familiar from earlier chapters. But in the international context these issues gain added significance, as we will see, so more focused discussion is required.

1. The Garment Industry in Bangladesh

The labels in your clothes might be from famous companies in the Western world. But often, those clothes are made by factories in developing countries, where labor is cheap. One of the countries with especially cheap labor is Bangladesh.

Western multinationals – major retailers like H&M, Walmart, and The Gap – do not make clothes. They design clothes, and they contract out their manufacturing to factories in places like Bangladesh. The working conditions in these factories are very poor.

Workers often work 12 or more hours per day and 6 or more days per week. They spend most of this time bent over sewing machines in hot, crowded spaces with poor ventilation. Despite the difficulty of their work, they are paid very little for it. The average monthly wage of a worker in the garment industry in Bangladesh is a mere 95 US dollars. The cost of living in Bangladesh is of course very low, but by some calculations a true living wage in the country – a wage that is sufficient for the worker to meet her basic needs and provide adequate support for her dependents – is in excess of 200 US dollars per month. Safety precautions are often ignored. Factory owners have been known to lock exit doors to ensure that workers do not steal merchandise. This is cheaper than installing cameras or hiring security guards. But when fires break out, as they sometimes do, this has deadly results.

One of the worst industrial accidents in recent history occurred in Bangladesh. On April 24, 2013, the Rana Plaza building collapsed, killing more than 1100 workers and injuring hundreds more. Rana Plaza was a poorly built structure, being used for a purpose for which it was not designed. Workers had

DOI: 10.4324/9781351016872-11

complained about cracks in the building's walls the day before it collapsed, but the owner insisted that the building was safe and ordered them to keep working. When the power went out in the district, the building's generators came on. The structure could not handle the strain and the building imploded, burying thousands of workers under thousands of tons of concrete.

People sometimes complain about working conditions in developed countries. They will say that workers don't get paid enough or that their working conditions are unpleasant or unsafe. You may have made complaints like this about your own jobs. These complaints may be justified. But it is clear that the working conditions in places like Bangladesh are much worse. U.S. workers get paid a lot more than their Bangladeshi counterparts. Retail workers in the U.S. – who are among the lowest-paid U.S. workers – work on average 30 hours per week and make a bit less than $30,000 per year. U.S. workplaces are both more pleasant and safer than Bangladeshi workplaces. Building and fire codes, among other regulations, are much stricter and enforced much more rigorously in the U.S. If you were a low-wage worker, you would be a lot better off in the U.S. than in Bangladesh.

2. Cultural Relativism

What should we make of the working conditions in factories in Bangladesh? What should we say about them compared to the working conditions in American workplaces? You might grant that working conditions in Bangladesh are different than working conditions in the U.S. But, you might also say, this is merely a difference, and not a wrong. In making this point, you might be making a general point about morality and culture. You might be claiming that morality is relative to culture. This view is called "cultural relativism," and in this section we critically examine it.

2.1. What Is Cultural Relativism?

According to cultural relativism, the right thing to do in a culture is what the culture thinks is right, which depends on what is normal and acceptable in the culture. The wrong thing to do in a culture is what the culture thinks is wrong, which depends on what is abnormal or unacceptable in the culture. On this view, there is no "extra-cultural" standard of rightness, and so no making sense of the claim that the practices of some cultures are superior to those of others. Bangladesh has its way of doing things, and that way is right for the people of Bangladesh, and the U.S. has its way of doing things, and that way is right for the people of the U.S. We can say that Bangladesh and the U.S. do things differently when it comes to labor standards. But we cannot say that one culture's way of doing things is better than another culture's way of doing things. That would imply the existence of a standard of rightness that exists outside of a particular culture, and according to cultural relativism, no such standard exists.

In Chapter 2 we considered various skeptical hypotheses about ethics. We considered the ideas that ethical statements are all false or do not try to express a statement that is true or false. You might think that cultural relativism is just one more kind of skepticism about morality. But we need to be careful here. Cultural relativists agree with skeptics that there is no objective or universal morality, or morality that is external to or independent of culture. But cultural relativists do not say that there is *no* morality. They think that morality exists and is culture-dependent. What is morally right in a certain culture depends on the actual practices of that culture, and this can differ across cultures. If cultural relativism had a slogan, it might be "When in Rome, do as the Romans."

Cultural relativism has, at least at first glance, some appealing features. First, it does a good job of accounting for differences in moral beliefs and practices. The fact is, there are differences – across time and place – in what people think is morally permissible, and these differences seem to be culturally based. Right now in the U.S., most people would say plural marriage – a marriage featuring one man and multiple women, or one woman and multiple men – is wrong. But plural marriage used to be common around the world and in fact is still practiced in certain parts of Africa and the Middle East today. To take another example, for a long time in human history, most people thought slavery was a normal part of life. Your tribe conquered another tribe in a battle, and of course you would take the people you conquered as your slaves. Now, of course, almost everyone thinks that slavery is abhorrent.

These differences are largely differences *among* cultures, not *within* cultures. In general, people in the same culture have similar beliefs about morality. The cultural relativist accounts for this fact by tying morality to culture. Moreover, the cultural relativist has an explanation for why there is disagreement among cultures about morality, namely, there is no standard of moral rightness outside of the culture to constrain a culture's choice of morality. Cultures have the freedom to choose different ways of living, and different cultures make different choices.

Another thing about cultural relativism that seems attractive is its apparently "non-judgmental" attitude toward other cultures. The world is full of different people and different ways of doing things. You might think that the correct attitude to have about people who do things differently than you is tolerance. Some cultures think plural marriage is an acceptable way of living, and other cultures think it is unacceptable. Bangladesh has adopted certain standards when it comes to labor conditions, and the U.S. has adopted other standards. You might think that we shouldn't judge how other people live their lives or arrange their economies. You might further think that we shouldn't interfere with how other people choose to live. "Live and let live," you might say.

Cultural relativism seems in tune with this sort of worldview. Suppose you got a B+ on your last exam. Your friend got a C+. This means that you got most of the answers correct, and your friend got fewer answers correct. But suppose that there were no correct answers. There are just the answers that you gave, the answers that your friend gave, the answers that other people gave, and so on. Then we couldn't judge that your friend did worse on the exam than you. Cultural relativism says that when we compare the morality of two different societies, there are no correct answers. The morality of one society cannot be better or worse than that of another; it can only be different. If there is no external standard, then judgment about the relative superiority of one society over another is impossible. Cultural relativism seems to provide support for the idea that we should not judge. We should live and let live.

2.2. Criticisms of Cultural Relativism

Should we accept cultural relativism? The features that make it seem attractive at first may not be so attractive upon closer inspection.

Consider first the idea that it does a good job of accounting for differences in moral beliefs and practices. Moral beliefs and practices do seem culturally determined. The culture you are born in seems to determine, in large part, your beliefs about morality. Since people are born into different cultures, it is no surprise that people have different beliefs about morality.

This line of reasoning is confused. In particular, it confuses explanation with truth. The fact that people are born in different places and at different times might explain why people have different beliefs about morality, but it doesn't prove those beliefs are true. The fact that you were born into a society where plural marriage is common and accepted and I was born into a society where it is neither common nor accepted may explain why you believe what you do about plural marriage and I believe what I do about plural marriage. But it does not prove that you are right to think what you do about it and that I am right to think what I do about it.

Many beliefs are "culturally determined," in the sense that they are the product of a certain time and place. But we shouldn't think that, because a belief is culturally determined, it is true – or just as true as a different, contradictory culturally determined belief. Consider beliefs about the shape of the world. People born into societies in which everyone thinks the world is flat will probably think the world is flat, and people born into societies in which everyone thinks the world is a sphere will probably think the world is a sphere. We can easily explain why people believe what they do in these societies. This is what everyone around them believes, and this is what they have been told by their parents and teachers. But this doesn't mean that what people in flat earth societies believe about the shape of the world is true, or just as true as what people in the spherical earth societies believe about the shape of the world. Indeed, it seems quite clear that people in flat earth societies are wrong. We don't need to blame them for being wrong. It may not be their fault that they are wrong. But they are still wrong.

The same goes for beliefs about morality. Culture may explain why people believe what they do. But culture doesn't prove that those beliefs are true. As the case of beliefs about the shape of the world shows, a belief may be culturally based but false.

But are beliefs about morality *really like* beliefs about the shape of the world? Are there objective moral facts in the way that there are objective scientific facts? If so, why is there a greater diversity of moral beliefs than scientific beliefs? Engagement with these questions would take us back to the kind of skepticism about ethics we discussed in Chapter 2. Let's not repeat ourselves, but instead remind ourselves of two things. First, you probably already think that there are some objective moral facts. For example, if your teacher assigned grades at random, without assessing your work, you would think that is wrong – really, objectively wrong. Second, standards of proof in ethics are different than standards of proof in science. We should not conclude that there are no moral facts because we cannot prove them in the same way that we prove scientific facts.

The other feature of cultural relativism that people find attractive is its apparently non-judgmental nature. Cultural relativism says that there is no objective moral truth, and one culture's moral beliefs are not better or worse than any other culture's, so we should just live and let live. That is, we should tolerate those who think differently than us.

Tolerance is an attractive ideal. Social media is filled with self-important people judging others for how they live, often without understanding. It might seem like a good idea to avoid this sort of behavior. "Judge not," says the Bible. But this advice is not implied by cultural relativism. Indeed, it is inconsistent with it. Cultural relativists say that the right thing to do in a society is what the society thinks is right. So cultural relativists would say that you should tolerate others if, in your society, it is considered right to tolerate others, that is, if tolerance is normal and acceptable in your society. But they would say that you should *not* tolerate others if, in your society, it is considered wrong to tolerate others, that is, if tolerance is abnormal or unacceptable in your society. To claim that we should tolerate others is to make an objective moral claim. It is to claim that we should tolerate others, period, without checking to see what is normal in our society. To make a claim like this is to commit yourself to an objective morality.

In the previous section, we considered arguments in favor of cultural relativism. Now we have seen that these arguments are problematic. We also reminded ourselves that we tend to think that there are at least some objective moral truths. What now?

Should we conclude that there is a single true morality for everyone and all times, which must be expressed in the same rules for everyone? If that is true, then the U.S.'s labor standards and Bangladesh's labor standards both cannot be morally acceptable, because they are different. Perhaps they both are wrong, but they both cannot be right.

This view – call it ethical absolutism – may seem just as unattractive as cultural relativism. We might reject the idea that whatever a culture does is right for that culture. We might think that some things, like slavery and forced labor, are always wrong, whether or not they are culturally accepted. But we might be reluctant to think that everyone should live by the very same set of moral rules. Plural marriage isn't accepted in our culture, but perhaps it is not wrong for everyone. The labor standards in Bangladesh would not be accepted in the U.S., but perhaps they are not wrong for Bangladesh.

2.3. A Middle Path

One prominent view in business ethics tries to strike a balance between cultural relativism and ethical absolutism. The contemporary American business ethicists Thomas Donaldson and Thomas Dunfee support an "integrative social contracts" approach to business ethics. The contract they describe is hypothetical. It is a set of rules for business activity that they think all businesspeople would agree to upon reflection, given the chance. On their view, there are certain moral rules – they call them "hypernorms" – that all business activity must adhere to. These are minimum standards and include rules against such things as lying, promise-breaking, and corruption. Above this minimum, businesspeople have "moral free space" to decide how to act. Businesspeople cannot do just anything they want, however. Their actions must be informed by relevant social and economic facts.

Consider nepotism, or the practice of giving preference to people who you are related to, especially when making hiring decisions. Nepotism is regarded as wrong in most societies. It is thought that firms should hire people based on their qualifications, not based on who they are related to. But before condemning a firm for nepotism, Donaldson and Dunfee say, we should consider what is normal in the society in which the firm operates and, in particular, what role families play in that society. Nepotism may be something that we should tolerate in some contexts. The same goes for labor standards. Before condemning a factory for low labor standards, Donaldson and Dunfee say, we need to ask what the level of economic development is in the society in which the factory operates. Measures to protect workers' safety cost money and may be unaffordable in poor countries. Certain working conditions may be too low for anyone, but above this minimum firms have the freedom to fit labor standards to the conditions in which they find themselves.

Donaldson and Dunfee's integrative social contracts theory may strike you as a reasonable way to think about things, one that avoids the extremes of both cultural relativism and ethical absolutism. But notice that it doesn't really solve our problems. We haven't identified the contours of moral free space or how firms should find their place in it. Instead, integrative social contracts theory confirms that doing business ethics across borders is a tricky business. It tells us that we shouldn't accept whatever the rules happen to be in a different culture, but also that we cannot just apply the rules from our own culture to a different culture. Integrative social contracts theory tells us to do business ethics in a way that is sensitive, but not beholden, to social and economic differences across cultures. It is an invitation to keep thinking about business ethics, and that is what we will do.

3. Labor Conditions

In the Bangladeshi garment industry, many people work exceedingly long hours under harsh conditions for low pay. Is there anything wrong with this? Should their working conditions be improved? If so, who has the responsibility to improve them?

Factories in places like Bangladesh are sometimes called "sweatshops." We will try to avoid this terminology. To label a factory a "sweatshop" is to make an implicit judgment about it: that it is bad. (There is no such thing as "good sweatshop.") But this is what we are trying to figure out. We shouldn't start by assuming they are bad. So as much as possible we will avoid the language of sweatshops in favor of the more neutral language of "overseas factories."

We will be focusing on the poor working conditions, the lack of proper health and safety protocols, and the very low pay in overseas factories. Our question is whether there is something wrong about them. Now you might recall that we discussed working conditions and pay in Chapter 7, when we discussed ethical issues in the firm. Why are we discussing these issues again here?

In fact, this separation is somewhat arbitrary. The geographical location of a factory does not alter what should be said about its working conditions. We will see that some of the same values at issue in Chapter 7 – especially freedom and welfare – are relevant to debates about working conditions in overseas factories. But scholarly discussions about labor standards in developed countries like the U.S. usually proceed independently from discussions about labor standards in developing countries like Bangladesh. In discussing these issues separately, we are traveling well-worn paths. There is another, principled reason for this distinction. That is, social and economic conditions are very different in developed and developing nations. Compared to developed nations, multinational corporations have a lot more power in developing nations. For many business ethicists, this has required starting the debate in a different place and following the arguments in different directions.

3.1. Understanding the Problem

Before we start evaluating labor standards in Bangladesh, we should understand why they are so low there. It might be tempting to think that labor standards are so low because Bangladeshi factory owners are greedy, and they don't care about their workers. They keep all the money for themselves and spend no money on employees, either for safety improvements or wages.

That answer might comfort you. It tells you that the problem is with particular individuals in a faraway land. But it is almost surely false. Bangladeshi factory owners are probably no more greedy than anyone else. So why are things the way they are in the garment industry in Bangladesh? At the risk of oversimplifying, the answer is competition and poverty.

The garment industry is competitive. If factories in Bangladesh are going to win contracts from Western multinationals like H&M, Walmart, and The Gap to produce clothing, they are going to have to do it for low prices. People like you and me don't want to pay a lot for our clothes. But if factories in Bangladesh offer Western multinationals low prices, they will only be able to offer workers low wages, and they won't be able to provide nice working conditions. The competitiveness of the garment industry in Bangladesh makes it difficult for individual factory owners to raise wages or improve working conditions. To do so, they will have to increase the prices they charge Western multinationals, and this may cause them to lose business to other factories.

In addition to competition, the other reason that working conditions in Bangladesh are as bad as they are is that, in Bangladesh, people are poor. They don't have good options when it comes to making money. As a result, they are willing to take jobs that offer extremely low pay and poor working conditions. This point is worth emphasizing. Bangladeshis are not being rounded up and forced to sew. They take jobs in garment factories voluntarily. To be sure, these jobs are not good jobs. You and I would very much like not to have them. But they are the best jobs many people in Bangladesh can get. If you and I were desperate enough, we would take them too.

3.2. Respect for Workers

An early critique of labor conditions in overseas factories appealed to the idea of respect for persons, especially as found in Kant. You may recall from Chapter 3 that Kant said that we should treat human beings as ends in themselves and not merely as means. While there is debate about what exactly Kant meant by this, a popular interpretation of it is that workers should be *respected* (treatment as an end) and should not be *used* (treatment as a mere means).

Workers are not tools, like machines. It is wrong to try to "use them up and throw them away" as one would a machine. Workers are human beings with thoughts and feelings and plans of their own. This demands superior forms of treatment. According to Denis Arnold and Norman Bowie, the two contemporary business ethicists who developed this argument, to respect workers, employers must obey the law, not practice or tolerate coercion; observe some minimum health and safety standards; and pay workers living wages. Few would disagree with the suggestions that employers should obey the law and not coerce people. The real interest of this view lies in the claim that respecting workers requires observing some minimum health and safety standards and paying workers living wages.

This view faces both practical and theoretical obstacles. On a practical level, it is not obvious how the idea of respect for workers, which is quite vague, can be translated into specific health and safety regulations or specific amounts of pay. Does "respect" require factories in Bangladesh to be air-conditioned? Or will a series of strong fans be enough? Does respect require workers to be paid $195 per month? Or does respect begin at $200?

This may be unfair to Arnold and Bowie. Perhaps all they want to say is that you can't just assume that there is no problem with certain labor conditions because people agree to them. We have to consider independently whether those conditions are respectful.

This brings us to the theoretical worry. It is not clear that Arnold and Bowie have understood the concept of respect in the right way. They believe that certain options – work under certain conditions – must be closed off to people – because those options are incompatible with respect for persons. But others claim that respect for people requires allowing them to make their own choices. According to these writers, it is disrespectful to try to close off options for other people.

As an illustration, suppose that you decide that you wanted to make a living as a cheerleader for a professional sports team. Your parents tell you: "That is a degrading activity." Perhaps they even cite Kant. "We refuse to let you do this," they tell you. Is this respectful? We might think not. It might be fine for parents to tell a small child what to do or how to live. The child doesn't know any better. But it is quite a different thing for parents to tell a grown adult what to do or how to live. Respecting people can sometimes mean letting them decide for themselves and not substituting your judgment for theirs. For this reason, we might think that respecting people means allowing them to choose to work in overseas factories, even ones that offer poor health and safety conditions and low wages. This does not mean that all choices are equally morally significant, however. We might want to be sure that workers know what they are getting into before choosing. Indeed, we might think that respecting workers' faculties of choice requires giving them this information. But once they have it, then we might think that workers should be permitted to decide for themselves.

3.3. Exploitation

Another common critique of overseas factories is that workers are exploited in them. We have emphasized that people take jobs in these factories because they don't have better options. This, some say, is what exploitation is all about.

We encountered the concept of exploitation in Chapter 5, when we discussed kidney sales, and again in Chapter 6, when we discussed price gouging. It will be useful to refresh our memories. To exploit someone is to take unfair advantage of them. Perhaps a bit more specifically, we can say that one person E (employer) exploits another person W (worker) when E extracts an excessive benefit from W in a situation where W cannot reasonably refuse E's offer.

Suppose that Wilma's boat has capsized in the middle of a large lake. Wilma has a life vest on, but the lake is cold and she is beginning to suffer from hypothermia. The sun is about to set and once it does, no one will be able to find her. She will die. Eddie happens to be out on the lake for a bit of sightseeing. He sees Wilma and offers to rescue her, but for a high price: $20,000. Wilma doesn't want to die, so she takes the deal. Eddie stretches an oar out to Wilma and she grabs it and lifts herself onto Eddie's boat. When they arrive back on land Wilma pays Eddie $20,000.

In this example, Wilma and Eddie enter into a business arrangement. Eddie saves Wilma's life, and Wilma pays him $20,000. This transaction is exploitative. Eddie benefits excessively. He gets $20,000 simply for extending an oar into the chilly waters and allowing Wilma to hitch a ride back to shore (where Eddie was going anyway). The reason that Eddie is able to benefit excessively is that Wilma cannot reasonably refuse his offer. Wilma has no decent alternative. It's either pay Eddie $20,000 or die.

It might be claimed that the situation of employers and workers in overseas factories is similar to the rescue case we've just described. In Bangladesh, many people have no other decent alternative to working in the garment industry. People who cannot find work in a factory may return to a life of poverty in the countryside; they may beg on the streets; they may become sex workers. Employers are able to use this fact, it might be said, to extract an excessive benefit from workers. In long shifts in cheaply built factories for low pay, workers churn out thousands of pieces per day.

Are workers exploited in Bangladesh? That depends on how much their work is really worth. In the rescue case, our judgment that Eddie exploits Wilma depends on the idea that the true value of what Eddie does to rescue Wilma – extending an oar and giving her a ride – is low, but the reward he gets for it is high. He is able to get a high reward because there is no one else around, and Wilma is desperate. In a normal situation (say, where there are a lot of other boats around), Eddie could only get a small amount of money for his efforts. It is not clear that this mirrors the situation of employers and workers in the Bangladeshi garment industry. It is true that workers produce thousands of pieces per day, while working in poor conditions for low pay. But this work may just not be worth all that much. Note that, unlike in the rescue case, there are lots of potential employers in Bangladesh, and they all offer poor working conditions and low pay. Unless they are colluding with each other to keep wages low, this suggests that employees' labor is accurately valued. So while factory owners are certainly benefitting from their interactions with employees, they might not be benefitting excessively.

This hardly settles the matter. What we need is a theory of fairness in wages. Only then we will be able to compare the true value of their work with what they actually get paid. Until we have such a theory, the objection from exploitation is unsubstantiated.

But now suppose, for the sake of argument, that workers in Bangladeshi garment factories are exploited. Suppose employers benefit excessively or disproportionately from the employment relationship. Even so, this must be a case of mutually beneficial, as opposed to harmful, exploitation. In harmful exploitation, the exploiter benefits while the person who is exploited suffers. Someone who swindles you out of money harmfully exploits you. Slaves are harmfully exploited. But in mutually beneficial exploitation, both parties benefit. The rescue case is one of mutually beneficial exploitation. Eddie is obviously better off after his interaction with Wilma. He is $20,000 richer. But Wilma is better off too. She is alive instead of dead. In the case of employers and factory workers in Bangladesh, both parties also benefit from the relationship. It may be obvious that employers benefit, but a moment's thought shows that factory workers benefit too. If they didn't, they wouldn't have taken the job.

Usually, we say that exploitation is wrong. It is wrong to swindle someone out of their money or make them into your slave. But is mutually beneficial exploitation wrong? A factory owner might defend himself as follows: "Yes, I exploit people. But I also benefit them. I offer them jobs, which are better than their alternatives. What would you have me do? I can only win contracts if I pay low wages and offer poor working conditions. If I improve working conditions and raise wages, then I will lose contracts, and I will go out of business. My workers will then be even worse off." Is there anything wrong with the factory owner's reasoning?

The scholarly debate about this question often comes down to a contest between the "nonworseness principle" and the "interaction principle." According to the nonworseness principle, a consensual, mutually beneficial interaction between two people cannot be worse than the absence of such an interaction, assuming that there are no negative effects on third parties. Factory owners in Bangladesh interact with workers by hiring them. Even if this interaction is exploitative, defenders of the nonworseness principle claim, it isn't worse than if factory owners didn't interact with workers, that is, didn't hire (and exploit) them. Defenders of the interaction principle resist this claim. They think that, once you decide to interact with a person, you acquire an obligation to treat them according to certain standards – an obligation you would not have if you decided not to interact with them. You cannot claim that you are morally in the clear simply because you are benefiting that person. Defenders of the interaction principle think that if factory owners in Bangladesh hire workers – and so initiate an interaction – it may not be enough simply to make their lives better. They must do more. How much "more," of course, is a matter of intense debate.

3.4. Why It Is Sometimes Hard to Make Things Better

So far we have considered two objections to labor conditions in overseas factories, based on respect and exploitation. We have also considered what might be said in reply to these objections. You might be thinking that the debate is missing the point. The point, you might think, is that labor conditions in overseas factories are bad. Why can't someone just make them better?

We noted that it is difficult for an individual factory owner to make things better. If the owner makes things better for workers – by raising wages or improving working conditions – he will probably have to charge higher prices, and he may lose business to another factory.

What if the government steps in? You might think that the government should raise the minimum wage and establish better workplace health and safety regulations. The government of Bangladesh has in fact passed some regulations recently, though not as many as some activists would like. But the government is reluctant to do too much, for the same reason that individual factory owners are reluctant to do too much. It will cause Western multinationals to go elsewhere. Just as the garment industry is competitive intra-nationally (i.e., inside countries), it is competitive internationally (i.e., between countries). If Bangladesh raises its labor standards too high, then Western multinationals will do business with factories in places like Ethiopia or Myanmar.

There is a more general problem here, and that has to do with economics. When the price of something goes up, demand tends to go down. So when the price of labor goes up, either because factory owners raise wages or because governments raise the minimum wage, demand for labor goes down. This means people will work fewer hours, or fewer people will be employed, or both. To be sure, some workers will enjoy the benefits of higher wages, but some will lose out, because they will lose their jobs or their hours will be reduced.

At least that is the standard story. Some have argued that, when it comes to labor, things are more complicated. Economists have studied whether increases in the minimum wage have "disemployment effects." The evidence is mixed. While large increases in the minimum wage lead to lower employment, small increases may not. Why is this? One explanation appeals to "efficiency wages." When workers are paid more (or are otherwise treated better), they may work harder. Labor becomes more expensive, but also more productive. Another reason that paying workers more may not lead to unemployment appeals to the "market for virtue." Some consumers are willing to pay more to purchase goods from retailers who treat their workers well. If this is right, then the higher cost of workers' labor doesn't result in lower revenues. Instead, it can be passed along to consumers.

Whatever the outcome of this debate, some efforts have been made to try to improve things for workers in overseas factories. In the 1990s, Nike was subject to severe criticism for the labor practices of its suppliers in Indonesia and Vietnam. They have since spent millions of dollars developing and holding suppliers accountable for meeting strict health and safety standards. More recently, in response to the Rana Plaza tragedy, Western multinational corporations banded together to try to bring about change in Bangladeshi garment factories. Out of Europe came the Accord on Fire and Building Safety in Bangladesh, joined by corporations such as H&M and adidas. Out of North America came the Alliance for Bangladesh Worker Safety, joined by corporations such as The Gap and Macy's. These organizations created detailed sets of health and safety regulations, and members pledged to do business only with factories that met them, often at considerable expense to themselves. (Initially there was an effort to create a single organization, but it fell apart over disagreement about the legal status of the agreement. The Accord is a legally binding document; the Alliance is not.)

What we might learn from this is that change is possible. But change tends to happen only when the most powerful economic actors in the developing world decide things should change. In the developing world, these are typically large Western multinational corporations. What makes them decide to change things? This question does not admit of a simple answer. But it seems clear that one reason that corporations decide to act is that they see economic advantage in acting – or perhaps more precisely, they see economic disadvantage in not acting. Nike was the target of organized protests, including boycotts on college campuses. Eventually it decided to work with rather than resist those who challenged its labor practices. Rana Plaza was above all a human tragedy, but it was also a public relations disaster for the hundreds of companies whose products are made in Bangladesh. Signatories to the Accord and Alliance wanted to avoid a similar situation in the future.

This goes to a final question that we might consider when it comes to "making things better" in the developing world. If we arrive at the judgment that conditions in factories in Bangladesh are bad and should be improved, whose responsibility is it to improve them? Is it the factory owners in Bangladesh? Is it the government of Bangladesh? Is it large multinationals – retailers like H&M and Macy's – who wield outsize economic power in Bangladesh? What about us, the consumers of these products? Recent history suggests that retailers act only when the public demands that they act. If retailers try to make things better unilaterally, then they may put themselves at a competitive disadvantage. Like it or not, most consumers in the Western world seem to want cheap clothes. You might think, for some of the reasons given earlier, that no one is acting wrongly in places like Bangladesh. But if you think they are, then you might conclude that ultimate responsibility for the wrongness lies with us.

4. Corruption and Bribery

The Rana Plaza collapsed when its generators came on. The building couldn't handle the strain. Was the problem that people in Bangladesh don't know how to construct buildings that can be used safely for industrial purposes? No. The problem was that this particular building was not designed for industrial use. According to a report issued by the government of Bangladesh, the top three floors of the Rana Plaza – which supported thousands of workers along with the massive generators – were not part of the original design of the building and had been constructed illegally. The structure as a whole did not meet a variety of building codes. To be clear, it did not meet Bangladesh's own building codes, never mind the stricter building codes you might find in a more developed country.

How did this happen? How did such a building ever get built in the first place, and why was it allowed to be used as a garment factory? We may never know all of the details, but part of the answer is corruption. According to the same government report, Sohel Rana – the owner of the Rana Plaza – bribed local officials to get construction permits.

Bribery and other forms of corruption are illegal everywhere, but common in many parts of the developing world. The United Nations estimates that about $2.5 trillion is lost to corruption worldwide every year. $1 trillion is paid in bribes. The case of Rana Plaza shows that corruption can result not just in economic losses but in the loss of human lives. In this section we consider what responsibilities businesspeople have with respect to bribery and other forms of corruption.

4.1. Bribery, Facilitation Payments, and Extortion

Let us begin by introducing some concepts that will help us to think through the issues. Some characters are also necessary. There is a factory owner whom we will call "Frances" and a government official who we will call "Gary." Suppose Frances wants government approval to turn part of a building she owns into a garment factory. This approval comes in the form of a permit, which only Gary can provide.

Suppose that Frances's building does not conform to the building codes for factories. It is made out of weak materials and lacks enough light and ventilation to offer workers a safe and healthy environment. Frances offers Gary $5,000 to give her the permit anyway. In this case, Frances is offering Gary a *bribe*. She is offering him money to do something that he should not be doing. Gary should not be giving Frances a permit, since her building is not up to code.

Now suppose that Frances's building does conform to the building codes for factories. It is made out of strong materials and has plenty of light and ventilation for workers. Despite this, Gary demands payment of $5,000 for issuing Frances a permit. In this case, Gary is *extorting* Frances. He is asking for money to do something that he should be doing. If Frances pays Gary the money, then she is making a *facilitation payment*. Gary should be giving Frances a permit, since her building is up to code.

Bribes and facilitation payments are sometimes conflated, but it is important to distinguish them. The law treats bribes differently than facilitation payments. While bribery is illegal everywhere, facilitation payments are sometimes legally permissible. Bribes and facilitation payments are also different morally. We are likely to be angry at people who pay bribes. They cheat and they corrupt others in the process. By contrast, we might feel bad for people who make facilitation payments. They are being squeezed for money by someone who has no right to squeeze them.

4.2. Bribery Is Wrong. But Why?

Despite its ubiquity, especially in the developing world, most people agree that bribery is wrong. It is worth thinking about why it is wrong. We'll start with bribery and then consider the trickier case of extortion and facilitation payments.

A variety of reasons has been given for thinking that bribery is wrong. It has been claimed that bribery involves deception; that it entrenches ruling elites; that it is anti-democratic; and that it undermines trust in government and corporate officials. All of these things may be true. But the most fundamental problem with bribery – the problem that lies at the root of all of these other problems – is to be found simply in a proper understanding of what bribery is. Bribery is an attempt to get people to do something that they have a duty not to do. It is wrong for people to violate their duties and wrong to try to get people to violate their duties.

This answer, it might seem, just pushes the inquiry further back. Where do these duties come from, and why is violating them wrong? There are a variety of possible answers to these questions. The most common answers appeal to agreements and harm. Certain duties are associated with certain roles and positions, and when you take on those roles and positions, you agree to perform those duties. Not performing them often causes harm.

When Gary agrees to be a building inspector for a town, he agrees – implicitly if not explicitly – to make decisions about which structures to give permits to "on the merits." That is, he should award permits to buildings that meet the building codes, not to buildings that do not meet the codes. That is the job of a building inspector. What happens if Gary violates the duty to award permits in this way? The answer will appeal to the reason for having the rules in the first place. The rules are there to protect workers from harm. If they are not followed, then people might get hurt.

The case of Rana Plaza provides a dramatic example. Government officials were enticed by Sohel Rana to ignore their duty to award permits only to structurally sound buildings, and the result was a tragic loss of life. Other examples of bribery are less dramatic but have the same basic structure. In the 1970s, executives at Lockheed Martin paid approximately $12 million in bribes to persuade executives at All Nippon Airways (ANA) to purchase a fleet of Lockheed Martin's L-1011 Tristar airplanes instead of rival McDonnell Douglass's DC-10s. Executives at ANA had a duty to make purchasing decisions on the basis of what was best for their firm. This is what they agreed to do, or were entrusted to do, when they became executives. Instead, they made purchasing decisions on the basis of what was best for themselves. The result was that ANA paid inflated prices for inferior airplanes. More recently, in the early 2000s, the German company Siemens was discovered to have paid more than $1.4 billion in bribes to officials around the world to win government contracts. Government officials – like Gary in our fictional case – have a duty to award contracts on the merits, that is, on the basis of which firm offers the best combination of quality and price. Siemens' executives were able to get them to ignore this duty. As a result, people in developing countries got less for their money than they should have.

As these examples show, the "bad consequences" associated with bribery are not always harms in absolute sense. Government officials in Bangladesh made workers' lives worse in an absolute sense when they accepted bribes from Sohel Rana. But officials at ANA made workers' lives worse only in a relative sense. The airplanes they bought from Lockheed worked. Without the bribe, however, they would have gotten better airplanes, paid less for them, or both. The same is true of Siemens. People were helped by their efforts, but not as much as they should have been.

The problem with bribery is not just that resources are misused at a certain point in time, but that the wrong message is sent to the market. When government officials in Nigeria (and Bangladesh, Argentina, Venezuela, China, Russia, Israel, and more) took bribes from Siemens executives, they communicated to the market that the way to compete for their business is not by offering value for money, but by offering large bribes. The virtue of the free market, as we saw in Chapter 4, is that it gives people incentives to use resources efficiently. You are only going to survive in business if you give people good value for money. If you give them something that doesn't work, or that costs too much, then you will go out of business. When bribery is rampant, instead of competing by seeing who can offer the best value for money, businesspeople compete by seeing who can offer the largest bribes. Under these conditions, only a select few government officials and powerful corporations win. Everyone else in society loses. In recognition of this fact, economic organizations such as the World Bank and the International Monetary Fund have tied support for governments in developing countries – in the form of loans, advice, and training – to commitments to anti-bribery initiatives. The goal is to ensure that these organizations' resources go to the people who need them, not corrupt government officials.

4.3. Extortion and Facilitation Payments

So far we have been talking about the wrongness of bribery. What about facilitation payments? The fundamental problem with bribery, we said, is that it involves the violation of a duty. When duties are violated, this can have bad consequences. This account of the wrongness of bribery does not apply to the case of facilitation payments. When you make a facilitation payment, you are paying a person in order to get him to perform his duty. You are trying to get him to follow, as opposed to break, the rules. Insofar as performing a duty has good consequences, you are helping to bring them about.

Suppose again that Frances's building is up to code, but Gary asks her for a $5,000 payment to issue her the permit. Frances sees no other way to get the permit, and she needs it to open her business, so she pays him the $5,000. When Frances pays Gary, she incentivizes him to do what he should be doing, which is issuing her a permit. Gary should do this because this is what the rules require – rules that are designed to keep workers safe.

Does this mean that facilitation payments pose no ethical problems? Hardly. There is certainly something wrong with what Gary does. Gary extorts Frances. He threatens Frances with a harmful consequence – the denial of a needed permit – unless Frances pays him money. Gary has no right to deny Frances the permit, given the state of her building.

What about what Frances does? As noted, we might feel sorry for Frances. She has done everything right but is being denied the permit. Yet we might not hold her blameless for paying Gary. It is true that when Frances pays Gary she helps to bring about the correct outcome, which is the issuing of the permit. But she also helps to keep alive a system in which corrupt officials enrich themselves at the expense of innocent others. If Gary is able to extract money from Frances, he will likely try to extract money from other innocent victims. And if Gary is able to extract money from many innocent victims, then Gary's fellow government officials are likely to try the same. Thus, we might say that Frances deserves some blame for paying Gary, because it helps to perpetuate a system in which many people get extorted. In this system, money is directed away from valuable economic projects into the pockets of government officials.

Our judgment in this case may depend on how difficult it is for Frances to refuse Gary's attempts at extortion. Suppose Frances can pay him now and get the permit today. Or she can sue the town for a permit. Suppose that this would take Frances a few weeks and cost her legal fees of $10,000, but she could get it in the end. If Frances can afford $10,000, we might think that she should pursue this strategy. If, however, Frances cannot afford it, and she has to either pay $5,000 or lose her business, then we might think it is permissible for her to make the facilitation payment.

The case of the Swedish company IKEA in Russia provides a useful illustration. Corruption in Russia is rampant – government officials routinely demand facilitation payments to perform even the most basic tasks – and IKEA's efforts to resist it are well documented. In 2000, executives at a local power company in Moscow demanded a payment to keep the electricity on for an IKEA store's grand opening. IKEA refused and resorted to renting dozens of enormous generators to power the store instead. This cost IKEA significant aggravation and expense, but they decided it was worth it.

You too might think IKEA made the right choice, but your judgment may depend on certain facts about IKEA. One is that IKEA was capable of making this choice. IKEA is an enormous company with vast resources at its disposal. It can afford to work around corrupt Russian officials. A second is that IKEA is a prominent firm and can set a powerful example for other firms to follow. You might think differently if the retailer were an unknown company and could not afford to do what IKEA did. In general, you might think that whether a company is permitted to make facilitation payment depends on the wealth and prominence of the company, and this will vary from company to company and from time to time.

4.4. But Everyone Is Doing It!

In the ideal world, there would be no bribery, extortion, or facilitation payments. But we don't live in the ideal world. In our world, and especially in the developing world, these practices are common. Does this fact change what the responsibilities of businesspeople are?

A. Carl Kotchian thinks it does. He was president of Lockheed Martin in the 1970s when it bribed ANA officials in Japan (and other officials in the Netherlands, West Germany, and Saudi Arabia) to sell airplanes. Kotchian said that that was just how things were done at the time. Everyone was trying to win business through bribes. If he didn't bribe, there would be no chance that he could win. He also thought that he had an obligation to Lockheed Martin's employees and shareholders to try to make sales and keep the company in business. So he thought that he had not just a permission but a duty to bribe. While Kotchian was eventually forced to step down from his position as president of Lockheed Martin over multiple bribery scandals, he never expressed any regret for acting as he did.

Does Kotchian have a point? The first thing to note is that Kotchian was right. Everyone *was* bribing. In fact, while bribery has never been expressly permitted anywhere, governments have long recognized that firms pay bribes. Until recently, bribes were treated as a legitimate business expense for tax purposes in the U.S. and Europe. The second thing to note is that Kotchian's bribes weren't yet illegal in the U.S. The Foreign Corrupt Practices Act (FCPA), which forbids officials of U.S. companies from bribing foreign officials, was passed in 1977 (largely in response to the outcry over Kotchian's and other U.S. firms' actions). But what about the moral status of his actions?

We should dismiss the idea that corporate executives are permitted to bribe officials because they have a duty to do what is best for their firms. The duty to do what is best for one's firm is limited by what's morally permissible. Burning down a rival's factory may be good for one's firm because it reduces competition. But no one thinks that this makes burning down a rival's factory permissible. To claim that executives have a duty to bribe officials because this would be best for their firms is to assume that bribery is permissible, but this is what is under consideration.

We should also recognize that "everyone's doing it," even when true, is not a license to do just any "it." If everyone were robbing other people, or assaulting them in the street, it would still not be permissible for you to rob other people or assault them in the street.

But what about the claim that if Kotchian didn't bribe, he couldn't win? This idea has some promise. The business world is, by design, competitive. Companies compete with each other to make sales to consumers. The point of competition is to identify, incentivize, and reward excellence – in this case, excellence at making airplanes. But for this to happen the competition must be fair. Minimally, there needs to be a level playing field. Kotchian might be understood to be saying that if everyone else is bribing, then it would be unfair to require him not to bribe. It would create a non-level playing field. It would be like having a 100-meter dash where everyone is on the starting line, except for one runner, who is asked to start from 20 meters behind the starting line.

But what exactly is the moral status of Kotchian's bribes? Should we say that, under the circumstances, Kotchian did the right thing? We might not want to go that far. Here it is useful to introduce a distinction between justification and excuse. To say that an action is *justified* is to say that it is the right thing to do, all things considered. To say that an action is *excused* is to say that it is the wrong thing to do, but the actor is not to be blamed for doing it.

Suppose that someone is attacking your innocent friend. You jump to his rescue, tackling the assailant to the ground. It is not normally permissible for you to tackle someone to the ground. But in this case your action was justified. It was the right thing to do, because you prevent an innocent person from being harmed. Now suppose that you tackle someone to the ground who you think is attacking your friend. In fact, this person was not attacking your friend. He and your friend were acting out a scene from the movie *Creed*. But you had no reason to think that they were just acting; they were doing it on the quad in the middle of the afternoon, dressed in their usual attire. In this case your action is excused. It is wrong to tackle an innocent person to the ground, but you reasonably believed that the person was not innocent, so you should not be blamed for what you did.

Armed with this distinction, we can ask: was Kotchian's behavior justified? That is, was it the right thing to do, all things considered? Or was it the wrong thing to do, but excused, because of the competitive pressure that he was under?

Using the example of the 100-meter dash, you might be tempted to claim that Kotchian's behavior was justified. The point of this business competition is to select the best maker of airplanes, and this can only happen when the playing field is level. In the same way, if you want to discover who the fastest runner is in a race, all the runners need to start in the same place. A runner who was placed behind other runners, you might say, would be justified in moving himself up to where the other runners are. By this logic, you might conclude, Kotchian is justified in paying the bribe, to "move himself up" into the same position as the other airplane manufacturers.

The analogy on which this argument relies is problematic. In a running race, it doesn't really matter whether the runners start from one point on the track or a different point. What matters is that they start in the same place. But it does matter whether people bribe or don't bribe. Bribery involves the violation of a duty, and this violation often has harmful consequences. When the executives of ANA solicited bribes from airplane manufacturers, they effectively siphoned money out of the company into their own pockets. Instead of getting better airplanes at a lower cost, they paid more for worse airplanes. The difference went to ANA executives. At the same time, we can understand why Kotchian felt he had to pay bribes. It was the only way to stay in business in the industry at that time. If this argument is right, then we should say not that Kotchian's behavior was justified; we should say it was excused. He did not do the right thing, but we don't blame him for doing what he did.

This is not, however, the end of the story. Bribery and other forms of corruption are a cancer on market exchange. Maybe in some circumstances we should excuse people who bribe, but we can also ask whether there is anything that they can do to fight it. What if Kotchian went to the press and complained that he – and everyone else in his industry – was being shaken down for bribes by corrupt government officials? What if he proactively complained to the U.S. Congress that he could not do business in foreign countries without paying bribes? Did he ever *try* to refuse to make corrupt payments – like IKEA's executives – and see if he could manage without them?

Corruption is a difficult problem. Ultimately, it will not be solved by the actions of any single business or businessperson, no matter how heroic. It will take the concerted action of the world community. We noted that economic organizations such as the World Bank and International Monetary Fund are taking steps to curb corruption, by tying their support for governments to anti-corruption efforts. Perhaps the most important organization fighting corruption today is Transparency International, which has more than 100 chapters in countries around the world. Their mission is to understand why corruption occurs and what is necessary to fight against it. There is little debate these days about whether corruption is wrong. The question now is how best to get rid of it.

5. Divestment

People who do business across national boundaries can encounter morally compromised environments and activities. They can find poverty, danger, injustice, and corruption. We've seen that Western multinationals have found this in the garment industry in Bangladesh.

We have considered reasons for thinking that some of this might be tolerated. Different cultural traditions and levels of economic development might license businesspeople to observe different rules abroad than they would at home. In some cases, we might excuse some bad behavior by businesspeople as the necessary price of doing business in compromised environments. But not any bad behavior should be tolerated. Some situations are so compromised that, instead of trying to do business in the situation, firms should simply walk away. In this section we consider this issue, commonly known as the problem of "divestment."

To invest in something is to contribute resources to it. To divest is to take resources away from it. In this sense, divestment happens anytime someone sells a share of stock, which happens billions of times per day on the world's stock exchanges. But "divestment" has come to have a moral connotation. When people talk about divestment, they are talking about withdrawing from a business environment or activity because it is morally compromised.

In this chapter we have focused on the garment industry in Bangladesh. While this industry is morally compromised (by poverty, injustice, and corruption), things are not so challenging that Western businesses are seriously thinking about divesting. So new examples are needed.

One can be found in the 1980s in Apartheid South Africa. Apartheid was a social and economic system in which blacks and whites lived separately – 'apartheid' is an Afrikaans word meaning 'apart-hood' – and unequally. Indeed, blacks in South Africa lived terribly under Apartheid. They had no political representation and minimal rights. Whites controlled all of South Africa's major social and economic institutions and held the vast majority of its wealth, despite constituting less than 20% of the total population. As international awareness of Apartheid grew, foreign firms and institutions came under pressure to divest from South Africa. Some, like Pepsi-Cola, did; others, like Coca-Cola, did not.

More recently, there has been debate about whether institutions should divest from the fossil fuel industry. Scientists agree that the climate is changing in ways that are likely to cause serious harm, and carbon emissions from fossil fuels are a major contributor to this change. In response, some institutions, including universities such as Stanford and Syracuse, have divested themselves of stock in corporations that produce fossil fuels, such as BP, Chevron, and ExxonMobil.

Divestment is an extreme decision, an option of last resort. Yet it may be justified in some cases. In this section we consider reasons that firms and other economic agents need to think about as they decide whether to divest from a morally problematic business environment or activity. When making any choice, it is natural to consider both its costs and its benefits. So it goes with divestment. In the next two sections we consider the types of costs and benefits that are thought to attend divestment decisions.

Our discussion will touch on several of the ideas examined in Chapter 10, in our investigation of ethical consumerism. There we considered reasons for and against boycotts. Divestment is a sort of boycott, except the agents withdrawing resources are typically producers and not consumers.

5.1. Costs

One potential cost of divestment is to the agent who divests. If you invested in a thing, it is probably because you thought that doing so would be to your advantage financially. This is why universities and other institutions invest a portion of their capital in fossil fuel companies, namely, because those companies have been profitable. If you now divest, then you are doing something that you think is against your financial interest. Pepsi and Coca-Cola entered the South African market because they thought that it would be profitable. To withdraw from the market would represent a cost to their businesses.

You might object that divestment is not guaranteed to result in a financial loss. If a firm divests from a morally compromised situation, you might think that it can "sell" this behavior to the public as an example of corporate social responsibility and be rewarded for it.

The experiences of Coca-Cola and Pepsi-Cola in South Africa provide a cautionary tale for this sort of thinking. Pepsi-Cola withdrew completely from South Africa. By contrast, Coca-Cola found a way to get its products on South African shelves. Coca-Cola sold its bottling plants to South Africans. Then they allowed the new owners to purchase Coca-Cola products manufactured in neighboring countries and sell them under the Coca-Cola label in South Africa. Coca-Cola products were still on the shelves in South Africa, and Coca-Cola was still making money from their sale. But the entity doing the selling was an independent South African company. Pepsi-Cola reintroduced its products to South Africa in

1994 when Apartheid ended – to great fanfare and with support from American and South African celebrities – but its market share never recovered.

The lesson you might draw from this is that consumers care less about corporate social responsibility than you might think. Or we might conclude that the 1980s were a long time ago, and people are a lot more aware of ethical issues than they used to be. None of this is to suggest, of course, that an agent's decision to divest should depend entirely on whether divestment is in that agent's financial interest. Doing the right thing sometimes requires sacrificing one's personal interests.

We have been talking about the costs to the agent doing the divesting. There are also costs to third parties, who may be innocent. When investors withdraw resources from a business, the business may have to cut costs elsewhere. For example, it may have to fire employees. You might think that there is no problem here if those employees are engaged in activities that are morally problematic. Perhaps this is the case with employees who are involved in the production of fossil fuels. They are helping to produce the bad outcomes. But the situation in South Africa was surely different. If a foreign firm pulls out of the country, then its workers, including its black workers, will lose their jobs. And the workers may have been doing nothing at all wrong. This is one of the reasons that some people opposed divestment in South Africa. They thought that the worst effects of divestment would be felt by poor black workers, not whites in the political power structure.

Whether these costs are prohibitively expensive depends on how long they last. Supporters of divestment in South Africa conceded that divestment would hurt workers, including poor black workers. But they thought that this pain would be temporary and would be worth bearing to achieve the goal of bringing down the Apartheid regime. This would be good for blacks in the end.

5.2. Benefits

Divestment can have costs, to both the agent who divests and third parties, who may be innocent of any wrongdoing. What about the benefits of divestment? The point of divestment is to bring about desirable social change. The point of divestment in South Africa was to bring about an end to Apartheid. The point of divestment in the fossil fuel industry is to reduce the consumption of fossil fuels, thereby slowing the rate of climate change.

The way that divestment is supposed to work is to starve organizations of resources. Almost every business needs some financing, either in the form of equity or debt. A similar result applies for economies. Most modern economies would go into a serious recession, if not collapse completely, if all foreign investment dried up. If they come to believe that having a certain social policy will result in foreign firms not investing, then they will change that policy.

Does divestment actually work to produce social change? The divestment movement against the fossil fuel industry hasn't had much effect. But this movement is still in its infancy, so that is not surprising. Only a tiny fraction of assets under management has been withdrawn from fossil fuel companies. What about the case of Apartheid South Africa? In one study, researchers found that significant events in the disinvestment campaign against South Africa (e.g., divestment announcements, currency sanctions, and trade embargoes) had no discernible impact on South African financial markets. The Apartheid regime was eventually dismantled, but this appears to have been due more to political than economic pressure.

What this suggests is that, for divestment movements to succeed, many agents need to work together and divest all at once. But for familiar reasons, this is difficult to do. Like a boycott, discussed in the previous chapter, divestment has the structure of a collective action problem, and these are notoriously hard to solve. As noted, it is usually costly for individual agents to divest. At the same time, achieving the goals of divestment doesn't depend on the contributions of any one agent. Think of it this way. If almost all foreign firms divest from an economy, then it isn't necessary for your firm to divest. The result doesn't depend on you. At the same time, if very few firms divest, then the socially valuable result will not be achieved. It makes no sense for you to divest in these circumstances; your effort will be wasted. So whatever other firms do, you have a reason not to divest. And of course this reasoning is available to every individual firm. This structure poses a challenge to divestment movements. Thus, we should not be surprised that there are few examples of successful divestment movements around.

It might seem that we are letting firms off the hook too easily. A lesson we learned in the discussion of corruption and bribery is relevant here. Not all firms are the same. Whether you have an obligation to divest may depend on the kind of firm your firm is. Prominent firms may set an example for others to follow. If a prominent firm decides to divest, then it might help other firms to summon the courage to divest. If that firm decides instead not to divest, then it might give other firms cover to follow its lead. The same goes for costs. Firms that face steeper costs for divesting have a less powerful obligation to divest than firms who can do so at relatively little cost. We can also put this point in terms of ability to pay. Firms that can absorb the costs of divestment have a stronger obligation to divest than firms for which divestment would threaten their existence. For this reason, we might think that Pepsi-Cola did the right thing when it decided to divest. It probably convinced some other firms to divest also. And while it was a costly decision, it was a cost that Pepsi-Cola could bear. While Pepsi-Cola still doesn't do much business in South Africa, it remains a large and thriving company overall.

As we consider the costs and benefits of divestment, a question to keep in mind is, if not divestment, then what? You might think the alternative is business as usual. So the investor in the fossil fuel company simply leaves her money invested with the company and goes about her day. Or the firm continues to do business in a morally compromised community like Apartheid South Africa without making any trouble for the community. But in fact there is another option: constructive engagement. The person who has invested money with the fossil fuel company can complain about what the firm is doing and push for change. The firm is more likely to listen to the complaints of its investors than those of generic members of the public. Similarly, firms operating in morally compromised countries can use their economic power to push for change. The country is more likely to listen to the firm that has an operation in the country than to a generic firm outside of it.

In fact, when calls for divestment from Apartheid South Africa were loudest in the 1980s, the U.S. President and U.K. Prime Minister, Ronald Reagan and Margaret Thatcher, respectively, recommended a policy of constructive engagement as opposed to divestment. They did so on consequentialist grounds, arguing that constructive engagement was more likely to produce desirable social change than divestment. (They also worried that a sudden overthrow of the Apartheid regime would lead to a takeover of the South African state by communists, and they were deeply antagonistic to communism.) It may be best to see constructive engagement as a precursor to divestment. Activists should try to engage with problematic industries and governments first. Then, if those industries and governments prove unwilling to listen or change, divestment may be necessary.

5.3. Complicity

So far we have considered divestment through the lens of costs and benefits. But for some people this is the wrong way to think about divestment. The way to think about divestment, they say, is in terms of complicity. Something bad is going on in the world, and the point of divestment is to make sure that you are not part of it. Fossil fuel companies are contributing to a major environmental harm. The government of Apartheid South Africa was responsible for oppressing and persecuting blacks. These activities require money. The point of an agent's divestment, it might be said, is to make sure that the agent herself is not the source of this money. You might say, when you divest: "It is important for me that I do not contribute to these harms."

It might seem hard to understand the logic here. If divesting is costly for me, someone might say, then the only reason it makes sense to divest is if it does some good for others. Pepsi-Cola took its products off the shelves in South Africa, but that just meant that Coca-Cola sold more. Pepsi-Cola was worse off, and the Apartheid regime wasn't damaged. What was the point of that?

But it often matters to agents not just whether good or bad outcomes obtain in the world, but whether they themselves produce those outcomes. Ask yourself which would be worse, helping to produce an outcome that is bad or simply witnessing an outcome of equal badness? You might say that helping to produce the bad outcome is worse. We might understand this answer in terms of integrity. The person with integrity is united as opposed to divided. In particular, there is a match between her values and her actions. The person with integrity acts in accordance with her values; her actions give expression to her values. If you think oppression and domination are wrong, and yet you participate in an economic system in which there is widespread oppression and domination, you are not acting with integrity. You are a hypocrite. You contribute to a system that produces outcomes that are opposed to your values. If you think people should reduce their use of fossil fuels to slow down the speed of climate change, and yet you invest your money in fossil fuel companies, then you are helping to speed up climate change, the opposite of the result you say you want.

Now we might recognize reasons why it might be permissible for you to do business in a country with a morally bankrupt political system or invest your money in a company that harms the environment. Maybe you will work "from the inside" to solve the problems. Or maybe you have no other decent options. But unless you have some excuse, your integrity will be threatened.

6. Chapter Summary

In this chapter we considered ethical issues that arise when business is conducted across national boundaries. We noted that labor standards are different and, in particular, lower in developing countries like Bangladesh than in developed countries like the U.S. We asked whether it is possible to say that one country's labor standards are morally better or worse than another's. Cultural relativists say it is impossible. Against this, it is hard to accept that all morality is culturally determined. Yet it goes too far to say that all cultures should adopt the same moral code, including the same labor standards. It is desirable to find a principled middle ground.

What should we say about the labor conditions in places like Bangladesh? One key concept in the debate about this question is respect. Some argue that respect for workers requires improving the conditions in which they work. Others argue that respect requires allowing workers to choose to work in poor conditions, as opposed to having decisions about their working conditions made for them by Western critics. Another key concept is exploitation. Some claim that workers in places like Bangladesh are being exploited, and this exploitation must stop. Others point out that there are worse things than being exploited, like being unemployed.

Corruption is rampant in the developing world, and this can lead to tragedy, as we saw in the case of the Rana Plaza. When you bribe someone, you pay them to do something that they should not be doing, like granting permission to operate a factory inside a structurally unsound building. People who accept bribes violate the duties associated with their positions, duties that they agree to discharge when taking them up. Extortion is different. Here the moral wrong lies primarily with the official, who threatens the businessperson with harm to collect a benefit he has no right to collect. But the businessperson may not be entirely off the hook morally. If he makes the facilitation payment, he helps to perpetuate a practice in which officials enrich themselves at the expense of innocent parties. "Everyone's doing it!" is a common refrain when it comes to corruption. Too often this is true. There is a lot of corruption, especially in the developing world. We considered whether this is a justification for engaging in corrupt behavior, or merely an excuse, and when this excuse might be available to a firm.

At some point a businessperson might decide to walk away from a morally bankrupt society or industry rather than to do business in it. We considered the costs and benefits of divestment, both for the agent who divests and for third parties. In theory, divestment works to produce desirable social change, but in practice these benefits can be elusive. Divestment only works if many agents cooperate, but each agent has an incentive to free ride on others' efforts. Costs and benefits are one way of analyzing the problem of divestment, but it can also be analyzed in terms of complicity. The question is not only what the effects of divestment are, on you and others, but what you help to do by not divesting. Divestment may be necessary to preserve your integrity.

7. Study Questions

1. Do cultural relativists think that there is no morality? Explain your answer.
2. Some people are attracted to cultural relativism because they think it gives the right answer when it comes to tolerating differences. Why is this answer confused?
3. Can you think of a business practice in another culture that should be tolerated as simply different? Can you think of a business practice in another culture that should be judged as wrong? How do you draw the line?
4. Almost everyone agrees that people should be respected. But there is disagreement about what this means for factory workers in developing countries. Explain the disagreement.
5. Are workers in the garment industry in Bangladesh exploited? If so, what can, and what should, be done about it?
6. What is the difference between paying a bribe and making a facilitation payment?
7. Why is bribery wrong? Is asking for a facilitation payment wrong? What about making a facilitation payment?
8. Do you think A. Carl Kotchian was justified in paying bribes to foreign officials to sell airplanes? Do you think his actions can be excused? How?

9. Why is it difficult for divestment movements to succeed?
10. Do you think Pepsi-Cola did the right thing when it divested from South Africa in the 1980s? What would you say about Coca-Cola's actions?

Additional Readings

Arnold, D. G., & Bowie, N. E. (2003). Sweatshops and respect for persons. *Business Ethics Quarterly, 13*(2), 221–242.

Cragg, W. (2018). Corruption, bribery, and moral norms across national boundaries. In E. Heath, B. Kaldis, & A. Marcoux (Eds.), *The Routledge companion to business ethics* (pp. 573–589). New York: Routledge.

Donaldson, T. (1989). Disinvestment. In his *The ethics of international business* (pp. 129–144). New York: Oxford University Press.

Donaldson, T. (1996). Values in tension: Ethics away from home. *Harvard Business Review, 74*(5), 48–62.

Donaldson, T., & Dunfee, T. W. (1999). *Ties that bind: A social contracts approach to business ethics*. Cambridge, MA: Harvard Business Press.

Heath, J. (2018). 'But everyone else is doing it': Competition and business self-regulation. *Journal of Social Philosophy, 49*(4), 516–535.

MacAskill, W. (2015, October 20). Does divestment work? *The New Yorker*. www.newyorker.com/business/currency/does-divestment-work

Manik, J. A., & Yardley, J. (2013, April 25). Building collapse in Bangladesh leaves scores dead. *New York Times*. www.nytimes.com/2013/04/25/world/asia/bangladesh-building-collapse.html

Rachels, J., & Rachels, S. (2019). *The elements of moral philosophy*. New York: McGraw-Hill Education.

Zwolinski, M. (2007). Sweatshops, choice, and exploitation. *Business Ethics Quarterly, 17*(4), 689–727.

Index